W9-BQL-568

MAJOR ISSUES IN AMERICAN HISTORY

General Editor
A. S. EISENSTADT, Brooklyn College

Conducting the Diplomacy of the New Nation, 1793–1815
Patrick C. T. White

The Negro Question: From Slavery to Caste, 1863–1910
Otto H. Olsen

Creating an American Empire, 1865–1914
Milton Plesur

The New Immigration
John J. Appel

Reforming American Life in the Progressive Era
H. Landon Warner

The Uncertain World of Normalcy: The 1920s
Paul A. Carter

THE UNCERTAIN
WORLD OF NORMALCY:
THE 1920s

A JEROME S. OZER BOOK
published by PITMAN PUBLISHING CORPORATION
*New York * Toronto * London * Tel Aviv*

THE UNCERTAIN WORLD OF NORMALCY: THE 1920s

EDITED BY

Paul A. Carter

Northern Illinois University

Library of Congress Catalog Card No. 77 – 133007

Designed by Lenni Schur

Manufactured in the United States of America

THIS BOOK IS FOR ROBERT KENNEDY CARTER, BORN JANUARY 15, 1969.

For man has moved from stone to bronze and steam,
And learned to love a larger fire glow;
New eons bring to dawn a brighter dream,
And old ones shudder as they turn to go.
It may be that the frightened, bursting earth
Is giving shining brotherhood its birth.

MANFRED A. CARTER
Evergreen Branches (Hampden, Maine, 1949)
Reprinted in *Blue and Strange*
(Dallas, 1955), p. 10

FOREWORD

The study of history in our classrooms too often proceeds merely from the perspective of the present. Hindsight becomes the great arbiter for settling the past's problems. In our standard textbooks, we judge rather than encounter the past; we instruct it with lessons learned from later developments. In such textbooks, the study of history tends to become a tidy arrangement of certain consequences that arose out of certain causes. As a result, the student can grasp only meagerly the sense that every past was its own present, alive with its own problems, wavering among the alternatives for solving these problems, uncertain about the future. With the security of hindsight and distance, the student is not sufficiently able to consider that a decade he sees as *then* was once a vital and challenging *now,* that its roads into the future were many, that there was nothing inevitable about the one it followed, and that many voices spoke and many forces were at work in affecting its decision to travel one road or another.

The study of American history has tended in recent decades, in yet another way, to remove the classroom from the past itself. It is not merely that we have been proceeding, in our textbooks, to perceive the past from a perspective that is settled and certain, but also that, in our supplementary materials, we have been reading not the past itself but how our major historians are perennially changing their interpretations of it. In this way, too, we are supplanting a study of the past with a study of latter-day commentators on it and, all too often, of commentators on the commentators. The original, vital language of the past itself has, it is fair to say, lost a good deal in the translation.

The *Major Issues in American History* series undertakes above all to restore the fresh, lively contact between the student of the past and the past he is studying. Each of the volumes in the series consists of fifteen or more essays written by earlier generations of Americans on issues of great importance in their times. The different volumes of the series tap a variety of primary sources, but mainly the rich store of our great periodical literature, in which the foremost leaders of American life, our publicists, literary figures, and statesmen addressed themselves to the major problems confronting their respective eras. The men and women who speak in these selections offer various reasons or qualifications for doing so: their intimate knowledge of the problem they are speaking of, their sophisticated perception of its nature, their deep persuasion about its urgency, their strong convictions about how to resolve it.

The selections in each volume seek to lay out the larger dimensions of the major issue with which it is concerned, to recapture the sense of the issue's contemporaneity and urgency, and to afford answers to questions such as the following: What are the nature and significance of the issue? How and why did the issue arise? How should it be resolved? What alternatives are there to achieve its resolution, and what difficulties does the pursuit of each of these alternatives present? Every age is alive with problems, doubts, and controversies, and the selections in each of the volumes seek to convey what these were, in the full measure of the immediacy and liveliness with which the age experienced them. In sum, the central aim of the series is to vitalize the study of the American past by means of *important contemporary essays on major issues.*

Each of the volumes has been edited by a specialist on the issue with which the volume is concerned. Each volume has several principal features designed to enhance its use by the student in his pursuit of a meaningful, rewarding study of the American past. The editor's introductory essay undertakes to present the issue in a broader perspective, indicating how it arose, what were its essential themes and substance, how the controversy it engendered proceeded, what proposals were made for its resolution, how it was ultimately settled, and what were its impact and historical significance. The headnotes for each of the selections extend the introductory essay, offering details about the author of the selection, what occasioned its writing, what the other sides of the controversy were, and the specific historical context in which the selection appeared. The bibliographical essay at the end of the volume offers a critical appraisal of the literature, primary and secondary, dealing with the issue under discussion. Selective rather than comprehensive, it affords the student the basis for a further exploration of the subject. Each volume has, moreover, a chronology which sets the major issue in the context of its times, relating it to the principal events of the age. It is a special point of the series, finally, that the selections have, wherever possible, been reprinted in their entirety. It is important that a spokesman of an earlier age be permitted to present his views in all their completeness and that the student give the past the full hearing it merits.

The *Major Issues in American History* series is meant for use in both basic and advanced courses in American history. The series extends the study of the American past in several ways. It takes the student beyond the confines of the textbook, with its pat formulations and neat divisions, to the reality of the past. Without in any way discounting the importance of what they are saying, it also takes the student beyond the perennial controversies among latter-day and recent historians about what the past signified. It sets the student down in the lively context of a major issue or crisis which earlier Americans had to face, and it compels him to take his place among them in facing and resolving it. Above all, it encourages him to venture out on his own into the realm of the American past and to develop those qualities of perception and judgment that make the study of history the challenging enterprise it is.

A. S. EISENSTADT
Brooklyn College

CONTENTS

A SELECTIVE CHRONOLOGY

1919 Prohibition Amendment takes effect with the passage of the Volstead Act.

1920 Final defeat of the Versailles Treaty by the Senate.
Warren Harding elected President.
Publication of *Main Street* by Sinclair Lewis and *This Side of Paradise* by F. Scott Fitzgerald.

1921 Postwar boom turns into brief depression.
Beginning of rapid proliferation of radio broadcasting stations.
Creation of Veterans Bureau and Bureau of the Budget.
Emergency Quota Law restricts immigration.
Washington Conference begins; major naval powers agree to reduce tonnage.

1922 Mussolini marches on Rome.
First experiments with Technicolor and radar.
Publication of *The Waste Land* by T. S. Eliot and *Civilization in the United States* by Harold Stearns.

1923 Warren Harding dies in office; succeeded by Calvin Coolidge.
Frank Lloyd Wright's Imperial Hotel survives Tokyo earthquake.
United States Steel reduces twelve-hour day.
H. L. Mencken becomes editor of the *American Mercury.*

1924 Teapot Dome investigations disclose corruption in Harding administration.
Coolidge reelected.
Second Ku Klux Klan reaches zenith of its political power.
Dawes Plan attempts to underwrite German reparations.
First performances of *What Price Glory?* by Maxwell Anderson and Laurence Stallings and *Desire Under the Elms* by Eugene O'Neill.

1925 William Jennings Bryan faces Clarence Darrow in the Scopes trial.
Publication of *Manhattan Transfer* by John Dos Passos and *An American Tragedy* by Theodore Dreiser.
Appearance of Charlie Chaplin in *The Gold Rush* and Harold Lloyd in *The Freshman.*

1926 Court-martial of General "Billy" Mitchell, critic of U.S. air power.
Collapse of Florida real estate boom.
Senate approves United States membership in World Court, but with reservations which prevent admission.
Publication of *The Sun Also Rises* by Ernest Hemingway.
First public presentation of "talking pictures."

1927 Charles Lindbergh's solo transatlantic flight.
Execution of Sacco and Vanzetti.
Ford ceases production of "Model T" automobile.

1928 Al Smith loses to Herbert Hoover in presidential election, but carries twelve largest U.S. cities.
George Gershwin composes *An American in Paris.*
Wall Street "bull market" at its peak.
Final defeat of McNary-Haugen bill for farm relief.

1929 St. Valentine's Day Massacre in Chicago.
Textile strike in North Carolina.
Publication of *The Modern Temper* by Joseph Wood Krutch and *Little Caesar* by W. R. Burnett.
Stock market crash.

The older generation had certainly pretty well ruined this world before passing it on to us. They give us this Thing, knocked to pieces, leaky, red-hot, threatening to blow up; and then they are surprised that we don't accept it with the same attitude of pretty, decorous enthusiasm with which they received it, 'way back in the eighteen-nineties, nicely painted, smoothly running, practically fool-proof. "So simple that a child can run it!" But the child couldn't steer it. He hit every possible telegraph-pole, some of them twice, and ended with a head-on collision for which we shall have to pay the fines and damages. Now, with loving pride, they turn over their wreck to us.

"These Wild Young People," by One of Them
(*Atlantic Monthly*, September, 1920)

It is one of the happy illusions of the youthful that they represent full bloom and that everything beyond them is decay.

They burst upon the scene and accept all the legacies, for which we have toiled, as personal property to which they are entitled because of their all-round superiority to any other living objects in sight.

We have smothered them with riches and blinded them with revelations, and then we are surprised because they differ from the little gawks and ignorami who circulated around the school house back in Hickory Creek, when Pa smoked cheroots and Ma owned a cashmere shawl.

GEORGE ADE, "Today's Amazing Crop of Eighteen-Year-Old Roués and Nineteen-Year-Old Vamps"
(*American Magazine*, March, 1922)

INTRODUCTION

From the physical and social wreckage of the past, certain historical fragments have been retrieved. The monumental statuary at Abu Simbel was sawn into blocks and thereby saved from the rising waters of the Nile. London Bridge was taken down and rebuilt, stone by stone, in the desert of Arizona. Public-spirited citizens of Manhattan kept the remorseless redevelopers from tearing down Carnegie Hall. And a resident of Vancouver, British Columbia purchased from the National Wrecking Company of Chicago the brick wall in front of which, on Saint Valentine's Day of 1929, seven men had stood and been shot. It may say more about the temper of the year the purchase was made (1968) than it does about that of 1929 that a food-company executive should have bought so grisly and expensive a relic for reconstruction in his den. But his act was a forcible reminder that the Twenties, once so near to us psychically that a book about them became a best seller under the title *Only Yesterday,* had become "antiquity." Between the parents who founded their families under the cloud of Hiroshima and their children who struggled into selfhood in the shadow of Vietnam there stretched a much-discussed "generation gap," but still further beyond that gulf stood the grandparents, whose living experience had become shrouded in legend. The undergraduate of the Sixties, upon hearing a professor lecture on "the Lost Generation," does not ordinarily seem to have gone home afterward and asked, "But, Grandma, did he mean *you?*"

It was easy to forget, moreover, that those grandparents had had to hurdle a "generation gap" of their own. "The mothers and fathers and uncles and aunts of the youth of both sexes between twenty and thirty" who in the year 1915 were launching their own businesses and professional careers, Randolph Bourne wrote, were unworthy of their children's loyalty. Complacent, selfish, and hypocritical, the older generation had "grown weary of thinking.... It tends more and more to treat human beings as moving masses of matter instead of as personalities.... The older generation has stamped, through all its agencies of family, church, and school, upon the younger generation, just those seductive ideals which would preserve its position.... Its influence is profoundly pernicious." Even as Bourne wrote these words, the seductive ideals of the older generation were hurling the younger at each other's throats by the millions, in the shell-churned muck that the green fields of France, by the grace of modern technology, had become. Henry F. May, in his book *The End of American Innocence,* is quite right to have pointed out that disillusionment such as Bourne expressed antedated the First World War, and therefore that the war did not "cause" the rebelliousness associated with the Twenties; but for many participants in that rebellion the war was what clinched it. The older generation had forfeited any claim to moral authority because its own ideals – or ingrained hatreds and systematic stupidities rationalized as ideals – had brought on the war, and then had trapped the younger generation into paying the price of their elders' folly.

Young men who had been through the maelstrom themselves were understandably a bit self-righteous on this point. As a volunteer ambulance driver at the front, twenty-one year old John Dos Passos thought himself and his friends "frightfully decent – all young men are frightfully decent. If we only governed the world instead of the swagbellied old fogies that do.... Down with the middleaged!" Four years later on the night train up to Tiflis from Batum in the U.S.S.R. he heard enthusiastic young Bolsheviks talk excitedly of the brave new world they were building: "food and schools, peace and freedom for all, except for the damn *burzoi* that were causing them so much trouble" – and, Dos Passos reflected afterward, "In the summer of 1921 it would have been hard to find a war veteran who wouldn't have endorsed that program."

They didn't all come out of the War wanting to govern the world. Some of them chose to stand aside and treat it as a bad joke, or to turn their backs on it in quest of some private Grail – excellence in writing, or courage in the bull ring, or perfection in sex. Nor did all of them blame the troubles of the times on the middle-aged; many joined the American Legion and cheered Colonel Theodore Roosevelt, Jr. when he cried: "You will always find us ready to stand for the ideals of this country handed down by our fathers ... Bolshevists, the I.W.W. and red flag Socialists I see as criminals, to be treated as such." (In any case, revolutionary ideals do not always derive from a "generation gap"; disagreeing with Bourne, the young insurgent might rather have felt that his radicalism confirmed his basic family loyalties, in the spirit expressed in 1929 by an American champion of Soviet Communism,

Mike Gold: "Mother! Momma! . . . I must remain faithful to the poor because I can't be faithless to you."). And there were quiet back eddies where the upheavals of the time seem scarcely to have raised a ripple. Rosemary Park, in more recent years Vice-Chancellor of UCLA, once told a convocation audience that when she entered college in 1924 "a burning issue was whether one complied with a college regulation and wore a hat in Harvard Square":

> As far as we knew, we could discuss anything we liked on campus. The university was a free market of ideas, but there were no very profound ones about. Young instructors told us they had been reprimanded for referring in class to a Viennese psychiatrist, Sigmund Freud, and in our history classes or in art and literature, modern as an historical term stopped at 1850. . . . The University . . . was rightly removed from the vulgarities and disputes of the outer world, and its task was to develop the standards by which we came to understand and to evaluate what was beyond — it was a good and quiet university.[1]

College, of course, embraced a far smaller proportion of the student-aged population then than it does now; the great majority of Americans in the Twenties had never lived in the kind of cloister Miss Park described, and their firsthand encounters with the vulgarities and disputes of the outer world *might* have bred in them a greater realism than was manifested by the inmates of the ivied halls — but the sweeping dogmatisms, sometimes radical, usually conservative, with which "self-made men" were wont to meet the challenges of the day make me doubt this. It would seem rather that "innocence" — in the meaning Henry May has attached to the term — far from having altogether ended in the First World War, had an extraordinary persistence into the Twenties. We find it all the way across the social and political spectrum, from Warren Harding declaring that the "Spirit of '76" was counter-revolutionary ("If revolution insists upon overturning established order let other peoples make the tragic experiment. There is no place for it in America") to Michael Gold declaring that another people's experiment in revolutionary overturn had created in the Soviet Union a land where man's inhumanity to man was unknown.

Echoes of that innocent spirit ring through several of the essays included in this volume, as it does through other of the period's media. Even so disillusioning an experience as war itself could be sentimentalized; witness the first Academy Award-winning motion picture ever made, *Wings* (1928), in which well-groomed young men went off in their quaint Spad biplanes "on the high seas of heaven" (as one of that silent film's titles put it), in pursuit of the wolfishly grinning Count von Kellermann and his Flying Circus. Sometimes, such is the documentary force of cinema, the monstrousness of the war did break through; this observer found the close-ups of tanks clattering over the

[1] Rosemary Park, "Whose World?," *The Key Reporter,* XXXIII (Summer, 1968), p. 2.

trenches still genuinely terrifying. The picture also captured the ecstasy men felt in being airborne, at a time when powered flight was an experience still relatively fresh and new. But the First World War as portrayed by Richard Arlen, Buddy Rogers, Clara Bow, and even the six doom-haunted minutes onscreen of a youthful Gary Cooper, was hardly the war experienced by e. e. cummings and John Dos Passos and Ernest Hemingway, nor was it the war visually captured in films of the Thirties such as *All Quiet on the Western Front* or *Grand Illusion.* It would be all too easy for the modern reader to condescend to such testimonies from the Twenties. But innocence can also engender keenness of vision, like that of the small child who — naïvely unaware of his elders' complicated reasons for believing otherwise — insisted that the emperor really had no clothes on. Ingenuous and ill-informed the writers of the Twenties sometimes were, but at their best they could be embarrassingly observant; and they were in the habit of asking questions in a way that forced the respondent to commit himself to a "yes" or "no" rather than to take refuge in one of the seven types of ambiguity. The so-called Lost Generation seemed almost perversely aware that the phrase "There are no easy answers" can itself be the easiest of answers.

As a result they lived in a sharply polarized universe of ideas. Political controversialists of a later day, for example, except for a handful on the far Right and the nihilist Left, might have begun by affirming that democracy was a "good thing," and then disagreed passionately as to how it was to be achieved; but in the Twenties the controversy extended to the democratic principle itself. If some Americans followed John Dewey and the progressive educators in their earnest conviction that learning could be a democratic and universal enterprise, others concluded from the psychologists' tests of "innate" mental ability just then coming into vogue that some people are inherently uneducable and therefore that egalitarian democracy is a fraud.

Polarities of this extreme kind meet the investigator of the Twenties at every turn. The name of William Jennings Bryan, for example, was still a household word for millions of Americans in the Twenties, but the name of Albert Einstein had almost equal incantatory power. The jaunty hymns to sex in the springtime by e. e. cummings and the dark broodings about wounded hawks by Robinson Jeffers were equally authentic poetic expressions of the age. Both the expatriate and the Rotarian, both the founders of the American Legion and the founders of the Communist Party, both the member of the American Civil Liberties Union and the member of the Ku Klux Klan were *typical* of the spirit of those years. Small wonder that the student and teacher of American history have so often met in the lecture on the Twenties their classroom Waterloo!

If we turn to foreign commentators upon the American scene in the Twenties we find their witness as divided as our own. Isoroku

Yamamoto, the man who planned the Pearl Harbor attack, was in the United States from 1925 to 1927 as Japanese naval attaché; still earlier as a Harvard student he had hitchhiked from Boston down to Mexico. On the basis of his experiences here he later warned the students of his old Middle School in Japan: "It is a mistake to regard the Americans as luxury-loving and weak. I can tell you Americans are full of the spirit of justice, fight and adventure . . . Lindbergh's solo crossing of the Atlantic is the sort of valiant act which is normal for them" – a different assessment indeed from that of many other judges, both foreign and domestic, of the American national character. To the dismay of the busy note taker, the decade 1919–1929 perversely defies generalization.

Were the Twenties in America – or in Japan, or in France, or in Weimar Germany, or in Mussolini's Italy, or in Ramsay MacDonald's Britain, for we are dealing here with an international experience – a revolutionary epoch devoted to smashing old idols and clearing away the rubble so that men could build anew? If so, the revolution was somehow heralded in Japan by state Shinto and in the United States by Republican landslides. Or, were the Twenties instead an age of repression, marked by fear, conformism, and downright stuffiness? One then recalls the slogan of the *New Yorker* magazine, founded in 1925: "Not for the old lady from Dubuque," a strong reminder that much could be said and done in 1925 that could not have been said and done, or even imagined, in 1875.

Said and done, yes, our note taker may concede; but in what spirit? Did men and women act and work and love in the Twenties under a pall of despair – able at times to enjoy the spectacle with H. L. Mencken, collecting his specimens of Americana for the *American Mercury,* or Anita Loos, collecting specimens of another sort in her best-selling *Gentlemen Prefer Blondes* – but aware nonetheless that the world they had known before 1914 had come to an end? Newspaper critic and reporter Lewis Gannett did not remember it that way; in 1940, recalling the good times he had had in the Twenties working for *The Nation,* he wrote: "It is almost impossible to believe today that a world could ever have seemed so full of hope." Nor did John Dos Passos remember his New York nights in the Twenties with regrets: "There is a time in a man's life when every evening is a prelude," he wrote in his memoir *The Best Times* (1966). "Toward five o'clock the air begins to tingle. It's tonight if you drink enough, talk enough, walk far enough, that the train of magical events will begin." Was then the Jazz Age a joyous, optimistic era, when men believed the world was their oyster and the sky the limit? At once one thinks of *The Waste Land,* of the vogue for Spengler, and of "all the sad young men" – or, at another level in the "literary Establishment," of H. P. Lovecraft, who opened one of the horror stories he wrote during the Twenties with a paragraph that outdid Joseph Wood Krutch at his most rueful:

> The most merciful thing in all the world, I think, is the inability of the human mind to correlate all its contents. We live on a placid island of ignorance in the midst of black seas of infinity, and it was not meant that we should voyage far. The sciences, each straining in its own direction, have hitherto harmed us little; but some day the piecing together of dissociated knowledge will open up such terrifying vistas of reality, and of our frightful position therein, that we shall either go mad from the revelation or flee from the deadly light into the peace and safety of a new dark age.[2]

But the apocalyptic grimness of reflections like these is set off, in the reactions of people who lived through the Twenties, by moments of rollicksome humor. "I am glad that, however serious, we are never solemn in these essays," Harold Stearns wrote in the preface to *Civilization in the United States* (1922). ". . . it would be a humourless person indeed who could not read many of them, even when the thrusts are at himself, with that laughter which Rabelais tells us is proper to the man." On what they considered the proper occasion, critical-minded Americans in the Jazz Age could be deadly serious. When Heywood Broun, the crusading columnist for the New York *World,* learned that the last appeal for clemency for Sacco and Vanzetti had been rejected, he immediately sat down at the typewriter and rolled off a column of smoking-hot prose that shortly thereafter cost him his job. But Broun was also a member in good standing of the Thanatopsis Literary and Inside Straight Poker Club, and if he cried out in anger over Sacco and Vanzetti he also cried out with delight over Babe Ruth. In fact, when the Harold Stearns volume appeared Broun gave it an adverse review, precisely because he felt that the contributors to *Civilization in the United States* had slid downhill from seriousness into solemnity. "Lost" though the generation of the Twenties sometimes called themselves, the tone of their protests seems by comparison far less grim than that of some of their spiritual descendants.

Still, to anyone who has lived through the quarrels of more recent decades, the cries of those who were young – and not so young – in the Twenties can sound hauntingly familiar. Even so dated, so over-and-done-with a controversy of the Twenties as the one about Prohibition turns out upon examination to have a surprisingly modern sound. The moral fury aroused over the Eighteenth Amendment, pro and con, so incomprehensible to a later generation, may have become more intelligible to us since the invention of LSD. We too have discovered that people can get excited about the connection between morality and chemistry. Moreover, the Prohibition issue was connected with larger questions of social control. "Enforcement of law and obedience to law," said Calvin Coolidge apropos of the Volstead Act, "are not

[2] H. P. Lovecraft, "The Call of Cthulhu," *Weird Tales,* February, 1928.

matters of choice in this republic," a *leitmotiv* that was destined to be heard again.

It is easy enough to find evidence to substantiate the argument that the Twenties contained in embryo the portents of our own age. The literary world of the Twenties, for example, showed the same sharp divergences that one found in politics, religion, or education, ranging as it did from the radical stylistic innovations of Dos Passos and Hemingway to the old-fashioned craftsmanship of Willa Cather and Edith Wharton; but it was precisely "the complexity and depth of Jazz Age fiction," Frederick J. Hoffman concluded in a posthumously published essay, that had given to subsequent generations "the attitudes toward modern reality that it is now possible for us to take." This view of the postwar decade has been vigorously contested, most notably by Bernard De Voto in *The Literary Fallacy.* Nevertheless, and especially beyond the boundaries of formal literature, it is quite possible that in proclaiming the Twenties to have been "the true sign of beginnings in our own century" Hoffman was right.

One reason why *Middletown,* published in 1929, has come back into vogue as collateral reading in college classrooms may be that Robert and Helen Lynd reported in that book not only what a medium-sized Midwestern city was like in the Twenties but also what American society as a whole was likely to become. The automobile already exercised its tyranny over the family budget ("I'll go without food before I'll see us give up the car," declared one working-class wife in Middletown); the "realtor," that demiurge of the suburbs, was already plying his trade; and even though television was not yet on the scene the recreational pursuits of Middletonians were already "largely passive, i.e., looking at or listening to something or talking or playing cards or riding in an auto; the leisure of virtually all women and of most men over thirty is mostly spent sitting down." And as for those under thirty, and still younger, what the Lynds found out about Middletown's schools, where teachers, paid about as well as retail clerks, taught a miscellany of unrelated information quite irrelevant to "life as Middletown adults live it," suggests that in 1929 it was already possible in American cities for young people to grow up absurd. Here in 1929 was a culture which clearly foreshadowed the oncoming consumer civilization.

"We have had the alternative of humanizing the industrial city or dehumanizing the population," wrote Lewis Mumford as a contributor to Harold Stearns's compendium on *Civilization in the United States;* "so far we have dehumanized the population." Four decades later, Mumford continued his argument unbroken as he told a worried Senate Committee: "Unless human needs and human interactions and human responses are the first consideration, the city, in any valid sense, cannot be said to exist." In the same fashion, forty-five years after the publication of *Civilization in the United States,* contributors to a *Partisan*

Review symposium on "What's Happening to America?" were able to pick up the chorus without missing a beat. Our industrial cities were still inhuman, our adult population was still hopelessly implicated in the "system," and whatever grounds there were for hope in the future still lay, if anywhere, in the activities of the young.

But had it not always been so? A century ago the Boston Brahmin John Fiske was already writing that the chief difference between ancient Athens and modern America was our speed and nervous tension, and much in the national character that we are inclined to think of as new or unique in the twentieth century ("other-directedness," for example) can be found in abundance in writings on America published as long ago as the Age of Jackson – in Cooper, Tocqueville, or Harriet Martineau. Moreover, in reading essays such as the ones which comprise this volume one must constantly be on the alert for those traits of the Twenties which did not simply foreshadow what was to come. Otherwise we constrain men and women who were alive in their own day, with their own sense of immediacy and purpose, to make themselves intelligible on our terms rather than theirs. In this sense it is quite true that "history is a pack of tricks we play upon the dead," and sometimes – given the continuing presence into a much later day of citizens still usefully at work whose adult lives have also spanned the Twenties, such as Walter Lippmann, Margaret Mead, Edmund Wilson, Georgia O'Keeffe, and Jack Benny – upon the living as well.

The last of many ironies in the Twenties was the way it ended, as Clio rang down the curtain on the decade with a great Crash. We know, of course, that Coolidge prosperity was not all it seemed to be on the surface; any tenant farmer or Negro could have testified otherwise. And we know that the spirit of the times would inevitably have changed, with or without a depression; for example, there is evidence that by the end of 1928 Mencken's *American Mercury* had already lost much of its characteristic *élan*. Nevertheless, writes John Kenneth Galbraith, "Some years, like some poets and politicians and some lovely women, are singled out for fame far beyond the common lot, and 1929 was clearly such a year. Like 1066, 1776, and 1914, it is a year that everyone remembers." For twenty years afterward, as J. P. Marquand had the central character observe in his novel* *Point of No Return* (1949), otherwise reasonable people kept on discussing the details of the stock-market disaster "apparently for the same reason that old ladies enjoyed describing surgical operations and sessions with their dentists. There was a snob value in boasting of old pain." And the result was inevitable. The conflicts and anxieties of the years preceding the Crash were either repudiated, in the style of the tough young leftists of the Thirties, or they were blotted out in nostalgia. The dateline 1914, before which the world was assumed to have been relaxed, peaceful, and secure, was moved up to 1929.

Were the Twenties, then, historically not an exceptional period after all? Frederick Lewis Allen lived to confess in 1946 that he had illustrated some of the trends of the Twenties with "rather extreme, though authentic, examples of odd or excited behavior" in his classic *Only Yesterday,* noting that "one could gather just such preposterous examples of American behavior today." And Professor David Burner has recently suggested that most of the wildness we associate with the period can be localized in the single year 1919; once the special hysterias arising directly from the First World War had spent themselves, the bitter social polarities found in this country during the last days of the Wilson Administration gave place to a "deep-rooted consensus that easily outlasted the conflict of the postwar months," in a "victory for the middle elements in American life."[3] In short, then, the *zeitgeist* was exactly what Warren Harding said it was: Normalcy.

Who has the right of it here? Will the conflicts of the Twenties smooth down into consensus over the long perspective of history, as Professor Burner seems to imply? Will they appear in retrospect as signposts on a scenic but exasperating detour from the main high road of our history? Or will they be diagnosed eventually as the birthpangs of a new historical epoch, perhaps even of a planet-wide new social order? Mindful of our own generation's dictum that "the medium is the message" – which is only a new way of stating the sound old doctrine that we cannot sever content from form – I have sought answers to these questions by plunging into the most readily available to us of that period's many lively media, the files of its magazines. The results of that investigation are laid before you in this anthology.

[3] David Burner, "1919: Prelude to Normalcy," in John Braeman et. al., *Change and Continuity in Twentieth-Century America: the 1920's,* (Columbus, 1968), p. 30.

PART I

PRIVATE REALITIES AND PUBLIC MYTHS

To traverse the world men must have maps of the world. Their persistent difficulty is to secure maps on which their own need, or someone else's need, has not sketched in the coast of Bohemia. . . . For the most part we do not first see, and then define, we define first and then see. In the great blooming, buzzing confusion of the outer world we pick out what our culture has already defined for us, and we tend to perceive that which we have picked out in the form stereotyped for us by our culture.

WALTER LIPPMANN
Public Opinion (1922)

1
THUNDER ON THE LEFT

Mike Gold learned his proletarian politics in a first-hand fashion that most literary radicals of his day could not match, having dropped out of school at the age of twelve to work variously as a night porter, driver, carpenter's helper, section gang laborer, shipping clerk, office boy, and factory hand. Two sketches vividly describing his Lower East Side tenement upbringing appeared in H. L. Mencken's *American Mercury,* and the same milieu inspired his 1930 novel *Jews Without Money,* the merits of which are being rediscovered in our own time. Confirmed in his outlook by a visit to Russia in 1924, Mike Gold – unlike some of the other writers on the Left – never apostasized, continuing as an active journalistic advocate for the American Communist Party until his death in 1967.

The modern reader, in whose mind the decade 1919–1929 ends with a depression but begins with prosperity, may be surprised at the extent of America's economic dislocations in the *early* Twenties. Would a detailed historical treatment of the period – for example, Irving Bernstein's *The Lean Years: A History of the American Worker, 1920–1933* (Boston, 1960) – retroactively vindicate the judgment of Mike Gold in 1921? Were the men specifically portrayed in this essay truly representative as "human documents of the famine in America," or were they a special case? The reader must be wary of his own present-day political convictions in responding to such questions.

In any event, the magazine which first published this essay earned praise from men who totally rejected its politics. Mencken, for example, told *The Liberator's* staff they were producing "the best magazine in America," though the Baltimore Tory thought Bolshevism "chimerical and more than a little dishonest." Launched in March of 1918 by Max and Crystal Eastman, *The Liberator* was a reincarnation of *The Masses,* which the postal authorities had harassed to death for its opposition to Woodrow Wilson's war to end all wars. Like its predecessor, *The Liberator* (at least until it became a formal Communist Party organ in 1922) was a rare blend of artistic freedom and political militancy. It published stories by Sherwood Anderson, poems by e. e. cummings, drawings by George Grosz – and revolutionary greetings from Big Bill Haywood, Bela Kun, and Lenin.

THE AMERICAN FAMINE

Michael Gold

Who can understand that calamity known as unemployment? Who can understand the famine of six millions of men and women in the midst of the heaped-up riches of the richest nation in the world? Who can understand the simple fact that men go mad with hunger and women's hearts break, and children die of starvation while all around them are the opulent cities, the huge factories and bursting granaries and warehouses of our civilization?

The Russian famine is not hard to understand. Seven years of war, revolution, and the Allied blockade, aided by the mindless fury of the Sun, have combined to slay millions of innocents. It was almost inevitable. The wonder is that the whole Russian nation is not wandering up and down the gray river-banks, stark-eyed and ghastly, nibbling at dusty leaves and grass and looking to the western horizon for the help that does not come.

Yes, it is a sacred wonder that there are millions of men and women still in Russia who build locomotives and tractors, and teach the peasants, and organize vast industries for the future, and dream and work, and love, and hope, and fight under the Red Flag for the great brotherhood that shall yet descend upon this sad earth.

But who can understand the famine in America?

It is here again, this mysterious plague of unemployment that breaks out every seven years in the capitalist world. No crops have failed; no factories have burned down; no blockade has been built against us; no epidemic has swept away millions of our workers. Everything remains as it was two or three years ago, yet seven million men and women, and their dependents, must starve.

FROM *The Liberator,* IV, no. 11 (November, 1921), pp. 5-11. Reprinted by permission of Max Eastman.

The rich are holding the usual pompous conferences, and are hiring thinkers to smear the crime of unemployment over with long words and statistics. The poor are holding their conferences on every street corner and in every wind-swept park, but they seem as futile as the rich. After all, the thing has happened, and it will happen again. It is the lash of some unknown God whom we have neglected to propitiate. It is magic. It will soon pass away, and rich and poor will heave a sigh of relief and settle down as before until the next crisis.

Who can understand the recurrent crises of unemployment in America? And who can wait until the last great crisis, when the poor will be forced to see that there is no door out of their misery, but the Revolution, and the thinkers of the rich will be at the end of their palliatives?

Unemployment is nothing but poverty. It is the demonstration that working men are slaves, are wage slaves, and cannot live but at the consent of a master. During an unemployment crisis the skeleton in the closet of capitalism stalks through the land with horrible gestures. Poverty, which is meek, becomes unemployment, which is bitter and reckless, and that is why the rich discuss it, as they do not discuss poverty.

Ah! how it punctures, like a surgeon's lance, the pussy sac of capitalistic hypocrisy! They can ignore the state of the poor no longer; they can offer no more spiritual remedies, no more tonic of "Americanization," no more settlement houses or "profit-sharing" schemes. Starving men are realists, and want jobs and bread, and society while it remains competitive, will never be able to guarantee them.

In every unemployment crisis that I can remember the same flurry of relief work and unemployment schemes of liberal thinkers has rushed through the capitalist world. The present unemployment famine in America has shown the familiar symptoms of capitalist panic, inefficiency and down-right dirty thievery. All the old familiar faces have been seen. There have been the road-building propagandists, the free-lodging-house Samaritans, the Christian soup-line superintendents, the seasonal trade-standardization sharks, the federal employment agency Dr. Munyons, the high taxes howlers, the reduced freight-rate Lydia Pinkhams — all, all have given their song and dance before the footlights.

George M. Cohan says that "the American flag has saved many a bum show," but this is the bummest show in the world, and we are sick of the liberalistic and governmental performers in it. They seem so wise and serious; they burst into such epic pages of statistics; but they have never done anything to solve unemployment and they never can.

In less than ten years there will be another fierce, dreadful wave of unemployment — another American famine.

I am not a divinely-informed prophet who say this — any American workingman will give you the same information.

Yes, if a chart were made of the flow of capitalist bunk during the present emergency the curves would be found closely similar to those of the previous crises. They can do nothing — they do not wish to do anything. They have not the courage, the intelligence, or the passionate human love that can be stung to horror by the sight of seven millions of human beings starving in the midst of plenty. They are money-makers all — predatory, unscrupulous, vain, callous, money-mad, ignorant and hypocritical.

It is interesting to make up the chart of their blundering criminality in this present crisis. For months the labor newspapers had been speaking of unemployment. Workingmen knew what was happening, because it was happening to them. But the first day that it was noticed in the capitalistic press, so far as I can find, was on June 4th of this year. The Hoover Committee on Waste reported that more than a million men were out of work in free America. It also said, in passing, that between four and five million men had been jobless during January and February.

This was the prologue to the "bum" show that followed, and that is still being played on the national boards. The riot of hypocrisy that has broken loose in the six months since then! The ocean of drivel, ignorance and well-wishing folly! It has been a sordid spectacle, one fit to drive a simple, clean, honest, social-minded dog or wolf to baying at the moon.

June 6th — Department of Labor report says unemployment rose during May, and that no marked revival of business must be expected before the spring of 1922.

June 12th — The steel mills at Pittsburgh are now running at only 20 per cent of their capacity.

June 13th — The annual convention of the American Federation of Labor is about to open. Mr. Gompers outlines the major issues for the newspapers — unemployment, immigration, the open shop, railroad rates, and "the problem of Russian affairs, the cancer that is eating at the vitals of the world."

June 16th — President Hopkins of Dartmouth, in commencement address, "Urges Education to Curb Discontent." (*Tennyson and Browning for the men sleeping in the parks!*)

June 21st — From the Amherst College centennial, a headline reading: "Coolidge Urges Spiritual Values — Declares They Are the World's Only Reliance in Dealing With Present Problems."

July 3rd — The New York Times, which gives problems like unemployment half a column a week, devotes eleven eight-column pages to the Dempsey-Carpentier prize fight. *Half-a-million words!*

July 4th — The New York Times reprints the Declaration of Independence in a large ornamental box on its first page.

"We hold these truths to be self-evident, that all men were created free and equal, that they are endowed by their Creator with certain inalienable rights, that among these are Life, Liberty and the Pursuit of Happiness * * *"*

July 7th — Dr. Thomas W. Salmon tells a Senate committee that 400 ex-soldiers committed suicide in New York state in the previous year, and that most of them would be alive had they received the proper attention.

July 12th — Three hundred unemployed ex-service men in Bridgeport march on the city offices and ask for work. They get a speech.

August 5th — First news of the horrible famine in Russia. Every newspaper in America exults, crows, chortles, slobbers with glee, grows grave and moral, points the obvious lesson, that under American democracy such things could not happen.

But how about this?

August 8th — "A suicide wave has spread over the United States since the first of the year," according to Dr. Harry M. Warren, President of the Save-a-Life League. "In the first six months of this year there were no fewer than 6,509 suicides reported."

Unsettled economic conditions, with loss of employment and business failures, are blamed by Dr. Warren for the "wave."

"The League gets thousands of letters from different parts of the country telling of sorrows beyond endurance, and begging for any possible help," says Dr. Warren. "Quantities of inspirational literature which the League provides free of charge have been sent out, but more funds are needed." (*Inspirational literature for the starving unemployed father of a family about to shoot himself. Doctor, what he wants is a job!*)

August 23rd — Hundreds of American men and boys, unemployed, enlist in New York in the Spanish Foreign Legion to fight in Morocco in the shabby little imperialist war conducted by the ancient oppressor of Cuba. The men are to be paid 60 cents a day. Most of them, when interviewed by bright young reporters, divulged the fact that they did not care for fighting, were not looking for adventure, but were starving, and enlisted for the three meals a day. *(What strange brains the masters have developed in their yahoos! Men become desperate enough to kill themselves, to go to Africa to fight savage tribesmen in the desert, but they are not brave enough to stay at home and break the bonds of the rich which have condemned them to starvation. The victim shouts, "Long Live the King!" as the royal axe falls on his head.)*

August 30th — Mayor Hylan appoints a fine-looking set of civic statesmen on an Unemployment Committee to solve the great problem. John Sullivan, President of the local A. F. of L. council, is a prominent member. Splendiferous things are to be done. It is a crucial hour, says the Mayor; half a million men are out of jobs in the city, of whom 75,000 are ex-service men. Something must be done.

Sept. 1st — Bird S. Coler, of the Mayor's Committee, and Commissioner of Public Welfare, says no unemployed men need go hungry or without a place to sleep this winter. The city has provided for all.

Sept. 9th — Urbain Ledoux holds his first slave market auction of unemployed men on Boston Common.

Sept. 19th — Mayor Hylan calls on all patriotic citizens to help in the crisis, and suggests a Business Revival Week as a remedy for unemployment.

The Boston Labor Council deplored Ledoux's auction block, and asked Mayor Peters to forbid the use of the Common again.

Sept. 20th — Ledoux comes to New York and the police club and break up his meetings. President Harding announces a great unemployment conference in Washington, for which he names all the social workers, professors, bankers, mayors, business men, lawyers and labor leaders who usually go in for this form of parlor game. Gompers and Schwab are members of the pleasant, bunk-shooting party.

Sept. 21st — Forty men being given sandwiches and cake in Bryant Park by six benevolent old women are clubbed and beaten by the police, and several of the old ladies are knocked down.

Sept. 27th — Opening of the grand unemployment conference at Washington. Harding makes a speech in his best manner, filled with his usual weird, mysterious circumlocutions, his small town pomposities, bar-room nobilities, Sunday-school pieties. The high spots:

"There is always unemployment. Under the most fortunate conditions, I am told, there are one and a half millions in the United States who are not at work."

"You are not asked to solve the long controverted problems of our social system. We have builded the America of to-day on the fundamentals of economic, industrial and political life which have made us what we are and the temple requires no remaking now."

(In other words, the Conference is solemnly instructed to do nothing, since capitalism must not be tampered with in any way, and unemployment is a fundamental and necessary part of it.)

Sept. 27th — Ledoux goes to Washington with a party of unemployed to see the President. He asks Harding to publish the names of those who made more than 100 per cent profit during the war. "Mr. Harding was most kind and courteous, and listened sympathetically, but he said it was impossible to do this under the present laws." Ledoux also asked the President to issue a proclamation appealing to the generosity of the rich in help to the jobless, but the President listened sympathetically to this also, and said it would be done only as a last resort.

Sept. 28-29-30 — The Conference still meets at Washington. It still discusses the ten or twelve stock solutions of unemployment that can be found in any liberal journal, and need not be repeated here. It adjourns finally to October.

October 10th — The newspapers say that the conference may break up. Gompers threatens to resign, as he has learned the employers plan to carry through resolutions recommending the open shop and a general wage reduction as the only cure for unemployment. What was the conference called for? To solve unemployment. Who believed it would solve unemployment? The Christian Endeavor leagues, the settlement house Messiahs, the keeper of the general store at Tibb's Corners, Mr. Gompers, and about eighty millions of other faithful and newspaper-reading Americans, including the editors of the New Republic.

The American Association for Labor Legislation, the accredited mouthpiece of the most liberal elements in the country, offers a cure for unemployment as follows:

1. Federal employment agencies.
2. Great public works.
3. Regularization of industry.
4. Unemployment insurance.

But the New York Times says editorially, "a certain degree of unemployment is curative of many social disorders." And Harding says to the conference, "There has been vast unemployment before, and there will be again. There will be depression after inflation, just as surely as the tides ebb and flow, but we can mitigate, we can shorten duration, we can commit all America to relief."

Let us leave them, the sedentary swarm of politicians, uplifters, and place-seeking liberals, and go out into the open air again, where rain falls on starving men, and revolutions are made. Let the talkers mitigate, shorten duration, and commit all America to relief, while we seek the facts of life. Unemployment is not a thing in books, a matter of figures and graphic charts. It is the raw brutal terrible reality of starvation and cold and death. It is famine and desperation, and it must be felt as one feels the death of a friend if it is to be understood. The liberal intellectualistic attitude seems to be that one must not grow emotional over the social facts, but that one must study, ponder, collect data, write articles in the liberal journals and economists' reviews, read many books and attend many conferences. One must do nothing. To do anything is not a mark of serious thought. One must be genteel and restrained. One must not become what H. G. Wells calls the "Forgodsaker!"

Have any of these gentlemen ever really stood about in the freezing rain in thin rags, hungry, jobless, friendless, half-dead with worry? I have. Millions of men in this country are doing this to-day, and for them it is an emergency, not the academic problem it is for the liberals. The truth is, the college trained man who is always sure of a fair job, the minister, the lawyer, all the bourgeois thinkers, can never understand these proletarian problems as they must be understood. What the liberal movement needs in this country is what the Russian movement needed in the seventies, a return to the people. Let them get into labor unions, the factories, the mines, and the farm granges. Let them write directly to the people when they have anything to say. Upton Sinclair seems naive and full of infantile indiscretions of thought to the over-cultured, but he is the greatest propagandist in America to-day because he has always written to the masses, and not to the limited groups who read George Santayana and Thorstein Veblen.

So many fine articles, so many well-spun, well-balanced, well-informed glossy articles were written on unemployment in our liberal and radical weeklies; and then a man of simple, direct feelings appeared on the scene and did more in two weeks than the rest had done in ten years. Urbain Ledoux came and found great masses of men starving. He conceived a dramatic method of flinging their misery into the teeth of polite society, and he acted on it. His slave market was a great inspiration, and it has brought forth more fruit than could have been believed. No one will ever do anything for the unemployed until they organize themselves and force some sort of recognition from the society that tries to forget them. Ledoux saw this. His trip to the President, with his "human documents" and his demand for a list of the war profiteers was an event that rang from coast to coast as no article ever could. It was an act, and acts do something.

Ledoux is a follower of Abdul Bahai; he has many sweet, quaint, foolish metaphysical obsessions; he is an early Primitive in economics; he does not like to worry the authorities, has a deep respect for law and order, but nevertheless he is a man — a full-blooded, passionate, brave and impressive social man. And he knows the people. The American radicals can teach him economics, but he can teach them how to move the people.

"Human documents?" Yes, Ledoux is right; they are the truest books from which one can study the facts of the class struggle. One can controvert a theory, an article or a pamphlet, but who can answer the dumb eyes of a starving, jobless man? What Presidential rhetoric is there that can clothe and feed the forsaken millions, and give them friends and warmth and a human and happy place in life? What have statistics to say on a cold night to the men huddling in Bryant Park, and what message has Parsonry for the hollow bellies and aching hearts? What cheer brings Good Taste, that delicate scribe who fills the professional journals, and what east-wind nourishment are the multitudes to such from the valiant speeches that fill the congressional halls and aldermanic chambers of the nation?

Ah! liars, hypocrites, rogues, and sluggards! word-bedazzled office men and frock-coated congressional bores! wealthy pimps of the souls of men, financiers, bankers, statesmen, economists, professors, white-collared lackeys and fools! you are digging well, silly moles, at the foundations of your stately civilization. It will fall. These slow, suffering masses who drift about your cities and whom you insult, will awake some day and will rend you. Patience and ignorance are not eternal. Do not count on them forever. Justice is a pyre that must be heaped to the heavens before it bursts into flame. But O, the great leaping, red cleansing conflagration at the end; O, the holy ashes from which the Phoenix shall rise!

I went about New York for several days with Hugo Gellert, the artist, to see the human documents of the famine in America, to see the patient, ignorant men whom the rich are killing and taming in this periodical Spartan massacre of the helots. One morning we stood before a bread-line on the Bowery. The dawn had forced its way through the sullen wall of sky. There was a faint, bitter light in the city like that on drowned ships. The houses were stern and charred remnants against the sky; they were smouldering in gloom. The elevated roared by, strange dark Caliban rushing on the errands of man. All was old and bitter. Thousands of tired men and women, half-asleep and bloodless, were on their way to the factories. Wagons rattled by. It was the black, black city of New York, and before a mission of Jesus Christ, who died for Love, as Keats died for Beauty, and as Liebknecht died that there might be bread and peace in the world, three hundred men were shivering in line.

They had waited for an hour or more in the darkness and cold; they were soon to be rewarded with coffee and stale crullers. Who were they? Who make up the unemployed? Workers all; three huge ruddy lumberjacks from the Maine woods, standing proudly and somberly as dying trees; dozens of sailors, in their rough clothes; battered, emaciated factory hands, dazed old derelicts with white, unshaven chins and watery eyes; strong young men, veterans of the war, hanging their heads in shame, stokers, cooks, waiters, mechanics, farmers, drivers, clerks and longshoremen, the useful citizens of the world, the creators of wealth, the hard-handed architects of society.

They did not speak; they stood there with hands thrust deep in pockets, braced against the wind; they were dumb; each understood the other's shame; it was not necessary to say anything, one to the other. I, too, felt ashamed, as I stood and watched; for I had five dollars in my pockets, besides the certainty of a month's living.

These men had nothing.

The Bowery is a little city of the damned. It is the bottom of the whirlpool that sucks forever downward the frail boat of the wage worker. Here men come when they have failed in the economic struggle, when they have made a mis-step to one side or the other in the eternal tight-rope balancing over the precipice of hunger that is the proletarian life. Here they come when they are weakest, and seek Lethe in drink and dirt and shiftlessness. Here they come when they are sick and friendless, and need a quiet place to die.

There are 600,000 men out of work in the imperial city of New York, 75,000 of whom are veterans of the war for democracy, freedom, life, homes, wives, children, music, laughter, recreation, health, friendship — Jobs.

The Bowery is always full of homeless wanderers, but now it is crowded with these men. The unemployed swarm on every corner, and in all the missions and lousy lodging-houses, blue with pipe-smoke. We went into one of the missions that are scattered so freely under the hurtling elevated structure that mounts the Bowery. These are the missions of those who are rich and who preach humility and brotherly love to those who are poor. It was a long, bare room, with a reading table at which some men sat sleeping for the few hours before they would be turned out into the night. A smuggy, cheap shrine stood in one corner, and over the reading table was hung an American flag. A hundred men in working clothes and overalls sat about — silent and sullen. They did not speak — there is nothing to say when men are hungry. They sat and waited.

No watchful priest or attendant was about, and a drunken man had come in. He staggered about, a thick-set Swede with a raw, red face and blue, wondering babyish eyes, offering everyone a drink of rot-gut from a quart bottle. No one would take it. No one would joke with him, or answer him.

"Aw, c'm on, less all be happy," he pleaded. "C'm on, fellas, less be happy!"

But they were too hungry and sane to be happy in this way. Happiness does not come out of a bottle, nor is it found in a phrase. It will only come when men are free and creative, when they are never hungry or afraid, when the Red Flag waves over the whole wonderful earth, and there are no rich or poor.

Around Cooper Union, where the Bowery splits off into Fourth avenue, the unemployed sit on the benches under the shadow of the statue of Peter Cooper, who invented some marvelous machine or other that has reduced the burden of labor. They sit there every day and every night. They rarely speak. They sit and wait. They read old newspapers, and watch the busy people go by. They dream of nothing — they are hungry. They sit and wait.

There is the Bowery Y.M.C.A., a massive red-brick structure with hundreds of rooms and beds for those who have jobs and can pay. The unemployed flock here, too — we saw hundreds of them one night watching the free moving pictures that are provided for the starving. A handsome young bank president fights on the screen a villainous Wall Street broker for the hand of the most beautiful camel-hair-eye-browed heroine in the world. Ah, what a theme for the downcast hearts of starving men — what a banquet of comfort and joy! There was a big bulletin board in the lobby, with a bold legend chalked on it: "GOD FORGIVES AND FORGETS — WHY NOT YOU?"

A dapper little superintendent came up to us, looking at Hugo's portfolio with interest, as we were reading this masterpiece of the Christian brain.

"Ah, an artist!" he said with the ready professional smile, and he offered to shake our hands, but we turned away in contempt.

Forgive and forget!

It rained the next morning as we set out on our rounds, the city lay wrapped in a gray, weary smoke of rain. The faces of the houses were wet, the pavements underfoot were slimy as an eel, there was a chill wind that drove the rain. The damp must have penetrated through the paper-thin shoes of the homeless thousands, the wind must have cut through their greasy, wrinkled rags. Along the Bowery one saw knots of them flattened out against the walls of the damp buildings and cowering in doorways. They were still dumb – and they seemed even sadder and lonelier than yesterday; the gray wide chill solitude of the day, when there was not even the sun, and the city seemed a great cortege of mourning, oppressed these sad outcasts.

About Cooper Square they had abandoned the benches and were standing in doorways and under the sheltered entrance to the Cooper Union library. They were in the reading room, scores of them, gazing like slow-witted kine through the endless page of the meadow-wide newspapers; they did not read with intelligence, as do men of brains and perception such as ourselves, they were thinking of the coming night, when they would have to go out to find a bed and a crust somehow.

Hugo and I went to the Grand Central station where the American Land Brigade had established a farm employment bureau for ex-service men. About four hundred men had applied here daily for jobs, the papers said, and about thirty and forty a day got them. The bureau took up a great marble corridor on the west side of the station, a gigantic balcony overlooking the shuffle, the chaos, the movement and splendid excitement of the main floor of the station.

Hundreds of young men were here, all with the bronze service button in their lapels, many with the silver button that tells of heroic wounds. These were the boys who had been martyred for Wilson's ideals. These were the boys who had been roasted in a hell hotter than the insane creation imagined by the Christian priesthood. These were the boys who had shed blood for freedom. Now they stood about in beggar's rags, hungry and jobless, with the dumb, animal look that one sees everywhere in these faces. The nation that had sainted them, that had demanded the "supreme sacrifice" of them, now turned them away like mongrel dogs.

Scores of them were lying on the bare marble floor, sleeping in all this din. Others squatted about on their haunches, miserably conversing. Above them and around them was the huge, wonderful monument of American industrialism, the superb arch of ceiling, a blue sky dotted with golden stars, the great Romanesque square columns, tall as mountains, the marble floors and walls and balustrades, luxury unbounded. It was a fitting frame to their misery. It was American shallowness, putting all its ardor and idealism into steel and stone, and letting men decay. It was American hypocrisy, a gorgeous body in which beat a putrid and inhuman heart. At ten o'clock every night these veterans were put out of the marble corridor, and they too must find the crust of bread and the sleeping place somehow in the immense unfriendly city.

Scores of other ex-service men make a dwelling place these days of Bryant Park, which is a fine green square next to the wonderful Public Library at Fifth avenue and Forty-second street. Hundreds of the unemployed have made this park their rendezvous; the whole place can be seen crowded with hungry idle men every day, sprawling over the benches, sleeping on the grass, moving up and down the walks in close companionship like sheep in a storm. They have formed some sort of organization here, and have their own law-and-order committee and other representatives. Charitable men and women come here and distribute sandwiches and clothing occasionally, and Ledoux held some meetings with them, and once or twice even the men were afforded the good old lesson that the State is not the friend of the workers, and were clubbed by the police.

The cold, lustral rain that was still falling had driven all the men out of the park on this day into doorways and other shelters. Fifty of them were jammed as tightly as human beings can be jammed without adhering into a little recruiting tent on the grass. Five or six of them shivered under a beautiful marble fountain, and a bunch huddled under a noble statue of William Cullen Bryant, poet of Calm and Serenity. In the library reading rooms we found dozens of others, prowling about disconsolately, too distracted to read. The rain fell for about two hours more, and when we came out at least a hundred men were again promenading up and down the walks, for the grass and benches were still wet, and it was cold.

A group of them had gathered about a little runt of a Jew, a five-foot hobo without a collar, who had a droll, wise, shrewd face like a gargoyle's, and the most mischievous little brown eyes. The men loved him, he was their fun-maker and jester. They buffeted him about, they kicked him and slapped him affectionately and he laughed and dodged their rough blows.

"Come on, Shorty, make us a speech!" they cried.

"G'wan, I ain't the Mayor!"

"Come on, ye gotta, Shorty! Give us a speech!"

They stood him on a bench, and he grinned like a satyr, and put his hand in his old dusty coat, like a statesman.

"Ahem!" he began pompously, and the crowd rocked with glee.

Other men came running up for the fun that is the great heroic gesture of mankind in misery. Someone produced a long false beard that had been gotten God-knows-where. Another stuck his derby on Shorty, and a clean, middle-aged man, who looked like a respectable clerk, took out his precious glasses from their case and lent them to Shorty.

How they roared as they saw their favorite in this wonderful make-up! They could not contain their laughter; they slapped each other on the backs, and the tears came to their eyes.

"Give us a speech, Shorty!" they shouted.

"Gen'l'men," Shorty began, lifting a dirty hand, "attenshin. I'm goin' to undress you all on a great subjec'. Lissen; I'm a Bullshevik, and I wanta ye to vote for me, see?"

"Hooray!" the crowd roared.

"I'm goin' tuh speak on unemployments. You know what that woid means, donchyer? It means bein' a millionaire without any money, see? Well, I just come back from Washington, boys, where I seen President Harding. He wuz playin' gol-luf on his front lawn when I come up to see him, and when I told him I come from the Bryant Park boys he says he's too busy; he's only got time to see the boys from Fifth avenue. But then, when he found out that he used to buy his chewin'-tobacco from a rich uncle of mine that runs a tobacco store in Marion, Ohio, he seen me, 'cause he knew I wuz honest.

"I told him about the unemployments, and he lissened. Then he says, 'Shorty, I'm sorry to see you're hangin' out with that Bryant Park bunch. They're a bad lot, and they'll spoil ye. Ye're too good for them — "

Here the crowd hauled Shorty down with a great whoop of indignation and pummeled him amid uncontrolled laughter. Shorty dodged about like a cat; he came up on his feet every time; nothing would ever keep Shorty down for long. He was the perfect city gamin, and he was in his element here. They set him up on the bench again. He took out a few frayed green cigar store coupons and held them up between his fingers.

"Some kind gen'lmen has just given me a hundred dollars for the boys out of work," he said with a big grin. "Who'll give me another hundred?"

He read several telegrams from an old yellow pad someone handed up to him.

> Bryant Park Committee — Send a hundred boys over to Blake's restaurant for supper. Tell them to walk quietly by two and threes and make no noise. We don't like noise, especially the way they eat soup.
>
> (Signed)
>
> THE HOLY ROLLERS.

There were loud cheers.

"Another telegram, gen'l'men.

> Bryant Park Committee — Send two hundred fellers over here for a job Monday morning — seven o'clock — at the workhouse.
>
> (Signed)
>
> THE BOARD OF HEALTH.

"Yes, gen'l'men, they're doin' everything they can for us. They all got kind hearts, and some day they're goin' to give us the earth, yes, they are. An' I'm goin' to be President some day, and I'll give ye all jobs, and we'll have gol-luf parties on the White House lawn, yes, we will."

It was just fooling; it was the unconscious wisdom of the proletariat, that waits for its proper time to burst through all the shells and shams; it was Gavroche predicting the tumbrils, and they understood him, these men, though he did not know all he was saying, nor did they. The grim jests of the proletariat; they have tumbled down many a throne!

Someone said to me the other night:

"But how *do* these men live?"

I don't know; they live somehow; and many of them die.

I was coming through Union Square one night. A young fellow stepped out of a doorway and asked me for a cigarette. I gave it to him, and gave him some money, too. Then I talked with him for a moment. He was a young, clean-looking chap, with a strong, lean American face, and blue, friendly eyes in which the tears shone as he unburdened himself to me.

"God, I don't know how this'll end for me. I've been out of work four months now. Haven't eaten for two days. I can ask for a cigarette, but haven't got the nerve to ask for money. The cops would pick me up, anyway, and I'd rather starve out here than behind bars. Used to be a mechanic in the Altoona railroad shops, but there isn't a thing doin' anywhere. A thousand men for every job. I get to places at six in the morning and they're already taken, and a big mob hangin' around outside. God! it's hell! I never knew I could get so low!

"How do I live? I don't know; parks, handouts, that sort of stuff. Haven't eaten for two days now, and wuz just getting to the point where I didn't care. God, look at all those autos goin' by, hundreds of them all day. It makes me sick to look at 'em sometimes; people with money, and I don't know where I'm goin' to sleep to-night. I never knew the world could be like this!"

No one seems to know. He wrapped himself again in the obscurity of the door-way, and shivered in his lonely misery. Half a million men in the city, without friends, without women, without food and shelter, without a single one of the simple, warm, human earthy things that make Life bearable! And the city does not care. The preachers preach their sermons; the poets write their delicate lyrics; the business men sit in their fine offices, solemnly conducting the world's affairs; the politicians make fine speeches; the debutantes give their dances; the actors strut about the stages; the editorial writers ladle out words of wisdom; there is laughter, life, color, wine, wealth; the whole monstrous city moves down its primrose path, like a courtesan plying her trade in the very shadow of the cross on which the Son of Man is writhing.

How clean and brave it is in Russia! How much better to starve and die there! There no one hides the hunger of millions behind the folds of a flag! There no one feasts while his brother starves! There misery is inevitable, it is the cruelty of nature, which can be borne, not the cruelty of man to man!

And here nothing will come of it all. We will know hunger and famine again. "A certain amount of unemployment will always be with us," says the President. Over there they are working, fighting, building, striving to the last nerve to abolish hunger, to create a world out of this misery that will be fair, just and beautiful, with Life for all, even the lowest.

But here all is still dark.

2

A VOICE FOR THE SILENT MAJORITY

Far — very far! — from the Bowery scenes of Mike Gold's essay is the setting for the one which follows. It may be necessary to warn the reader in advance that this article was not intended as satire, so drastically has the reputation of its central character changed since it was written. Typical of this later assessment is Irving Stone's "Calvin Coolidge: A Study in Inertia," which appeared in Isabel Leighton's collection *The Aspirin Age* (1949). Other writers on Coolidge have expressed less personal animus toward their subject than Stone, who — typically, as a Californian — confused Coolidge's New England reserve with absence of feeling, but the general outlines of Stone's characterization have been widely accepted.

The author of the essay reprinted here, Myron Stearns, was a prolific free-lance magazine writer whose work appeared in outlets as diverse as *Harper's, Popular Mechanics, American Mercury,* and *World's Work* — but most frequently in the mass-circulation slick-paper giants: the *Saturday Evening Post, Ladies' Home Journal,* and especially *Collier's. McClure's Magazine,* which published the article reprinted here, was in the Twenties no longer the towering force it had been in the era of Theodore Roosevelt; it was in fact on the verge of expiring. Meanwhile its "muckraking" tradition had been transmuted into a benediction of America's business civilization (Ida Tarbell, for example, who in 1901 had filled many of its pages with her classic historical indictment of Standard Oil, was represented in the *McClure's* of 1925 with a laudatory serialized life of U. S. Steel's Judge Elbert Gary).

It would be easy, therefore, to pass over this article on Coolidge as commercial pandering, both by the writer and by the magazine. After all, other contemporary authors saw the man in the White House in quite another light even in his own day; one has but to think of Sinclair Lewis' meandering but highly quotable *The Man Who Knew Coolidge* (1928). Yet there may be something in this sketch of the President which the "debunkers," both in the Twenties and afterward, have missed. Transcripts of Coolidge's press conferences (see Quint and Ferrell, eds., *The Talkative President,* Amherst, 1964) suggest that Stearns' article had some ring of reality. Can it have been possible: a Coolidge with charisma?

GENTLEMEN, THE PRESIDENT!

A STUDY OF CALVIN COOLIDGE

Myron M. Stearns

The White House at Washington is not particularly conspicuous. Across a park, from the front, you can hardly see it at all. From the rear, where the ground is lower, it seems higher, beyond a low hedge and a wide stretch of lawn. It stands a little in front of the center of grounds the size of four city blocks, surrounded by fine trees. Perhaps the trees, here and there, make the tall pillars of the portico less noticeable. Across the street to the west, the great bulk of the State Department building, a relic of the wooden-gingerbread period of American architecture, rising almost from the sidewalk, is more prominent.

From the White House itself low wings have been built to the west and east, extending like long corridors across the grounds almost to the street. At the very tip of the west wing, right across the street from the big four-or-five story State Department building, the President has his offices.

There was an entirely different quality from an ordinary call in the message, "You're wanted on the phone by the White House."

FROM *McClure's Magazine,* New Series, I (June, 1925), pp. 44–56.

The black call-boy was a shade more deferential. A man within earshot looked quickly around to see who was getting the message. There is an inescapable limelight that surrounds every act, every slight contact, of the President of the United States. The prominence of his position, the potential power of his every act, makes itself felt.

Over the phone the president's Secretary, Mr. Sanders, told me to come around to the regular weekly conference with newspaper correspondents that day, and stay afterwards to talk.

There were perhaps forty newspaper men in the vestibule of the executive offices. A good many of them had canes and spats. They piled their coats and hats on the long table, on chairs, on the mantle-shelf, and made themselves familiarly at home. It occurred to me suddenly that it was through these men, Washington correspondents of their papers all over the country, that my impression of the President had come. Of necessity, they stand between the man in the White House and the rest of us at home who ordinarily have no chance to go to Washington, reporting his actions, translating his words, interpreting his often far-reaching decisions or his perhaps equally far-reaching silences.

At exactly four o'clock a door was opened and we all trooped into the President's private office.

The room is round. The carpet is green; comfortable leather lounging chairs are also green. Heavy draped hangings on the windows are still darker green. At one corner of the President's medium-sized desk stands a beautiful American flag, silk, on a standard as high as your shoulders. Mr. Coolidge stood behind the desk, with his back to the curving row of windows, waiting for the newspaper men to group themselves in a semi-circle before him. In his hand he held a thick bunch of papers.

To these correspondents it was all an old story. To me it was full of surprises.

The President was a taller man than I had expected. As tall as I am — about five feet ten. From cartoons and photographs I had gathered the impression of a man of medium height, or below. But he's not; he's above. He's a heavier man than I'd expected. The lower part of his face is quite full. Not a small man, at all. His hair is darker than I had thought it would be; in certain lights it shows the "sandy" quality often mentioned, but for the most part it seems merely light brown.

He began speaking, answering a suggestion written on one of the bunch of yellow pages he held in his hand. His voice was rather low, clear, and easy. He talked without any of the hesitation, or bitten-off sentences, that you would expect from a man who is supposed to be taciturn almost to the point of absolute silence. He spoke with easy confidence, with a smoothness that gave an impression of mastery, both of what he had to say and of how to say it. It was like a man telling his acquaintances of matters on which he happened to be thoroughly posted. He gestured from time to time as he spoke, and when he did the movements were easy, apparently unconscious, usually only with the hand, or arm below the elbow. When he came to a point where he referred to a suggested action – it was during his set-to with the Senate in the matter of the Warren appointment – as being not worth taking because it would be useful only to "put the Senate in a hole," he smiled, taking the newspaper men into his own humorous slant on the situation. He did not question the right of the Senate to criticize the action of the President of the United States; but it seemed to him that the matter of confirming the selection of his personal associates should not be made material for partisan politics. Stressing the point that this should not be made a partisan matter sounded quite reasonable. So did his other statements. When he came to the matter of calling another Disarmament Conference he spoke with the same easy reasonableness, as though world peace were a simple matter of the nations of the earth getting together and agreeing not to fight. Indeed, from first to last it was hard to find any point where one could either criticize or disagree; the handling of each matter was direct, reasonable and evidently sincere.

Before him the crowd of correspondents shifted slightly, moving from foot to foot, some raising and lowering themselves a trifle on their toes. Many were taking notes. Inside of two hours these quiet sentences would appear in headlines across the afternoon papers: "President Intends to Call Another Arms Conference," "President Will Re-Submit Warren's Name to Senate," "President Believes Cabinet Appointments Should Not Be Matter of Party Politics." At his side a short-hand reporter took down each word as it was spoken, to make sure there would be no garbling or misquoting of what was said by the "Spokesman for the White House" – for in these conferences the President is not directly quoted.

Apparently there was no mental hesitation or doubt in his mind concerning the important things he was saying so simply. It was wholly easy, natural, and confident.

By contrast the newspaper correspondents presented a far greater picture of tension. Used as they were to the situation, inured to listening to the presidential sentences, they had not the relaxed control of the man facing them in an everyday business suit, motionless except for the action of his lips and an occasional very slight rocking backwards and forwards on his toes. To me, having heard of Coolidge only at second hand, it seemed an impressive occasion, an impressive demonstration of fitness to fill a high office.

A question or two was asked, to be answered as readily as the speaking on the written notations, in an easy, simple, direct, and evidently sincere way. The man's confidence, his complete familiarity with his subject, was apparent. It was as though he was so sure of his ground that he could safely walk at random within the confines of his knowledge – even though each word might be quoted far and wide. It was quite reasonable. You felt that even though, from your own point of view, you might disagree with him, there would be always a certain reasonableness on his side – a direct method of approach and attack that would leave many people, at least, convinced, and on exactly the same grounds as he himself was convinced.

The President put the remaining papers on his desk, and nodded slightly. The interview was over. The President of the United States had spoken. The correspondents made their way out, putting their notes in their pockets. When they were gone, Mr. Sanders stepped up and introduced me to the President. His handshake was firm, but rather quick. Shaking hands, with presidents, gets to be a rather formal matter, I imagine, and Mr. Coolidge seems willing to have it over within the least possible time.

"Sit down," he said. He sat down himself, swung around in his swivel chair, crossed his legs, and leaned back. "Well," he said, "What can I do for you?"

The plan was for me to spend enough time with him to tell people about him intelligently. He seemed a little vague about it. What it would require, and what it would result in.

"The idea," I explained, "is for me to make a visit to you here, and tell what I see – just as if whoever reads about it had been here instead. How you look, and how you act, and what you do, and the way you spend your time. How the business of the office is carried on, and what life in the White House is like – possibly even a little about the way your mind works, and how you tackle a problem. Just common details, that will give people a chance to form opinions of their own, instead of having to take what *I* may think." That seemed to clear it up.

I spoke of a slight resemblance that Mr. Coolidge bore to a

man I'd met on one of the Atlantic boats a couple of years ago, an assistant of Mr. Frank Stearns, and wondered if the President happened to know him.

"Yes indeed," he said, "I know him well. Why, he's an Amherst man." And he gave the year. He knew my uncle, also an Amherst man, and gave *his* year. And still another. "Do you know," he said, "that in proportion to its size, Amherst has more men in *Who's Who* than any other college in the country?" He's kept a lot better track of his college than I have of mine, and is more interested in it. He was loath to change the subject; one idea would suggest another along the same line. It occurred to me that the action of his mind might be compared to the cutter yachts of thirty years ago, that came about slowly and seemed always loath to change their course – in sharp contrast to the later centerboard boats and "skimming-dish" models, that would spin into a new direction as easily as nothing at all.

It was hard to realize that this simple matter-of-fact man, with his quiet voice, his frequent smile, his eagerness to talk about his college or whatever else was interesting him, was the solemn Coolidge we've been told about, who is supposed to speak only in monosyllables.

"Come around in the morning," he said, "about nine o'clock, or whenever you feel like it, and we'll see if we can't fix it up. You can be in and out of the offices and get an idea of how things work."

So imagine yourself given the run, for the time being, of the President's executive offices, in the tip of the White House wing opposite the big State Department building – where decisions are made, and actions are taken, day after day, that affect your prosperity and well-being, and mine, and a hundred million more.

There was a small group of newspaper men outside the executive wing. There were two or three camera men, ready to take a snap of any notables who might be passing in or out. There was a good-natured sergeant in uniform at the door; he has seen newspaper men come and go, one after another – and presidents too. Inside the vestibule there was the desk of the rather important man who passed you further in, or kept you out, whom I hardly know how to describe except as one of the president's secretary's secretaries. He sends you in to Mr. Sanders, the President's Secretary, or calls out Mr. Clark, the president's private secretary, or possibly connects you with still another secretary. Then you get in to Mr. Sanders' office.

The President's Secretary, you realize, is a pretty important person. Don't confuse him with any idea of an ordinary secretary. Mr. Sanders was elected to Congress from Indiana in 1916. Mr. Slemp, his predecessor, is perhaps a still more striking example of "President's Secretary." He was also a member of congress, from Virginia. He graduated from college with a higher stand than any other student ever secured in the history of the institution. He is a millionaire. Steering people into the President or steering them away from him, indirectly influencing the whole course of government — the laws that govern us, the armies that defend us, our foreign relations, the taxes we pay — by assisting this contact and preventing that and smoothing out the other, means a good deal.

Mr. Sanders' office is larger than that of the President, square, finished in yellow, and with windows on two sides — one of them on the street. It connects through a corridor with the round green office of the President. On Mr. Sanders' big desk is a tall vase of beautiful roses, worthy of a bank president or motion picture magnate. On the wall opposite the desk is a large photograph of the President, carrying still further the motion picture touch, where the picture of the Big Boss usually hangs in the reception room.

The atmosphere of the big room is one of courteous hospitality. As frequently as practicable the different visitors are introduced to each other, carrying still further the impression of interest and friendliness. Many of the callers — in fact, the great majority — are elderly, gray-haired men. The list of appointments for the morning gives an idea of the scope of the vast influences of the President of the United States. It includes a bishop, several different congressmen, two senators, a foreign ambassador, a distinguished scientist, a high army officer, a financier, and the editorial writer of a Chicago paper, as well as a visiting delegation of women welfare-leaders, and a workman who is to be personally thanked by the President for some service rendered, I think in connection with the inaugural ceremonies. As the morning wears on, one or two of the appointments are canceled. A cabinet minister comes in without an appointment, asks to have a little of the President's time, gets it, and goes away. Most of the interviews are short; a few minutes up to — rarely — half an hour. At times Mr. Sanders' office has eight or ten people waiting, and there is a hum of conversation like an afternoon reception. At other times it empties, until you can hear the clock on the mantel-piece ticking in the silence. Occasionally there are conferences in whispers. They may concern matters of little moment; they may, on the other hand, touch delicate foreign relations that affect the course of nations.

I got into conversation with the visiting banker, to find out what manner of man he was. He had started in, he told me, in railroad work, and was a brakeman for several years. To-day his own boy is following almost in his footsteps, working each vacation to earn money for further study, preferring — as his father wishes it — also to make his own way. The lad's "Harvard fund" is now around $1,500. A younger brother is still a Boy Scout; the father has himself put in five years as scout-master.

If all the President's callers are as good scouts as that, he's lucky.

As the door of the corridor opens to let out departing visitors, Mr. Sanders ushers in the next man or group, introducing each one punctiliously.

Outside, in the vestibule, a crowd gathers as the morning ends. Between fifty and a hundred visitors who have been directed to the White House by their congressmen or Senators or other friends are on hand to look at and greet the most powerful man in the world. At 12:30 two doors opening directly into the President's office from the vestibule are opened and the line of visitors passes through, going in one and out of the other. Standing behind the President in his office, I again notice his height — well above that of the hand-shaker's average. The visitors pass through rapidly, to an accompaniment of "How do you do," "Glad to meet you," "How are you," or just nothing at all, from the President. There are more women than men in line, two to one. A little girl gets a longer handshake, and an extra smile. A baby on father's arm is not forgotten. When he gets old enough to understand he will be told how the President of the United States reached up and took his tiny fingers. One or two women pause long enough to deliver rapidly a carefully prepared sentence, before they are hurried along by the pressure in the line. Three schoolboys are the only ones who take a chance and look back. In all, there are seventy-eight people in line this morning. They have averaged a little more than one second apiece. The whole ceremony has taken less than two minutes.

The first morning I was in Mr. Sanders' office when the hand-shaking started, and the whole business was over and the vestibule cleared before I even found out that the thing had begun.

After the hand-shaking there is a breathing spell. In the outer office Mr. Sanders has a chance to dictate, or look over accumulated material, or get the appointment list for the following morning straightened out. In the inner office, the President has a chance to turn to his mail, the letters that have been sorted for him as being of sufficiently commanding importance to warrant taking his personal attention and the nation's time. This and other matters keep him at his desk, except for the short walk to the main body of the White House — he usually takes it outdoors — and lunch, until well into the afternoon.

At his desk, the President is almost motionless. A batch of letters is brought to him to go over. He picks up the one on top, glances through it in from three or four seconds to possibly half a minute, then makes a quick notation on it and puts it to one side. During the process his head, his body, his feet, do not move; where most people would shift in their chairs, turn their head, move about a bit, he does not. It is as though he had schooled his body to be "silent." He conserves energy, and he conserves time. Occasionally he writes longer directions across a page — two or three lines.

Signing documents takes a good deal of the President's time. There are hundreds of bills that require his signature before they are effective; when he vetoes a measure that the legislature branch of the government has passed, as was the case with the bonus bill, it is a matter of grave moment. With others, his signature means just as much. And then there are countless more of less consequence. To judge from appearances, signing things is one of the reasons for having a President.

The things to be signed — letters, bills, documents of any sort — are brought in by one of the secretaries and presented to the President. Mr. Coolidge comes to a position as definite as "present arms!" or "parade rest" — feet, knees, body, arms just so, pen already dipped in ink and waiting. The signing begins. As each "Calvin Coolidge" is finished, the secretary whisks the document from the top of the pile, and the pen hardly pauses. There is no sound in the room except the scratching of the pen, no motion except the President's hand, and the secretary's arm as it whisks the signed paper away and comes back for the next.

In a different way, it is almost an exact duplication of the hand-shaking ceremony. In each a system has been worked out that saves so many seconds apiece, so many hours a year.

Yet there is no nervous tension — no straining for speed. When the President swings his chair around to talk to you, and crosses his knees, he is at ease, comfortable, relaxed yet alert.

So much for the office.

"At dinner," the President's private secretary told me, "you will wear your dinner jacket." He took no chances.

To be sure, if you will flock with presidents, you have to wear dinner-jackets.

The White House rooms — it is hard to think of them as being under the same roof as the executive offices in the long, distant wing — are large and high. There are great oil paintings — George Washington, Martha Washington, Thomas Jefferson — and heavy curtains, and big pieces of plush furniture. Just the little party of Mr. and Mrs. Coolidge, and Mrs. Coolidge's mother, and a couple of guests, seem almost lost in the big rooms. Two dogs help make the environment less formal — Laddie Boy, the boisterous Airdale, and Rob Roy, a white collie.

The dining room is large like the rest. The table is round, with great spaces of green carpet around it, against which the white collie makes a beautiful picture. The White House servants, like the sergeants at the executive offices, in most instances "go with the place." Presidents come and presidents go, but the old darkies who help you off with your coat stay on.

Mrs. Coolidge is not quite so tall as her husband, and darker. Her hair has none of the "sandy" glint that the sun brings out in his. During the past year or so I have done a great deal of writing about schools; the work has brought me in contact with many teachers. Again and again, among the more earnest and enthusiastic and intelligent ones, I have met those who have in no small degree resembled the President's wife. As White House hostess, she takes the lead from her husband, almost as though there were a definite division of duties between them — the executive work and all pertaining to it falling to his exclusive share, while Mrs. Coolidge takes over the social side. Later, the President told me that this is in fact the case; that he leaves the White House arrangements so entirely to his wife that, except in a general way, he doesn't even know what the plans are or who the guests will be on any particular evening. On the other hand, he keeps to himself, just as definitely, the entire burden of his official duties, the nation's business and his own personal concern. Mrs. Coolidge knows no more of this work than he does of hers. At the table, he most nearly approaches the picture drawn of him as a silent man, leaving his wife, except for an occasional remark, to direct the conversation.

An excellent chowder; the President remarks on how good it is. Ham, sweet potatoes, spinach, and beets, with small home-grown rolls of the kind that my mother used to call "baking-powder biscuits." Then a green salad, excellent again, with cheese. And last, to be sure, true New England apple-pie before the small cups of coffee. A typical family-circle meal, with only the evening dress, the big room, and the fact that guests are usually, instead of only occasionally present, to differentiate it from thousands of others all over the land.

Four tall candlesticks give the table an air of distinction, the little yellow flames reflecting in points of light on the attractive jade ear-rings that Mrs. Coolidge wears. The meal is surprisingly free from formalities. The President eats rather quickly; he is through before the others. Mrs. Coolidge is a pleasant and thoughtful hostess. The servants, even, give an air of taking care of you, of looking out for your comfort rather than of strict attention to the proper form. One time, I remember, the collar of my coat was not turned over smoothly; the old doorman hurried after me to fix it before I got away.

After-dinner cigars are smoked upstairs in the President's study. Mrs. Coolidge and her mother go into another of the big rooms to listen to a radio concert. Usually the President and his guests join them in fifteen or twenty minutes; if the visitors are all men, though, friends of the President, or seeing him on any particular business, this is not the case. Then the study gradually gets bluish with smoke.

The President sits in a comfortable desk chair, tipped back, and occasionally puts his crossed feet on the corner of his desk. It is a position of easy, unconscious comfort. To me it suggests New England chairs, tipped back around the country grocery-store stove. The desk is large, with a good many books and papers on it, in piles. One big bunch of yellow papers is pasted over with newspaper clippings — one batch the general news of the day, another division the political items, another the editorial comment. Mr. Coolidge frequently passes up altogether the general news of the day — crimes and scandals and distressing accidents. He usually skims briefly through the political news and matters of international interest. The editorial comment he runs over more carefully than anything else. It is there that he finds both a running account of current events and their interpretation. The desk is not particularly orderly, as is the one in his office; it has too much on it. It suggests there are a good many things that he'd like to do, if he had the time — books he has decided to read, and so on. As in his office, a flag stands at the corner of the desk — and here there are two, the stars and stripes at one end, the President's flag at the other.

As in his office, the President talks freely, easily, without any of the marks of a silent or taciturn man. The talk runs to this and that, skimming political subjects, and glancing away again. Always he turned from one subject to another slowly, almost reluctantly; frequently, just as some one started to introduce a new topic, he would interrupt with a remark that carried farther some thought on the old one.

The talk turned to the development of children. "In the

country," he said, "the contrasts are sharper, and impressions are deeper, than in the city. Why, if a wagon came down the road when I was a boy, we noticed everything about it – what kind of wheels it had, and the horses, and the harness." And following up the same line of thought, he told of his own changing about; how he first went twelve miles away to preparatory school; then down to college; then studied law; then to Northampton; then up to Boston, in the state legislature; then governor; then to Washington, as Vice-President – until it seemed as though it were all just going to school, over and over again.

"The President of the United States" he refers to not infrequently. So does Mrs. Coolidge. Once, telling of driving an automobile to California with a full carload of family, I was asked if it wasn't pretty hard work. I admitted it was, but qualified it: "Doesn't having a good time usually mean hard work?"

"Now," said Mrs. Coolidge, "you're talking exactly like the President of the United States."

Whenever the dogs came into the room – they were usually together, egging each other on to start something – the President sternly ordered them away. They seemed to be doubtful as to whether he was absolutely in earnest or not, but ended by obeying. It was not until the third day of my acquaintance with him that I saw the reason for their hesitation – although I had guessed it before. Then, instead of ordering them away, he let them come to him, and tousled their heads, and made the white collie sit up and put up both his paws. "He's always wanting attention," the President said; "he's a regular nuisance." And he kept on petting him.

Once, the President turned to his desk during the conversation in his study, and started writing. Mr. Warren was his guest that evening, and kept on talking with me. Presently the President interrupted with a comment; he was following the conversation as closely as before. At the end of the evening he took from his pocket a note that would open certain doors for me.

"You'd better arm yourself with this," he said. He had thought ahead for my convenience. It was what he had written in the study.

The main hall on the second floor of the White House is twenty feet wide, and so long that it seems almost narrow. It has a red carpet, and at one point four or five stairs that take you to a slightly higher level. An electric elevator that works by push-buttons takes you upstairs or down. Mr. Coolidge pointed out to me the room President Lincoln used as his bedroom, and told me how, when he couldn't sleep, Lincoln had often taken a book and walked down the long hall to where his private secretary slept in the opposite corner of the house, and waked him up and read to him, sitting on the side of the bed.

The Coolidge family, when there are no guests, goes to bed rather early. The hours in the big White House are quiet hours – not like the busy ones during the day at the executive office. The President himself sleeps well, he tells me. "Though sometimes," he adds, "I wake up early, if there is a pressure of things I need to think about."

That is significant. Instead of lying awake and worrying, he wakes up early to attack additional problems.

Frequently the week-end is spent on the *Mayflower*, dropping down the Potomac Saturday afternoon, and coming back Sunday. In that case, church services are held on the boat. If the President stays in Washington, as during the time I was his guest, he goes to the First Congregational Church.

Every seat in the church is filled. Admission is only to pewholders, or by card. When the President's party comes in, at exactly 11 o'clock, the entire congregation rises, at a signal from the preacher.

It is a big, oblong room, this main body of the church, with a square-cut gallery along three sides – just such a plain, unornamented hall as my own father used to preach in, in New England forty years ago. The form of service, the music, the hymns, the announcements, all sound as familiar to me as during my boyhood. There is a big bouquet in front of the pulpit, red flowers mixed with yellows of different shades, and white, like a mammoth edition of one of the old-fashioned farm nosegays. The sermon is a plain, homely talk that takes for granted the religious verities and assumptions on which it is based. The singing of the choir, the playing of the organ, are also plain, rather pleasing, rather unfinished performances – music such as I again recall from the nineties. The responsive reading is a bit rapid, following words rather than meaning. It is impossible for me to avoid running over, in my mind, the circumstances that have allowed me, gradually, in a different part of the country, to drift away from this particular form of worship, and in the end question even many details of the creed itself. Obviously, the President has never chanced into such circumstances. He sits with an arm extended along the back of the pew, thoroughly at home.

On Sunday afternoon Mr. Coolidge talked with me steadily, for four hours – from three until seven. During that time he did most of the talking. Not continuously, to be sure, but as any conversation might run on, with pauses before another addition to the subject, and sometimes slightly longer gaps before a new topic came up. We went back to the days of Greece and Rome, and forward to speculate on the future of the race. During the first three quarters of an hour or so the President was sitting in an ordinary kitchen chair, knees crossed, while a New York sculptor gave corrective touches to a bust that had been brought to the finishing stages from a photograph. During that time the conversation was in measure three-cornered, although Mr. Baker was largely concentrated on his work. Afterwards the President took me for a walk of nearly three miles, and then we came back and talked an hour or two.

Here we have, apparently, a complete contradiction. A man with a reputation for silence such as no man in public life ever possessed, and a perfect willingness to talk freely, easily, for hours at a time. I believe the explanation lies in two things.

First, Mr. Coolidge, at times, "withdraws" into silence almost as a turtle draws back into his shell. I noticed a little of this at the table, and occasionally in his office. Much more marked instances, of course, have come to me second-hand. One story tells of a bet made between two men, one of whom was to sit next to the President at a large dinner, that he would not say three words during the entire meal. Towards the end of the evening, getting desperate because Mr. Coolidge had not yet spoken at all, the man next him told of the bet, ending: "He bet ten dollars you wouldn't say three words, but I bet you would." Mr. Coolidge, according to the story, considered the matter for some moments, then turned a little towards his companion. "You lose," he said. Two words. I take it the President doesn't feel it is worth while, on such occasions, to make the necessary effort to start a conversation; the smaller conventions get little attention from him, and "small talk" is the last thing you can imagine him bothering about. Or possibly under special circumstances certain small inhibitions become stronger, and do not seem worth overcoming until there is a more compelling purpose to be achieved. The second thing we talked about. The President told me that the newspaper men and other writers he had met were, as a whole, a fine crowd. But to make a story, to draw a picture, they might take some point and develop it, like cartoonists.

"Take economy," said the President. I forget whether the subject came up that Sunday afternoon, or during one of the talks in his office. "Saving money is never popular. If you go in for an economy program, you're almost sure to be held up as a penny-pincher. But it's necessary. Waste just creeps into government. It's easy to run along and just leave it there. It's easy to run an extravagant government. It's lots harder to run an economical one."

As we left the White House two secret service men, in plain clothes, slipped into their overcoats and unostentatiously followed us, a few steps behind. At street crossings, they came up on each side of us, and the four of us waited for a gap in the automobile traffic, just as anybody else would. When the street had been crossed they'd drop behind again. Ocacasionally some one recognized the President, and he would bow or lift his hat; but for the most part even those who passed close to us didn't notice him. Although it was a chilly day, he wore neither gloves nor overcoat, walking with a short, brisk step, and keeping his hands clasped behind him.

"Walking is about as good exercise as you can get," he explained to me later, when we were talking about his mechanical horse and how the story of it happened to get out. "And it takes less time than anything else. Of course, I'd like to ride a horse, but to do that, or play golf, means changing your clothes when you go out and when you come back. If I just walk, I'm getting the exercise I want as soon as I get outside the door, and in fifteen or twenty minutes I can be back and get to work again, feeling a lot better. Sometimes I simply walk around the White House grounds."

At one time the subject of government forestry, on which I had been doing some writing, came up, and I referred to the total area — 157 odd million acres. The President, without questioning my figure, was a little hesitant to accept it.

"I thought it was around a hundred and eighty million," he explained. He was right, at that. The gross area is more than 182,000,000. I had subtracted the amount of privately-owned land within the forest borders.

Once or twice, while talking, I ran against what seemed to me to be strong prejudices. In particular these came up in connection with certain men. Sometimes for, sometimes against. In one case I argued about it a little, but felt as though I had come against something that couldn't be attacked, any more than a phase of religion. Perhaps I was wrong. At any rate, on other things the President's mind seemed to work clearly, easily, accurately.

One other thing requires mention. Repeatedly at and near the White House, I came in contact with those whom the President has chosen to assist him in his work of administrating the government of the United States. He seems to lean towards the type that he represents himself — simple, direct, and extremely able, even if sometimes within certain circumscribed areas. Obviously, he has mastered the great art of organizing brain-power, man-power, effectively. He secures results that would be perhaps impossible for other men by choosing the men he needs, and then putting behind them his own faith, his own simple reliance, his own unwillingness to change, his own outstanding loyalty.

His power is almost unthinkable. When the selection of a new attorney-general came up, the whole matter of law enforcement and justice, our own respect for the government, our own attitude, and that of others towards us, and towards our lives and property, was involved. Matters of taxation, of economy, of tariff, touch the pockets of each of us. Five hundred million dollars annually is spent by the Army and Navy Departments for national defense, to protect us from possible foes; how is that expenditure made — wisely, or foolishly? It is the President, through his selection of the Secretaries of the Army and Navy, and shaping the policies they are to pursue, who, largely, decides. When we commute to the city, when we mail or receive a letter, when we pay the freight on a shipment of household goods, when we tour through the national parks or camp in national forests, we come in contact with the work of the Department of Commerce, or the Department of the Interior, or the Department of Agriculture — all directly affected and guided by the President himself.

He must know about telegraph and telephone and radio and railroads and commission men and motion picture censors, as well as about the government forests, and water power, and everyday morality. Through the State Department our entire future, our relation with other powers, our foreign policy, the likelihood of war or the possibility of peace, is at stake. Read, if you will, any of the messages that President Coolidge has sent to Congress, and see how much is involved — and, incidentally, how complete is the grasp which this quiet man has of his subject.

A kindly man, I found Calvin Coolidge, and considerate. Friendly, and easy to talk to — at least, it seems to me, for any one of similar heritage, understanding the same environment and its results. Above all, a competent man who can cooperate with able assistants, securing with them results that more spectacular men might never achieve. Able to come to the great work of government simply. Able to put a full day's work into every day without fuss or feathers. Accepting the doctrine of human fallibility, keeping himself free from worry and fit for work, attacking the involved and intricate matters of administration directly, with a quiet mind, a step at a time and the nearest one first. Possessing two, at least, of the attributes of true greatness — he is a simple man, and sincere.

3
THE COLOSSUS OF WILLOW RUN

The Germans, as usual, had a word for it: *Fordismus.* If you visited Rome, said a Soviet journalist, you called on the Pope; if you visited America, you went out to the Ford plant at Willow Run. With loving piety the widely read *American Magazine* for August, 1929, published a homily entitled "Henry Ford Talks to Young Men," and Aldous Huxley made the benighted inmates of his *Brave New World* pray to "Our Ford." More soberly Daniel Snowman, in a study of *America Since 1920* (New York, 1968), acknowledged that "As the first great mass-producer of automobiles, Ford might be said to have done more than any other person to alter out of recognition the society into which he had been born."

Arthur Pound, in the article reprinted here, did not so much "muckrake" or "debunk" Henry Ford and the Ford Motor Company as try to contain these phenomena within believable limits – both economic and human. Like other writers represented in this collection, Pound had a newspaper background. Two years prior to his essay on Ford, he wrote a series of papers for the *Atlantic*, collected in 1922 as *The Iron Man in Industry,* which introduced some readers for the first time to the sociological problem we now call "automation." After the Great Crash of 1929 Pound published other books on business enterprise, as well as poetry, a novel, and biographies (e.g., *Johnson of the Mohawks,* 1930). He was state historian of New York from 1940 to 1944.

When this article appeared in its pages, the *Atlantic Monthly* was enjoying rejuvenation. After a disastrous plunge in circulation in 1897 it had shown that capacity for self-renewal which persists in cold roast Boston, to the nation's and that city's own surprise. Ellery Sedgwick, its editor from 1909 to 1938, was independent enough of the Establishment prejudices of the *Atlantic's* hometown to print Felix Frankfurter's vindication of Sacco and Vanzetti, and to publish Ernest Hemingway's short story "Fifty Grand" after virtually every other leading American editor had turned it down. By 1930 James Truslow Adams would be attacking in an *Atlantic Monthly* article one of the magazine's own heroes and fathers, Ralph Waldo Emerson.

THE FORD MYTH

Arthur Pound

I

In a newspaper morgue the envelope filed under 'Ford, Henry' bulks larger than that devoted to any other private citizen. That measures his importance, for news is the breath of our communicating civilization. In that mass of clippings, the most significant is this: —

> WHITE SULPHUR SPRINGS, W. VA., *Sept. 27.* — In addressing the National Tax Association here to-day, Representative William R. Green, Republican, Iowa, declared that the present system of corporate taxation presents an easy way of avoiding taxation, adding that he did not believe the American people would permit this state of affairs to continue indefinitely. Mr. Green said Henry Ford was popularly supposed to have the largest income of any citizen in the country, and that while no one knows what income tax Ford pays, it is certain that it cannot be at all in proportion to his income.

Here begins an irrepressible conflict that will be news for many years to come. A member of Congress, ranking Republican on the revenue-hunting Ways and Means Committee and slated for the Chairmanship since Fordney's retirement, has talked to a serious audience of practical men about the Ford fortune. Let Mr. Ford laugh that off if he can; let him enlarge as he pleases upon wealth as a means to service, jobs, and enterprise. Nevertheless the talk will go on. Presently it will be heard in Congress, where the debate will centre, not upon whether the Ford fortune should be scotched, but whether it should be scotched as corporate profits, as income, or

FROM *The Atlantic Monthly,* CXXXIII (January, 1924), pp. 41–9.

as inheritance. Years hence treasury experts will still have the Ford fortune in mind while adjusting their tax brackets. This prospect should be enough to disqualify Henry Ford as a presidential possibility. He and the Government mean enough to each other already.

The Iowa Representative's speech reflects the beginning of a change, slight but meaningful, in the public attitude toward Mr. Ford and his possessions. Representatives seldom come by such trenchant ideas through sheer ratiocination. Instead, they pluck them out of street-corner conversations and general-store debates. Iowans must have been discussing the Ford fortune before Mr. Green mentioned it at White Sulphur Springs.

The latest estimate of the Ford wealth is $750,000,000. The assets of the Ford Motor Company, owned entirely by Mr. Ford and his son Edsel, were more than $536,000,000 last February. Since May the company has done the best business in its history, the cash item rising from $159,000,000 to more than $200,000,000 between February and May. Its domestic production of cars and trucks reached one new 'high' in the week ending August 7, and another in the week ending September 25, when production amounted to 41,769 cars and trucks and 1857 tractors. From January 1 to October 18, it produced 1,500,696 cars and trucks – almost as many as all other American manufacturers combined.

But domestic production of cars, trucks, and tractors is not the only source of the Ford wealth. There are Ford companies producing under other flags. Also, Mr. Ford owns all, or substantial parts, of companies that sell coal and transportation. The bulk of his property is in the Ford Motor Company. In the twelve months ending February 28, 1923, the company earned more than $119,000,000, after deducting $34,000,000 for taxes. This is 22 per cent on the $536,000,000 investment covered by the statement. In the current year the Fords are accumulating wealth at a rate close to $400,000 a day, or $150,000,000 a year. As corporate net income, moreover, this profit pays only 12½ per cent Federal tax. By leaving this profit in the corporation, instead of taking it out in dividends, the two Fords save at least 50 per cent additional tax that they would have to pay if the same sum were distributed as individual income to stockholders.

If Henry and Edsel Ford are not the richest father and son in America today, they soon will be. The enormous profits which Henry Ford ploughs back into the business, the pace at which he is extending his control of raw materials and his domination of supplies, his growing interest in water-powers and transportation, his exuberant health and zest for expansion, the morale of his labor forces and the competence of his technical staff, these predicate Ford production and profits beyond anything on record in American industry.

Great fortunes are usually accompanied by great expenditures, either for display or philanthropy. The Ford fortune is neither threatened by the one nor curtailed by the other. Mr. Ford has too much sense to play the rôle of a Croesus. Perhaps because he is too interested in life and work to know what ennui is, he has acquired none of the expensive habits of the rich. His favorite recreation is motor-camping with a few cronies. He spends less than many a wealthy unfortunate who keeps up appearances with a racing stable, an ocean-going yacht, and sundry houses strategically located with regard to the seasons and the social whirl. Just as Mr. Ford has no ambition to shine as a pillar of the turf, so likewise Mrs. Ford reveals no ambition to rank as a pillar of society.

Philanthropy does not retard materially the bulbous growth of the Ford fortune. The Fords may indulge in many quiet benefactions; and no doubt they meet the levies laid upon them in various drives, like other well-to-do citizens whose names and ratings are down in the books of their local charity organizations. But the public gifts of Henry Ford are small and few in proportion to his huge earnings. He built a hospital in Detroit — to date that is his chief contribution to the public-service plant of the city where he made his money. Derided as a 'pay-as-you-enter' hospital because it is self-sustaining, it nevertheless provides excellent hospital service at rates the average man can afford to pay. His purchases for public use of two literary shrines — John Burroughs's birthplace and Longfellow's 'Wayside Inn' — are graceful and pleasant acts; but not expensive when measured by the Ford ability to pay. He helps to support the Wild-Life-Protection Fund of the New York Zoölogical Society. Multiply the cost of these benefactions by ten and you would still be short of the Rockefeller or Carnegie gifts to public causes.

Unless Mr. Ford changes a deep-seated conviction, this situation is not likely to change. In *My Life and Work* he goes on record against charity and philanthropy. Also, he doubts the value of professional social service. Come what may, Henry Ford is unlikely to deluge the land with libraries, save heathen from hookworm, or provide palatial quarters for college undergraduates. Prominent solicitors often return from Dearborn with this message: 'We must wait till Edsel gets it.' There is no hint as yet that the Ford wealth is troubling the Ford conscience or burdening the Ford spirit.

Thus far Mr. Ford's rise to riches distresses few of us. No one abuses Henry Ford simply because he is rich; 'soap-boxers' do not rail against him and the radical press does not gird at him, as they rail and gird at many men of lesser wealth. His critics are mostly of two sorts: financiers and Jews — to Ford they seem to be one and the same. Neither group objects to his wealth and power, but merely to his talk. The common people extend a blanket blessing on all his works, in marked contrast to the hostility with which they have viewed other of the unco rich since the muckraking days of twenty years ago.

There are solid grounds for this approval, as well as mythical ones. Ford rose from commonplaceness 'on his own.' He 'stuck by the shop' when lesser industrialists fled from close touch with production and its human problems. He has raised wages, avoided strikes, and earned a reputation as a good boss — and good bosses are pearls of great price in industrial society. His company led in changing the 'automobile game' into the automotive industry — a dignified and solid business with substantial sales-depots, dependable service, and responsible managers.

But above all else Ford provided 'folks' with cheap motor-cars. When the automobile attacked America, the small producer needed the new means of transportation in order to hold his own in the world; otherwise he must inevitably have fallen back in competition with better-equipped forces. If there were no cheap cars to-day, American farmers would be well on their way to peasant consciousness.

These achievements, and the apparent ease of their execution sans special privilege, monopoly, or control of natural resources, have created a mass opinion that Henry Ford is a miracle man, a wonder-worker. To a complicated industry he brought a pioneer spirit which the sons and grandsons of pioneers were bound to respect. Fearless as any master scientist, this mechanic of genius, who seems to know tools and men equally well, carried mechanical production to its modern uttermost in devices that save time and drudgery. These aids to automatic production have their drawbacks, social and physical, but they obviously produce cheap goods, and by degrees they increase leisure for the masses.

Finally 'this man Ford,' as the first families of Detroit used to speak of him when he was on his way up, is scornful of many things, worthy and unworthy, that the common man scorns and to which the well-to-do defer at least in attitude. He scoffs at learning that has no earning power, at influence that is based only on affluence, at history, art, and many of those finer graces of life which, even in a democracy, as yet mean little to the masses. This plutocrat, sprung from the people, remains a rebel, conscious that much is wrong with the times, the world, and the country. In his own town he played a lone hand, refusing to sit in with the business oligarchy which, there as elsewhere in industrial communities, is the real seat of power. Bankers continued to be his pet aversion long after he became a banker himself. The American people could keep hold of such a man in spirit; could even, brooding upon him mystically, make him the central figure of a myth. In a world that daily became more of a puzzle for simple minds, here was a man of the people who could 'beat the big game.' Better than any man of his generation Henry Ford came to personify the dynamic democracy of naïve America.

Countless farmers think that, with Muscle Shoals in Ford's possession on easy terms, they would get cheap fertilizer on easy terms. Hard-pressed folk fancy that he could give them the benefits of cheap money without any of its disadvantages. Oil operators shiver at the thought of Ford going into oil in the present debilitated condition of that industry. Millions of wage-earners think that they are being abused because their employers do not meet the Ford scale of pay. There are shippers all over the country who imagine that Ford could give them cheaper railroad rates by reorganizing the country's railroad system, as easily as he reorganized the Detroit, Toledo and Ironton. To all these, Henry Ford is the good fairy to whom nothing is impossible.

Recently an Albany newspaper carried a story that illustrates neatly the power of the Ford myth. Its readers were assured that city and State officials were lying in wait for a certain exalted person, to impress upon him the necessity of having the Hudson River deepened at government expense. Once the sympathies of this worthy were enlisted, the United States simply could not refuse millions for improvements which would make their cities ocean ports. The citizens had visions of shiploads of Troy collars and Albany aspirin being loaded at their wharves for cities on the seven seas. And who was the personage to be waited upon thus humbly? You expect the answer, 'Henry Ford.' Not so; no such luck. Mr.

Leibold, if you please, the secretary to the great man. Thus does the hero's reflected glory elevate the underling. Convert Mr. Leibold, and Mr. Leibold can convert Mr. Ford, and Mr. Ford can convert the Board of Army Engineers and the Committee on Appropriations and whoever else needs to be converted. Presumably the meeting came off properly, because Mr. Ford, who incidentally owns a factory and water-power at Green Island, recently advised the Government to proceed with the improvement. If it does, Green Island will be conveniently near the head of navigation.

It is easy enough to pick holes in the Ford myth. Instead of rising singlehanded to success, Mr. Ford had the devoted aid of a group of notable men in the Ford Motor Company's early years. One of them, a master advertiser, made Ford 'first-page news' by exploiting his 'five-dollar-a-day profit-sharing plan' in 1914. Another laid the foundation of a system of office administration that remains a marvel of business efficiency long after his departure. There are dozens of 'Ford alumni,' as Dean Marquis calls them, filling high positions in the business world, whose contributions to the Ford Motor Company's success must have been large. Of course, these men grew under Ford; yet no doubt Ford grew also because of those associations. Nevertheless the semi-autobiographical story of Ford's business rise contains no mention of them. Mr. Ford does not share authority; neither does he share the limelight.

A good deal of Mr. Ford's popularity on Main Street and Mill Street are due to his open dislike for Wall Street. Clashes between industrialists and financiers are common enough in industrial society to suggest incompatibility between those who deal in goods and those who deal in credits. In the new industry of automobile-making, this temperamental conflict between innovating and conservative forces was bound to crop out, and did so, not only in Mr. Ford's case but in the cases of other manufacturers whose vision ran ahead of their resources. But with Ford the prejudice has hardened into an obsession, persisting unabated after he has become a money power in his own right, loaning millions to the city of Detroit with a nonchalance that contrasts oddly with the ceremony that attends Wall Street operations.

The attack goes on even after Wall Street has surrendered, hailing Ford 'comrade' with as much brotherly feeling as the spokesmen of that somewhat inhibited section can muster. The *Wall Street Journal* recently called him, in admiration that is almost affection, 'Wall Street's Shock-Absorber.' There is reality in the phrase. Ford advocates openly ideas that Wall Street loves but, out of deference to public opinion, is constrained to keep in the background. When Ford says that labor unions are excellent devices for killing time, Wall Street chuckles. When Ford says that the Interstate Commerce Commission should be discarded, Wall Street beams. When Ford put forth his Muscle Shoals offer, Wall Street gasped at its sheer audacity. It reminded the old-timers of Jay Gould at his best. When Mr. Ford gets to hammering Wall Street, and then goes on to hammering international bankers and Jews indiscriminately, he reminds one of AE's Irish orator who was forever trying to bring up a large family of words on a small income of ideas.

III

Neither Mr. Ford nor his most enthusiastic admirers mention the most important factor in the extraordinary Ford success — the market. America at the opening of the twentieth century was the net result of political and economic influences ancient in origin and mixed in effect. Centuries of enterprise, thrift, labor, invention, political struggle, and legal interpretation — to say nothing of several wars — had to be lived through before this continent was ripe for the automobile. Before Ford cars could become as common as autumn leaves there had to be pipelines and railroads; and before these could come to pass there had to be Scotch inventors, Dutch bankers, Indian fighters, Pilgrims, conquistadors, feudal barons, Crusaders, martyrs, and all manner of other energetic, Westernizing persons, century without end. No Rockefeller; no Ford. No Stephenson; no Ford. No Caesar; no Ford!

One result of the travail of all these centuries was a rich country of distributed wealth and eager-minded inhabitants, politically well-organized, called the United States of America. A land of magnificent distances and rich natural resources, populated by persons hungry for new means of transportation and prepared to pay spot cash. Europe had steel and laboratories and capital and able mechanics; yet Europe could not develop cheap automobiles, for lack of enough buyers to support quantity production. The past prepared the stage for Henry Ford; and if he had not undertaken to satisfy the American appetite for cheap cars when he did, someone else would have done so in short order. When our most notable beneficiary of history scoffs at history, practitioners of that noble art can afford to smile sagely, as Tacitus might have smiled at the struttings of a barbarian king.

True believers in the Ford myth overlook, also, the luck of the Ford success. The man has been lucky as well as shrewd. He was lucky when his 'six' failed to attract the public, and he was driven back to the small car. He was lucky when W. C. Durant could not quite raise in cash the relatively few millions for which Mr. Ford stood ready to sell him the Ford Company in the early days of the industry, when Mr. Durant was amalgamating the General Motors Company. Ford was lucky again when the upward swing of the business cycle enabled his dealers to dispose of the goods he dumped upon them when, as he says in *My Life and Work,* he dug assets out of his factory rather than borrow money. This shifting of part of his debt burden to his dealers might have seriously embarrassed the wide-flung Ford sales-organization; actually it did its members good rather than harm. Yet no mind, however shrewd, could have foretold that the upward swing of the business cycle was so near at hand. Luck again.

Ford was even lucky in his one defeat, when he ran for the Senate in 1918, and was beaten by a few thousand votes in a campaign where his opponents used too much money. The motor king scored a moral victory, and was spared the tedium — for him torture — of sitting in the Senate. Ford is lucky in anything that lets him concentrate on the job which he so completely masters, and unlucky when he wanders into other mazy passages of this intricate experience we call life. Edison knows his Ford, Couzens knows his Ford.

The public may never outgrow the Ford myth entirely, but Mr. Ford himself outgrows it little by little, a piece here and a piece there. He seems to have outlived the Messianic mood, in which he felt 'called' to evangelize a sinful world even though at great expense.

This phase ended with the Peace-Ship fiasco. He admits now that the Peace Ship taught him a good deal about war. Except for tilting against international bankers (always unidentified), Mr. Ford no longer concerns himself greatly over international affairs.

Lately he has been growing in humor and also in insight into his own character. The Wood interview in *Collier's Weekly* is one of the most revealing of all Ford's many utterances. That and the Crowther book[1] give Ford's view of Ford better than all secondhand

[1] *My Life and Work,* by Henry Ford in collaboration with Samuel Crowther. New York: Doubleday Page & Company. 1923.

expositions. In the former our richest man says he is unfit for the presidency 'because he lacks a political mind.'

There are other equally good reasons why Henry Ford should never be President, but that is enough. Intelligent dictators do excellently well in business everywhere, and in European politics they seem to be quite the fashion just now; but hereabouts we still believe in checks and balances, constitutional rights and democratic processes, and other like intangibles which Mr. Ford, in order to secure efficiency in government, would have to shear away along with the red tape he so cordially detests. Therefore he says the country could not stomach him except in an emergency.

The moral is obvious. There is no present crisis equal to the penalty. Even the sale of that steam plant down in Alabama can hardly be magnified into a convincing emergency. Our politicians, if they value their places, will take care to avoid, for a few years to come, anything that savors of an emergency. Upon them the Ford boom serves notice: —

> 'N' Henry Ford 'll get you if you don't watch out.

IV

Economically, Ford is building something new in America, a self-contained business for practical purposes, personally owned, that has the strength and solidity of a vertical trust without its legal complications. It controls raw materials, manufacturing processes, and marketing in ever growing degree. Merely for self-protection it must continue to unify control until it approximates complete production from ores to automobiles. Whereas vertical trusts are usually consolidations of corporations drawn together for mutual support and protection, the Ford Motor Company is reaching the same end by purchase and development. When the process is completed, the company will stand, from the standpoint of industrial security and efficiency, in a class by itself in America, and rivaled in Europe only by Krupps.

It will not do to dismiss this achievement as transitory. It constitutes a notable contribution to the industrial strength of the country. Moreover, it is likely to last as long as any business unit of our time. I cannot imagine any sort of civilized America, under any kind of political and economic régime whatsoever, that could or would dispense with the flexible transportation that the motor-car provides. The industry will always be noticeably sensitive to the ups and downs of general trade, but its quick recovery from the post-war depression showed strong recuperative power. And the low-priced market, of course, is the most dependable. There may be revolutionary changes in design and means of propulsion. It is not to be expected that the Ford Company will ever break new ground in those directions; but presumably it will take up proved betterments in time to save its position, as it did in the case of the self-starter.

Finally, even if chronic pessimists on the automotive industry should be proved right by events, it does not follow that the Ford Motor Company would be ruined. The Ford Company is to-day a complex of industries, a vast machine-shop and assembly plant, with pendent chemical, metallurgical, mining, hydro-electric, forest, and textile activities. There will always be demand for coal, pig iron, wire, machined parts, wood, glass, acids, cloth, and electrical energy. The Fords produce all those things now, and can go on producing them, whether they are sold as automobiles and tractors or in some other form. The change would be costly, but not necessarily fatal. There is a tremendous vitality in broadly based industrial enterprises. Krupps grew great making munitions of war; but it did not perish when that market was cut off by fiat. Instead of quitting, it began beating its cannon metal into locomotives and other peace goods. Industry is the indispensable, 'key' activity of modern life.

Henry Ford, busy in his huge new plant at River Rouge, provides the unique spectacle of a man occupying his own monument. It is one likely to outwear many a graven pillar and may even outlast some political principles held sacrosanct at the moment.

This is not saying that the Ford Motor Company will continue indefinitely its present terrific pace of expansion. Every business is the measure of the man at the top, and every business tends to become stiff with age. Still, Henry Ford presumably has at least ten active years ahead of him, and he has given his company a momentum that will not be lost until long after he departs, even though it may not be fortunate enough to find his like as a leader. And ten years of wealth-accumulation, at the present rate of growth, would make Ford thrice a billionaire, with an income of more than a million dollars a day.

Therefore the Ford fortune and the Ford policies have important social bearings. Are the Fords to become merely another rich American family, following the usual course of our plutocracy from shirtsleeves to polo, and from cookstoves to coronets, in three generations? Is the Ford business destined to be merely another big business which, founded by an original individual with spirited if somewhat narrow ideas of public service, is destined to degenerate into an impersonal, profit-taking machine, amid the growing indifference of its employees and the waning regard of a disillusioned public?

These are questions that time alone can answer. But inasmuch as Mr. Ford has expressed himself emphatically upon some of the determining principles of his life, we may deduce, perhaps, whither he is driving by setting down the directions in which he appears determined not to be driven. The conclusions, of course, are purely speculative; there is always the chance that Henry Ford will do the unexpected. Still, sixty years and ten times as many millions are not conducive to vagaries.

V

The professed aims of Henry Ford's existence are to pay high wages and sell goods cheap. You might think an employer could easily avoid profits by so doing; but Mr. Ford does not agree. Every time he has lowered prices, he has tapped another layer of buyers and increased his sales. Whenever he has raised wages, he has increased efficiency of production. His volume is now so enormous that he could sell cars at close to cost and still reap large profits from the sale of parts only. So the manufacturing and merchandising policies which Henry Ford approves are no more likely to keep his fortune from growing than is philanthropy, which he disapproves.

Mr. Ford's explanation of his so-called 'profit-sharing' plan leaves me unconvinced. His men get high wages, part of which is listed as profits; but that there is any general disbursal of company profits on a grand scale to rank-and-file workers is not apparent. At least, the sums divided so far have not kept the Ford fortune from 'snowballing.'

At the time this profit-sharing plan was put through, great expectations were raised that the Ford Motor Company was destined to break new ground in the troubled sphere of industrial relations — great expectations never yet realized! They who believe that industrial difficulties cannot be solved altogether through authority; they who think that the wage system should be amended to allow the routine worker more voice in his destiny; they who give to the word 'coöperation' a humanitarian and spiritual emphasis — all these altruists are sadly disappointed in Henry Ford. Undeniably fair in his dealings with Labor, undeniably sage in discussing the practical psychology of toil, undeniably wise in his later policy of decentralizing production, still he does not grasp that in these latter years Labor has come by something it values above houses and gear and raiment — to wit: a vision of self-sufficiency, the promise of a new day when the Fords of this earth shall do Labor's bidding, not Labor theirs. Mr. Ford is deaf, dumb, and blind to the labor movement and all its implications. He is a benevolent despot, standing firm against collective bargaining in all forms; an autocrat who would be as unapproachable to a shop committee as he is, notoriously, to process-servers.

Yet Henry Ford has given the labor unions something they greatly needed — competition in well-doing. On a grand scale he has demonstrated that the way to beat unions is to do more for one's workers than the unions can win for them. The Ford organization is to-day an industrial clan. Its members are widely scattered in space and social position, and subject to all the myriad differences that make against solidarity in the human family. Nevertheless they are with the company and with its boss, in spirit. Critics, whether of high or low estate, have been sloughed off or shoved out, sometimes ruthlessly. Those who remain seem to be Ford's men in the sense that the Gregara were The MacGregor's men — come weal, come woe.

That morale is Henry Ford's best achievement. But in so far as this clan spirit is a reaction to the personality of a leader, it is likely to fade after the leader passes, unless it can be stabilized by definite concessions to coöperation in the forward-looking sense of the word. Perhaps any such contribution to the solution of industry's central problem is beyond him; perhaps he does not care to try. At any rate, he says nothing to show that this matter is on his mind, and plenty to indicate that it is not. The chances are that the thing will not be done.

When the Ford score is finally cast up, the prospect is, therefore, that this extraordinary man, for all his originality and excellent intentions, will be found to have added to our social scheme merely another swollen fortune and another big business unit. In that event, the fortune inevitably will come to be appraised, rightly or wrongly, as evidence of gluttonous appetite, a tainted hoard to be raided, upon need or envy, by an embarrassed or jealous State.

The business, by reason of its size and social importance, will become in time one more battle-ground for unionism, one more target for state control, one more argument for Socialism. Henry Ford is a superman who has ploughed a straight, deep furrow through the crust of custom; but another generation may reap stranger crops there than Ford ever dreamed he was planting.

Mr. Green of Iowa, for the moment personifying the sovereign State in its unending struggle with too masterful individuals, pointed an accusing finger at Mr. Ford one mild September day. The incident passed without much comment. Few noted the challenging gesture, as few mark the turn o' the tide. Yet the turn is as inevitable as the tide itself. This challenge, too, was inevitable, and registers, unless all signs fail, the high-water mark of popular favor for Ford. Now, unless the man be great beyond his words and works, the ebb is on.

4

AN APOLOGY FOR URBAN POLITICS

"Some of the perturbed Methodist clergymen in the South opposed to [Alfred E.] Smith's nomination" for President, wrote Charles Willis Thompson in *The Commonweal* for May 30, 1928, "unconsciously revealed what really moved them most profoundly . . . when they said he was 'New York minded.'" Later in that campaign year Thompson published in the *Catholic World* the article that follows, explaining the political institution which had nurtured Smith, an institution which to outlanders had always seemed a particularly fearsome creation of New York minded men.

Charles Willis Thompson had scored his first major newspaper beat in 1900 during the Boxer Rebellion when he learned that an Allied Expeditionary Force was marching on Peking, but his principal forte was domestic political reporting. He worked for the New York *World* and for the *Times* before turning free lance in 1922. As a New Yorker, as a Republican, and as a Catholic convert (in 1927), Thompson enjoyed an unusual perspective from which to view the activities of Manhattan's Democratic party machine. (Father James M. Gillis, who edited the *Catholic World* when this article appeared in its pages, was an early and perceptive opponent of both the Italian Fascist and the Nazi regimes, who later became also a vehement critic of the New Deal, the United Nations, and President Roosevelt and his family; *Commonweal* in 1955 described him as "a kind of ecclesiastical Robert Taft.")

Apart from questions of partisanship on the part either of Thompson or of his editor, how well does this assessment of Tammany in the Twenties stand the test of history? "Smith and Olvany and Walker are not the sort of leaders who are complacent in the presence of corruption," Thompson wrote in 1928, when Jimmy Walker — complacent to a degree matched only by Warren Harding — had already been Mayor of New York for three years. Walker's precipitous downfall in 1932, and the victory of Fiorello H. LaGuardia in the next mayoralty election, suggest that city WASPs and out-of-town bumpkins were not the only types who mistrusted the Tammany Wigwam. On the other hand, to judge a political organization *primarily* by the presence or absence of corruption may be to ask the wrong question. An earlier Tammany sachem, George Washington Plunkitt, had argued that in the long run the Republic might be less well served by civil-service reformers than by men who frankly "seen their opportunities, and took 'em."

THE TAMMANY MONSTER

Charles Willis Thompson

For the past three months my daughter and her husband have been hitch-hiking through the South and West. Everywhere they have been received with that friendly hospitality which is always ridiculously styled "Southern hospitality" or "Western hospitality" or some other kind of hospitality, according to the particular region the braggarts of their own good manners happen to hail from. The fact that the two wanderers come from New York always excites interest, and their kindly hosts ask them many questions about that alien congeries of cities; and high in the list is the invariable desire to have the visitors explain that mysterious and dreadful enigma, Tammany.

"Tammany and Wall Street are the same thing, aren't they?" is a question they have encountered over and over again in Iowa, Nebraska, Oklahoma, Kansas, and to some extent elsewhere.

That question gives a fair picture of the delusion about Tammany which exists in the minds of so many Americans. It is not a political organization; it is an ogre, a force for unimaginable evil; there is something about it indefinable, and hardly human. "Something troglodytic, shall we say?" as the puzzled lawyer ruminated in trying to account for the strange horror that possessed him at the sight of Mr. Hyde.

New York, to them, is the lair of obscene and extra-natural combinations of the literal hosts of hell. Another of these is Wall

FROM *The Catholic World,* CXXVIII (October, 1928), pp. 1-9. Reprinted by permission of the editor of *The Catholic World.*

Street, which is not a place of business but the witches' cave in which foul creatures plot ways to rob, magically, peaceful homes in the West and South. Long years of political denunciation of "Wall Street" and "Tammany" in those regions have resulted in an unconscious visualization, crystallization, incarnation, of these subterranean and malign Manhattan horrors; they have assumed an almost tangible shape in the imagination. As Wall Street reaches out in the night across thousands of miles to filch the sleeping farmer's wallet from under his pillow, so Tammany devours, in its filthy New York den, the virtue of boys and girls, and is this year reaching out hungrily for more victims. "Shall we guide his gory fingers where our helpless children play?" the question of eighty years ago, recurs again.

There are plenty who know better than this, but who imagine Tammany to be a political machine corrupt above all others, which after robbing New York for nearly one hundred and forty years is now seeking to control the Federal Government so that it can extend its robberies over the whole nation. They imagine it exists only for larceny and graft. They would scorn to be associated with the less informed farmers who ask, "Tammany and Wall Street are the same thing, aren't they?" but there is no reason for their scorn; they are in the same boat. Between believing that "Tammany" is an ogre, and believing that any city could be governed for one hundred and thirty-nine years by thieves, there is no intellectual difference whatever.

Men have a habit of personifying everything evil, and everything good. They personify the Reign of Terror by calling it "Robespierre" and heaping all its horrors on his head, though in fact Robespierre was not the fiercest of the Terrorists and was overthrown and killed by the more ruthless element. And when they think of corruption in politics, they embody it and call the monster "Tammany."

Its ill fame has reached across the ocean, and "Tammany" is the only American political organization which has become a part of the language; and of more than one language. Guglielmo Ferrero, the Italian historian, seeking to explain — to Romans, mind you — the nature of political organizations in Julius Caesar's day, simplifies it so they can grasp it; he explains that Caesar had a Tammany organization, and the Italians understand at once. Joseph McCabe, the British freethinker, is explaining Spanish politics to his readers, and wishes to find a word for *caciquismo* which every Briton will understand; so he says that *caciquismo* means the same thing as Tammany, and the English get the idea on the spot.

So fixed in popular "thought" is this personification of all political evils in "Tammany" that it is no longer necessary to use any adjectives; the word Tammany is enough; say that the villain you have in mind belongs to Tammany, and you have said all the hard things you need; you do not have to say "corrupt" or "wicked." Recently I read in the New York *Herald Tribune* a letter arguing that Governor Smith is not the favorite son of New York State, because New York has always voted against him. This seems surprising, but the writer explains; it has always voted against him except for a part of the State that need not be considered, that part lying south of Westchester County, because that section is "Tammany-controlled." It is not, therefore, to be counted at all; it is to be dismissed as not a part of the State. The letter writer seriously believes that the seven millions in the counties of New York, Queens, Kings, Richmond, and Bronx, which comprise the city, slavishly cast their votes as they are ordered by the spider in Manhattan, and submit joyfully to its larcenous rule. This writer is a New Yorker; the delusion exists even there, where any man who uses his eyes knows differently.

Actually, there is no such thing as Tammany. There is a Tammany Society, whose headquarters are in the building called Tammany Hall; but it is not a political organization. The thing people have in mind when they speak of "Tammany" is the Democratic organization of the County of New York, one of the five counties comprising the city. It is not an organization of masters and slaves, or of grafters and dupes; it is an organization like that in any other city, consisting of the enrolled voters of the party, good and bad, wise and foolish, rich and poor. It includes doctors and ministers, merchants and peddlers, bankers and laborers, settlement workers and immigrants, housewives and stenographers, saleswomen and women of fashion. Those who vote its ticket are a large majority of the millions who comprise the five counties in the City of New York.

How does it happen that since the year 1789 the greatest city in the country has submitted to — and rejoiced in — a government which for all that time has robbed it? Are there none of its residents who do not enjoy being robbed; none of its ministers, lawyers, teachers, workingmen, musicians, shopkeepers, engineers, truck farmers, who prefer honest government; or has an honest minority remained a minority for one hundred and thirty-nine years? And if the latter, how has civilization continued to exist there all that time? Crime did rule a city once, San Francisco; but in a few years a vigilance committee put a stop to it; if it had not, civilization would have perished there. Such things as the permanent rule of crime do not happen; never did.

Every large city is ruled by a machine. The word machine sounds sinister. What that word means, however, is the organization of a political party. Every political party has to be organized, like every other association from a debating club to a revival meeting. In each city there are honest and dishonest men, and so there are honest and dishonest men in each machine. When, in any city, the dishonest men get control of the machine for a time, it is said to be a crooked machine. "Tammany," whose real name is the New York Democratic organization, has sometimes been controlled by dishonest men and sometimes by honest ones; like the organizations in other cities. It has sometimes been as bad as others; sometimes worse; sometimes better; and so has the machine in every city in the land.

There were two periods in which Tammany was worse than any other machine except that of Philadelphia. Even this record was subsequently exceeded in Chicago, San Francisco and Terre Haute, but in these two periods Tammany stood almost alone in infamy. One was the time when Tweed was its first boss; the other was the time when Richard Croker was its third boss. It is an article of popular faith that Tammany has always been ruled by a boss, but it never was until 1866. Fernando Wood had come fairly near to being a boss, but never got to be more than the foremost figure among a group of leaders. The word "boss" was applied to Tweed because he ruled the machine and was the first man to do so; and he was a thief. The gang of bandits he controlled robbed the city for five years, and then were overthrown; for no city enjoys being robbed, in spite of the insistent delusion that New York has been an exception to that rule for one hundred and thirty-nine years.

Tweed fell in 1871, and the machine passed into the hands of John Kelly. The popular delusion is that Tammany has controlled the supine city all these years, but for the fifteen years of Kelly's rule it did not. The Democratic majority in New York was so large that there were several Democratic parties, the leading one being the County Democracy, with Tammany ranking second, Irving Hall third, and some flea-bite Democratic parties making nominations every year so as to sandbag an office or two out of one of the bigger organizations. The Republican Party, in those years, was too small and too contemptible morally to be considered at all.

Kelly, one of those who overthrew Tweed, was an honest man.

There were scandals during his fifteen years, but they were not Tammany's scandals. Of the Mayors elected, Ely, Wickham and Edson, though not Tammany men, recognized Tammany; Grace, Cooper and Hewitt were anti-Tammany Mayors, out and out. The worst scandal occurred in the closing days of Edson's administration, when the "Boodle Board of Aldermen" sold Broadway to Jake Sharp. When this franchise was being offered for sale by the boodlers, Boss Kelly sent orders to the few Tammany Aldermen that they must vote against the steal; and they did. The Republican and County Democracy Aldermen voted for it. That was Kelly's only connection with any scandal. A year and a half later he died.

He was succeeded in 1886 by Richard Croker, who organized graft into a system. He and his gang did not rob the treasury as Tweed did, but levied tribute on legitimate business, vice, crime, and amusements, and grew rich. It was, in my opinion, a vastly worse government than Tweed's, and it lasted longer. One revolt threw Croker out of power in 1894, but three years later he came back from Ireland, whither he had run at the approach of the storm, and resumed his bandit rule with more ferocity and rapacity than before; evidently seeing that the end was near and he must make hay while the sun shone. He had four years of unrestricted plunder; then he fell, and immediately decamped to Ireland to spend the rest of his life there. He had ruled the city, except for a three-year interregnum, for fifteen years. This was the worst spot in New York's municipal record; Tweed's five-year term of brazen theft was far less disgusting.

Murphy, who succeeded Croker, ruled longer than any other of Tammany's four bosses — twenty-two years. Under him Tammany gradually turned away into other paths. It figured in no scandals. Murphy's ideals may not have been very high at the beginning, but as he grew older he came to have a strong distaste for crookedness and repressed it wherever it showed its head; and from the first days of his bosship he had never encouraged it.

To succeed him a Judge named Olvany was taken from the bench. But to call Olvany a boss is merely to call him an official leader; he is just such a boss as Hiram Johnson is in California, as Murray Crane was in Massachusetts, as Thomas Taggart is in Indiana. The city of New York has been well governed, as compared with other cities.

In the thirty years that have seen the fall of Croker and the change in Tammany toward the honesty of his predecessor, Kelly, Philadelphia has been ruled by the Hog Combine, Dave Martin,

Israel Durham, the Gas Ring, Jim McNichol, Edwin H. Vare, and now William S. Vare. Its worst years were those under Mayor Ashbridge, whose effrontery outfaced Tweed's; though Mayor Smith was subsequently indicted for profiting by the importation of hired assassins to murder his opponents. The indictment languished, for Smith had nothing to do, himself, with this purchase of murder. There has been no variation in Philadelphia, as there has been in New York, in the character of the machine government. The morality of the machine has differed, but seemingly only according to the varieties in the characters of the several bosses who have run it. It gives a much better government under William S. Vare than it did under any of his predecessors; there have been no scandals under his rule.

In the same time San Francisco, after a period of execrable rule at the hands of its machine, reached its high point by sending Boss Ruef to the penitentiary. Terre Haute presented the country with the unique spectacle of a government which was entirely corrupt from top to bottom; and Canton broke another record by an alliance between government and the criminal classes which made the similar alliance under Croker seem quite amateurish. Chicago had one corrupt machine after another, with frequent intervals of decency, and at present rejoices in government by gangsters through its machine; it is ruled jointly by the Crowe machine and the Scarface Als. Indiana's officials, from Governor down, are filling up the jails. In all this time there has been no major scandal in New York; and no minor scandal that is chargeable to the Tammany organization.

And yet some Methodists of Little Rock, Arkansas, in bolting the nomination of Governor Smith, base their desertion of the Democratic Party largely on the ground that Tammany is "the rottenest den of political infamy that ever existed on American soil." It is not; it is an organization of all the Democrats of New York, who resemble other Democratic and Republican communities in being composed of the high-minded and the base; of men and women "most remarkable like you." Sometimes, as in San Francisco under Ruef, in Philadelphia under Ashbridge, in Indiana under its recent Governors, the base have got the upper hand in Tammany, and Tweed and Croker have ruled most vilely. Sometimes, as in Chicago under Brennan's brief sway, there has been an honest leader; and Kelly has compelled his men to stand firm against corruption in the great scandal of the time. Again, as in — but no, there is no exact parallel elsewhere for this — such a high-minded man as Smith has become the dominant figure, and has won for it the support of independents and reformers of all parties; a support they demonstrate yearly at the polls.

It is quite true that in this campaign the Republican newspapers have taken as a war-cry the phrase, "It is the same old Tammany," as corrupt as it was in 1871 and 1894. New York Republican journals are telling the uninformed West and South that there is no "new Tammany;" and there is not, if by a "new Tammany" is meant an organization composed entirely of virtuous men. It is, indeed, the same old Tammany; that is, it is the same old composite, like all other party organizations. This time, however, it is run by Smith and Olvany, not by Tweed and Croker, and there is a difference. The Republican Party did not become villainous when its rogues got the upper hand, under the Presidencies of Grant and Harding; nor did it become unanimously holy when its head was Roosevelt.

However, the argument is made that this year there are scandals in Tammany Hall. There are, as always happens in every city government, some grafters in office; and Tammany is rooting them out and cleaning them up, not because Tammany has become a band of reformers, but because Smith and Olvany and Walker are not the sort of leaders who are complacent in the presence of corruption. What these newspapers conceal from their readers in the West and South is that every one of these grafters has been exposed or prosecuted by "Tammany" officials; that among the leaders in the work of finding them out was a Health Commissioner named Harris; that their chief pursuer is a Commissioner of Accounts named Higgins; that the prosecutor of the Queens County grafters is a District Attorney named Newcombe.

I use the word "Tammany" here because that is the word always used by the newspapers making the charge. The fact is that each of the five counties which comprise New York City has its own independent organization. "Tammany," which is only a nickname derived from the fact that is official headquarters are in the building bearing that name, is the organization in New York County, one of the five. Admittedly the distinction is not acute in the case of Bronx County, which is a Tammany annex. But the organizations in Brooklyn and Queens are baronages which merely acknowledge the hegemony of Tammany and reserve their own rights. Brooklyn, under McCarren's leadership, held Tammany at arms' length and often compelled its submission; McCooey has been more placable, but only because under him Brooklyn gets what it wants. And the Queens organization, where the principal scandals have occurred, is not only not a part of Tammany but is antagonistic to it, and has been fighting Tammany for several years. So, when I call Newcombe a "Tammany" man I am not literal; he is a member of the Queens organization. But it is the word the Republican newspapers use in throwing dust in the eyes of the West and South; and, since they tell their credulous Methodist allies in Little Rock and elsewhere that the Connolly grafters are "the same old Tammany," as if all officeholders in the five counties were appointed by Tammany, I have to make my meaning clear by using the same word; if Connolly, the machine boss, is a "Tammany" man, then the District Attorney is one, too, having been elected by the same organization.

It goes a little further than that, though. Newcombe is, in fact, doing Tammany's work and realizing her hopes when he prosecutes the Queens grafters, and so, if anybody in Queens is to be labeled "Tammany," he deserves the name more than Boss Connolly (who has been indicted with Tammany's enthusiastic approval) does. Three years ago Tammany was obliged to put a rival organization in the field in Queens to fight Connolly at the Democratic primaries. It is rather comic to find Tammany saddled with the opprobrium of grafting done by the hostile Queens machine.

There is, of course, a great deal of insincerity in this banging and tom-tomming about "Tammany"; at least as much insincerity as honest ignorance. Those who wish to vote for Hoover for other reasons find it much easier to give the pretended reason, as ex-Senator Owen of Oklahoma did, that they "cannot stand Tammany"; it sounds rather heroic and very virtuous, and conveys the same meaning as "I cannot stand vice and crime." And so, if Smith were a Methodist, the bolting Methodists of Little Rock might not be saying that they have to bolt because Tammany is "the rottenest den of political infamy that ever existed on American soil."

Four years ago Mr. Owen could "stand Tammany." He could stand it so easily that he visited Governor Smith and asked him to turn Tammany's support over to him, Owen, when Smith's own nomination was seen to be impossible. The reporters were curious to find out what revelation had enlightened Mr. Owen about the "infamy" of Tammany in four years; and he referred them to a book by M. R. Werner entitled *Tammany Hall.* This book is being made use of to spread throughout the country the false belief that Tammany is, and always has been since 1789, "the rottenest den of political infamy that ever existed on American soil"; and no impartial person can read it without coming to the conviction that it was written and published for the purpose of spreading that false belief, and spreading it in the interest of the Republican Party.

This book, which is playing a part in this campaign, is cunningly and craftily written. It inculcates the belief that for one hundred and thirty-nine years Tammany's record has been uniform; that its first boss was Aaron Burr, "the first great grafter of a century ago," and that there has been a monotonous procession of piratical leaders leading the same pirate crew, down to and including Murphy. It is evidently designed for that great majority of the electorate which knows nothing of American history, for Burr was exactly as much a grafter as Hamilton or Jefferson; and not he but Tweed was the first boss of Tammany Hall. From this initial deception the author continues, weaving his web by suppression here, misrepresentation there, and exaggeration elsewhere, until the impression produced at the end of his book is one of horror that such infamies could have continued uninterruptedly in one city for one hundred and thirty-nine years. The book was brought out on the eve of the campaign, for a purpose sufficiently obvious; and that purpose is being carried out by the Republican Party despite Mr. Hoover's own earnest desire that this contest shall be fought honestly and without maligning his opponents.

The record of Tammany, rotten as it was under Tweed and Croker, is better on the whole than that of most other machines. It has even been positively, not relatively, better than the others during the period following Croker's flight; the twenty-two years of Murphy's leadership and the four years of Olvany's. It is in those twenty-six years that Philadelphia has suffered under Ashbridge, Durham, and the Gas Ring; that Chicago has progressed from the intolerable rule of Lundin and Thompson to government by the professionally criminal classes; that San Francisco has had to rise and send Boss Ruef to prison; that the city government of Terre Haute has gone to jail, that the criminal government of Canton has ruled by murder, that from Governor down Indiana has been administered by corruptionists. And in those twenty-six years there have been no scandals in New York, except the inevitable graftings of minor officials who have been caught and ousted by Tammany.

A charge often made, and now being used in the South and West, is that Tammany has "betrayed" every Democratic Presidential candidate. It has never betrayed one. The charge rests on the fact that Republican Presidents have carried the city. They have carried it because independent voters are probably more numerous in New York City than in most other cities. The popular conception of Tammany being that of a superhuman force of evil, it is supposed to carry the unresisting votes of the New York millions in its sulphurous pocket and cast them where it wills; but it does no such thing. The "Tammany" voters — that is, the majority of New York voters — vote as they please, and the organization can dictate their votes no more than any other organization can; much less effectively than Vare's machine in Philadelphia can, for instance. The only other conceivable foundation for the charge is that Kelly, half a century ago, was violently against the nominations of Tilden and Cleveland, and sulked in his tent for a while after those nominations, pretty much as ex-Governor Lowden did this year after the defeat of the farm relief program — and of his own nomination — by the Republicans at Kansas City.

What is the reason for singling out Tammany as worse than all other organizations in politics; as being something preternaturally powerful and diabolical, "something troglodytic, shall we say?" The constitution of men's minds is such that they must personify everything, political corruption included, and Tammany is a much more mouth-filling word than "the Democratic organization" of New York or any other city. It conjures up a creature having a physical structure and shape. "Imagination bodies forth the forms of thngs unknown." The word Tammany, to one seeking to incorporate and incarnate political corruption, "gives to airy nothing a local habitation and a name."

There is, too, in the mind's eye of the West and South, something alien in this sinister creature of the fancy. It is pictured as papist and priest-ridden. There are many who, when they speak of a "Catholic priest," do not think of him as a minister of God; they think of him as a cunning heeler scheming to carry out the orders of a Machiavellian political machine located in Rome and possessing superhuman knowledge of the smallest details of what goes on in every hamlet hereabouts. Tammany seems to them to be one of the agencies of this foreign political machine, always at work trying to undermine and overthrow the peace of humble and inoffensive communities in this and all other countries. By joining this mental picture of the crafty, scheming, political priest with that of the slimy monster from the pit called "Tammany," you can get at the state of mind of those who really think Governor Smith's defeat is a duty enjoined by God, and not properly a political matter at all.

Tammany — the Democratic organization of New York County — consists of Catholics, Protestants, Jews and infidels. Its District Attorney, Mr. Banton, is so good a Protestant that he sometimes occupies a pulpit; many of its leading officials and office-holders, including judges, are Protestants and Jews. Catholics in New York are mostly "Tammany men" — that is, Democrats — just as in

Philadelphia they are mostly members of the Vare Republican machine.

It is, however, curious to remember that in the beginning Tammany was not only a non-Catholic but practically an anti-Catholic organization. It was as nearly the home of "native Americanism" as any organization was in those days, before Maria Monkism and Know-Nothingism had excited passions which till then were sleeping. A hundred years ago the Tammany men were called Bucktails, and Fitz-Greene Halleck wrote his admirable song beginning:

> "There's a barrel of porter in Tammany Hall,
> And the Bucktails are swigging it all the night long."

It was something of an honor to belong to Tammany, if you were a Democrat. With the increase in immigration the Irish became powerful enough to change the Hall's attitude toward them; but so late as Tweed's time the ruling powers, including Tweed himself, were still native American and Protestant. Kelly, who died in 1886, was the first boss who was a Catholic. Not until 1888 did Tammany elect a Catholic Mayor. Since then it has nominated for Mayor four Catholics, four Protestants, and one Jew. However, in Nast's immensely influential cartoons he always depicted the Tammany voter as an Irish thug and criminal. That horrible bravo with the brute face and the pug nose, the shillelah and the whiskey bottle, is "Tammany" today in many a mind; and this though Nast's cartoons are unknown to most of those who visualize the creature.

To sum the argument up: For one hundred and thirty-nine years the chief city of the Union has been governed by thieves, has been bled white, has been robbed daily by its rulers, "a lying, perjured, rum-soaked and libidinous lot," to quote Dr. Parkhurst's famous sermon. And it has not been ruined. Constant robbery has not annoyed or offended it, and strange to say has not made it poor. On the contrary, it has prospered materially, and its average morality is at least the equal of that in pure bailiwicks like Chicago and Philadelphia. Generation after generation has been born, grown up, died, and given way to another, each in succession to be pitilessly milked and mulcted, each to be ruled incessantly and monotonously by the same "lying, perjured, rum-soaked and libidinous lot," directing their baleful activities from "the rottenest den of political infamy that ever existed on American soil." And the city still exists, still grows rich, though it has been their unresisting prey for one hundred and thirty-nine rapacious years.

PART II

". . .BUT SOME ARE MORE EQUAL THAN OTHERS"

'I have never yet met a man,' said Cardinal O'Connell, 'who understood in the least what Einstein is driving at.' No doubt His Eminence, searching his archi-episcopal province, might have found one in Cambridge, or even on Beacon Hill, but in South Boston, to which he may be presumed to have confined it, he did well to give it up as hopeless. Here I do not sniff at the South Boston mind: it is simply the ordinary mind of the human race. That mind is almost as resistant to knowledge as the most recalcitrant fire-clay.

H. L. MENCKEN
Treatise on the Gods (1930; rev. ed. 1946)

5

"IF YOU'RE BLACK, GO BACK"

"The yokels vote for the Hon. Mr. Balderdash," wrote H. L. Mencken in 1922, "not because they admire him, but because their only choice is between him and the Hon. James Bosh." Afro-Americans, from long years of viewing white America's political quarrels essentially as outside spectators, have often concurred. The NAACP's official journal *The Crisis: A Record of the Darker Races,* founded in 1910 and ably edited from that date until 1934 by W. E. Burghardt Du Bois, did take time out in 1924 from its task of chronicling the progress and plight of black Americans to endorse Robert M. La Follette for President; four years later, however, Du Bois declared: "It is certain that either Herbert Hoover or Al Smith is going to be elected President of the United States, and in our humble opinion, it does not matter a tinker's damn which of these gentlemen succeeds."

One political victory of 1928, Du Bois conceded, mattered a great deal: that of Oscar DePriest in the First Illinois Congressional District. Born in Alabama and educated in Kansas, DePriest had moved to Chicago in 1889, where he was elected to the Cook County Board of Commissioners and to the Chicago City Council. In 1928 he was a delegate to the Republican National Convention, and his election to the U. S. House of Representatives that year made DePriest the first Negro ever to sit in Congress from the North. Such was the background for a pleasant minor social event early in the Hoover Administration — and for the extraordinary reaction that followed. The sampling reprinted here may profitably be compared with press responses to similar encounters in other periods; that of Booker T. Washington and Theodore

Roosevelt in 1901, for example, or of Eartha Kitt and Lady Bird Johnson in 1967.

Congressman DePriest was returned to office in 1930 and 1932, surviving the downfall both of the Republican city machine in Chicago and of the Hoover regime in Washington. A casualty of the massive shift in Negro voting from the Republican to the Democratic party during the New Deal, he was defeated for reelection in 1934 by a black Democrat, and the First Congressional District of Illinois has ever since remained a black Democratic stronghold. Meanwhile Oscar DePriest remained active in Chicago Republican politics; he was a delegate to the 1936 GOP national convention, and in 1943 he was again elected a Chicago alderman.

Mrs. DePriest Drinks Tea

W. E. Burghardt Du Bois

Most of the facts in the following article are known to the public. The comment and reactions, however, have been partially concealed. For the sake of historical accuracy, and to the astonishment of our descendants, we are publishing the following article.

THE FACTS

Mrs. Oscar DePriest was a teacher of music before she was married. The DePriests have been married thirty-two years and have had two children: One son was drowned; the second, is married, and has a son.

Mrs. Hoover, the wife of the President, had been giving a series of teas to the wives of the members of both Houses of Congress during the extra session. She asked Mrs. DePriest by formal written invitation to attend a tea, at which were present the wives of the Secretary of War and the Attorney General, the niece of a Senator from Ohio, and the wives of Representatives from Pennsylvania, Indiana and Ohio. Mrs. DePriest said afterward: "I met a group of charming ladies. It was a most delightful afternoon."

These are the facts and they have been disputed only in one

FROM *The Crisis*, XXXVI (September, 1929). Reprinted with the permission of The Crisis Publishing Company.

case: The Tampa, Florida, *Life* declares that Mrs. DePriest "was never invited." That the affair was "informal and on the lawn," and that Mrs. DePriest "remained at the outer edge of the gathering where Negro servants were present. . . . She was not recognized by Mrs. Hoover or any of the ladies present on a social plane with the guests." This is, of course, a lie out of whole cloth similar to the apocryphal stories of Booker Washington's dinner, and done for Southern consumption. It is but one illustration of the extraordinary reaction which this tea has had over the country.

Two incidents followed the tea: The National Association for the Advancement of Colored People held a public musicale in Washington, to which Mr. DePriest invited his fellow Congressmen. At Cleveland during the annual meeting of the National Association, Mr. DePriest made some plain statements concerning the situation: he called the white Southerners "cowards and hypocrites"; he declared that he would take every right of a Congressman from the Congressional Barber Shop to tea at the White House; and that he would vote no appropriation to enforce the 18th Amendment until something was done to enforce the 14th and 15th.

THE REACTIONS

Let us now note the reaction of the nation.

First, certain prominent Southerners hasten to comment on the tea: Pat Harrison called the incident "as deplorable as it is astounding!" Senator Sheppard of Texas regarded the tea as "a step fraught with infinite danger to our white civilization." Congressman Green of Florida declared that "the social consciousness" of Americans was outraged, and promised not to attend any social functions at the White House or dine at the Congressional restaurant. Senator Simmons of North Carolina, who supported Hoover, regarded the affair as "exceedingly unfortunate," while Senator Overman, his colleague, said it was a "great blow to the social stability of the South."

Bishop DuBose of the Methodist Church, South, thinks the tea "has deliberately wrecked the fairest chance that has come to the nation in the past one hundred years."

Several Southern legislatures which were in session immediately took up the matter. The Florida House of Representatives declared the entertaining of Mrs. DePriest "both shameful and disgraceful, and if persisted in, will destroy the prestige of the Anglo-Saxon race." The Mississippi legislature condemned "unreservedly the tea as tending to destroy . . . racial integrity." Texas passed a resolution which the Governor signed explaining that he disapproved the tea but would not criticize Mrs. Hoover.

* * *

For the most part, the incident was seized upon by the regular Democrats of the South as proof that the Solid South could not be broken and that it was a mistake for Southerners to vote for Hoover. The Milan, Ga., *News,* likes "Hoover better than we thought we possibly could. We like him because he is the kind of President we suspected he would be. The social equality kind. And while we are not pleased with social equality, we endorse it for a Republican President. It is the thing that more nearly than anything else insures Southern democracy." The Winona, Miss., *Times* declared "this unfortunate incident will lose the Republican Party hundreds of thousands of votes that it had corralled during the last Presidential campaign." The Dothan, Ala., *Eagle* declared that Hoover "has no real regard for the feelings of Southern people," and that "The Republican Party has always sought to antagonize rather than cultivate the friendship of the people below the Potomac." The Roanoke, Va., *Times* says "that the tea and resulting talk is going to cost the Republican Party thousands of votes in Virginia in November and in other states next year." The Danville, Virginia, *Bee* calls upon Southern Democrats to settle minor differences, "and by their ballot cast in united strength, rebuke at the first opportunity a Republican administration which is sponsoring DePriest." The Birmingham *Age-Herald* says: "It will no longer be possible for the Hoovercrats to pooh-pooh the race issue." The Macclenny, Fla., *Reporter* calls the Hoover Democrat now a hybrid animal, "to be treated as our other hybrid, the mule – just ignored." The Opp, Ala., *News* says:

> The social venture of the First Lady of the nation having a Negro woman as her guest in the White House, looks ugly enough to we Southern people (sic) but if the mere social feature was all there was to it the matter wouldn't be half as grave as it is. Other and graver matters are sure to follow, however, for it is difficult enough at best to keep feelings between the races good here in the South. With such example as the recent White House tea, the problem becomes far more serious and approaches an impossibility.

The Concord, N.C., *Tribune* complains that Hoover "failed to name a Southerner to his cabinet; he likewise over-looked the Southern states when he named his Farm Board; he has entertained a Negro at the White House." It concludes that he has "no hopes of carrying the South again."

A few Northern papers touch this political aspect. The Hartford *Courant* says:

> the uncompromising attitude of Bishop Cannon and his friends have caused many Southern Democrats to feel that the transfer of political allegiance that was registered in November may become permanent. To these, the opportunity offered by the issue of 'social equality' to escape the penalties of their regularity and to restore the fortunes of the Democratic Party in the South is irresistible. In view of this low political activity, the attitude of President and Mrs. Hoover is doubly commendable. They have not sacrificed principle for expediency.

The Providence *Tribune* adds:

> One prejudice is set against another prejudice. It is enough to make decent, intelligent, fair-minded and honorable people hang their heads in shame for their fellow countrymen.

Certain Southern papers go beyond this purely political phase: They profess to see a deep plot: The Raleigh, N.C., *Times* declared that DePriest gets his "cue" from the White House, and that the Hoovers are desperately trying to revive the subsiding prejudice against the South as the supposed oppressor of the Negro race. The Tuscaloosa, Ala., *Journal* regards the tea as an opportunity for "incidentally and adroitly testing public sentiment without seeming to make it of fundamental importance."

Numbers of Southern people and leaders agree that the effect will be to harm and threaten the Negro. The Wilmington, N.C. *Star* declares that DePriest's speech has done more harm to the Negro race "than any ten men in the last century." The Double Springs, Ala., *Herald* thinks the tea will "tend to create false hopes in their black breasts," and will revive the Ku Klux Klan. The Pembroke, Ga., *Enterprise* looks forward to intermarriage and rape:

> If a vicious Negro happens to reason that if a Negro woman is good enough to be entertained by the wife of the President, he is good enough to enter your home and pay court to your white daughters, and you voted for Hoover, the old adage of 'chickens coming home

to roost' will stand up on its hind legs and look you squarely between the eyes.

If the next twelve months were to record a criminal assault on the persons of a hundred white girls, or even one, by Negro brutes, by reason of being emboldened by the unfortunate indiscretion of Mrs. Hoover, the white woman who voted for her husband can shoulder their share of the responsibility.

The Carnesville, Ga., *Herald* says: "When a Negro decides that he is on an equality with the white man, then he will not only seek the white man's daughter in marriage, he will seek to supplant him in every conceivable place and time."

The Monroe, Ga., *Tribune* says that the tea has done more to disturb relations between the white and black races "than anything that has occurred during the past twenty-five years."

The Durham, N.C., *Herald* says that DePriest "has done more to setback the efforts of the better thinking men and women of both races . . . than anything else in this generation." He has almost "undone the fine progress that has been made."

The Cordele, Ga., *Dispatch* is even wilder:

> Utterances like that of DePriest, if continued, will eventually mean racial destruction — at least, in this section of the country. That Negro may keep up his agitation until every black man and woman and child would be driven out and suffer untold hardships and privation. Lawful slavery — if it should ever exist again — would be a paradise as compared with the suffering that would be heaped upon every black man if the DePriests were allowed to continue dispensing racial arsenic. The whole power of the armies of the nation could not prevent it. White men would die resenting it — shed the last drop of blood exterminating such Negroes as DePriest.

* * *

Several Southern papers take occasion to reiterate the "fairness" of the South. The Memphis *Commercial Appeal,* for instance, says "that Negroes are lynched for the same crimes that white people are lynched," and that there "is no law in the statutes of any Southern state limiting the franchise of the Negro which does not apply equally to the white man."

The Dalton, Ga., *Citizen* says:

> The South is treating the Negro fairly. He owns his property. He goes to school at the state's expense. He votes when he qualifies.

Other papers just as flatly contradict this and see in the whole tea and talk a challenge to the nullification of the 14th and 15th Amendments and a comparison with the 18th. Northern papers like the Minneapolis *Evening Tribune* say: "We can't pick and choose the votes that we should revere, and if the South wants the 18th Amendment obeyed, it must accept the 14th and 15th."

The Syracuse *Post Standard* says: "The Constitution should be obeyed, although the South does not propose that it should be obeyed."

On the other hand, the Birmingham *Age-Herald* retorts that "those who voted for Hoover were told last year that trouble might be expected with regard to the 14th and 15th amendments if Mr. Hoover won. That trouble has come."

The Nashville *Tennessean* declares the 14th and 15th Amendments

> As a matter of fact, were never adopted by the necessary number of free and sovereign states. Their ratification was forced upon a helpless people by Negro and alien legislators sustained by federal bayonets. They were inspired in hate and born of a malicious purpose to wreck revenge upon the people of the South.

The Tampa, Fla., *Tribune* says:

> The election of DePriest and the recognition according him has done more to destroy friendly relations between the races than all the good work in that direction has accomplished in 50 years. It was bad enough to elect any kind of Negro to Congress; but when the one elected is of the loud-mouthed, braggart type of DePriest, it is intolerable.

The Jackson, Fla., *Blue Shirt* (the organ of the "white working class") talks plain English about the Negro vote:

> You might as well make up your mind that the niggers are not going to vote in the South and there are more ways than one to stop them and don't worry, we will stop them. When you try to encourage your race by trying to raise $200,000, you are just encouraging bloodshed and if you want to see your race wiped out in the South just keep up your work. The fight is coming in the South and there is no use of us playing the ostrich by hiding our heads in the sand, as race war is coming sure and I don't want my people to be caught unprepared and I hereby advise every white man to look up that old musket or that old rifle or even that old rusty revolver, and get it cleaned up.

The Tampa, Fla., *Times* adds:

Between DePriest and Tinkham, this business is not through yet. There is probability of much trouble over social equality between the races and over the 13th, 14th, 15th, and 18th Amendments to the constitution and their enforcement.

* * *

The attitude of Mrs. Hoover is not without defense even in the South.

The Bristol *Tennessean* says: "There is no more justification for the exclusion of a black man and his wife from such a function than there is to exclude a red, yellow, brown or white one."

Coleman Hill, columnist in the Macon, Va. *Telegraph* writes:

> How Mrs. Hoover's action can influence the future courses of private hosts and hostesses, I am absolutely unable to see. No law compels Mrs. Vanderbilt to invite the janitor of the Trinity church to her next supper; nor is the Idle Hour Club forced to accept Phil Towns or Lee Battle into membership. Mrs. Hoover did the gentle, the gracious, the courteous thing. Instead of glorying in her deed, the brotherhood of Southern political parasites has taken occasion to bow its heads — I quote the typical resolution of the Texas legislature — 'in shame and regret'.

One Southern Bishop, W. N. Ainsworth, has expressed similar sentiments.

The northern press is either paralyzed into silence or speaks like the Springfield *Republican*:

> The Hoovers function in the White House as the official symbols of government and government in this country cannot turn a blind eye on Negroes. Negroes cannot be eliminated, ignored or nullified. They are here to stay. The Hoovers deserve congratulations. They are showing the stuff they are made of.

6

A NUREMBERG LAW FOR AMERICA

Prejudices such as those recorded in the preceding selection were not confined to unlettered Southerners. Robert De Courcy Ward, Harvard '89, holder of the first chair of climatology at any American university, editor of the *American Meteorological Journal,* contributor to the *Britannica's* renowned Eleventh Edition, fellow of learned societies both here and abroad, and author of 330 professional papers, was an unquestioned member of the American academic Establishment. In 1894, the year he was first appointed instructor at Harvard, Ward founded the Immigration Restriction League; thirty years afterward he saw that organization's principles enacted into law, and wrote the following article.

Scientific Monthly, founded in 1915 as a companion to *Science* (the official journal of the American Association for the Advancement of Science), inherited the subscription list of the old *Popular Science Monthly* when that venerable journal was transmuted into a hobbies-and-mechanics magazine. The new monthly carried on its predecessor's insistence upon the relevance of science to general culture. Alongside articles on spectrum analysis, lace wing larvae, and the evolution of the stars, therefore, its first issue carried essays on "Overpopulation and the Living Standard"; "What Science Owes the Public"; and "Religion and Man's Origin." The magazine's files from the Twenties include an essay on "Science and Conduct," a sobering article on "The Agricultural Limits of our Population," and, in the very issue in which Ward's discourse on immigration appeared, Ira Woods Howerth's "Is There a Natural Law of Inequality?," which answered the racial elitists of the day (e.g., Lothrop Stoddard) with a resounding No.

On such questions the scientific community of the Twenties did not speak with one voice. Men like Franz Boas and Alês Hrdlicka were already engaged in research of a kind that would eventually overthrow the intellectual credibility of racism. The editor of *Scientific Monthly* itself, who had studied physiological psychology under Wundt at Leipzig and had done pioneering work in the field of "mental testing," drew back with scientific and humane caution from the biological inegalitarianism some of his colleagues were inferring from the recently developed "I.Q. test." (See J. McKeen Cattell, "The Interpretation of Intelligence Tests," *Scientific Monthly*, XVIII (May, 1924), 508–16.)

HIGHER MENTAL AND PHYSICAL STANDARDS FOR IMMIGRANTS

Robert DeC. Ward

The Immigration Act of 1924 established a new American immigration policy. It marked "the passing of the dominating factor of economics and established for the future American policy the basic elements of racial values and family stock quality."[1]

Within certain limits, which are rather vague because of an at present unknown number of "non-quota" immigrants, we have decided to admit only a limited number of new aliens, and the bulk of these are to be of the same racial stocks as those which originally settled and developed our country, founded our institutions, framed our constitution and to-day still make up the bulk of our population. Until we had set some sort of numerical limitation on immigration, better selection – mental, physical or economic – was impossible. That very important first step having finally been taken, it now becomes our duty, both to ourselves and to coming generations of Americans of whatever racial origin, to set higher mental and physical

FROM *Scientific Monthly*, XIX (November, 1924), pp. 533–47. Reprinted by permission of the American Association for the Advancement of Science.

[1] *Eugenical News*, July, 1924.

standards for all our future immigrants. It is an absolutely illogical and indefensible situation that our regulations governing the admission of animals and plants are to-day, and have been for years, far more stringent than our immigration laws, and have been more strictly enforced.

It is the aim of the present paper to consider briefly:

1. what legislation has already been enacted to exclude eugenically undesirable immigrants;
2. how these laws have worked, and
3. what further amendments have been suggested in order to bring about a better selection of immigrants on mental and physical grounds.

THE GENERAL IMMIGRATION ACT OF 1917

The general Immigration Act of 1917 enumerates all the classes of aliens which Congress has so far declared shall be excluded because eugenically undesirable. In respect to these classes the act of 1917 remains in force, not having been superseded by the new act of 1924. The aliens thus specifically debarred under Section 3 are the following: idiots, imbeciles, feeble-minded persons; epileptics; insane persons; persons who have had one or more attacks of insanity at any time previously; persons of constitutional psychopathic inferiority; persons with chronic alcoholism; persons afflicted with tuberculosis in any form or with a loathsome or dangerous contagious disease; persons not comprehended within any of the foregoing excluded classes who are found to be and are certified by the examining surgeon as being mentally or physically defective, such physical defect being of a nature which may affect the ability of such alien to earn a living. In order to prevent so far as possible the bringing or landing of any aliens belonging to the above excluded classes, certain fines are imposed upon the transportation companies in cases of violation of the law, if it appears to the satisfaction of the secretary of labor that any alien so brought was afflicted with any of the specified diseases or disabilities at the time of foreign embarkation, and that the existence of such disease or disability might have been detected by means of a competent medical examination at such time. In addition, the company has to pay a sum equal to that paid by the alien for his transportation from the initial point of departure to the port of arrival.

In order to determine whether any alien belongs to any of the excluded classes such alien may be kept on board ship or at an immigration station long enough to enable the medical officers to reach a definite conclusion in the matter.

The act specifically and definitely provides that the decision of a board of special inquiry (which acts on the cases of all aliens who do not appear to the examining inspector to be clearly and beyond a doubt entitled to land) "shall be based upon the certificate of the examining medical officer, and, except as provided in Section 21, shall be final as to the rejection of all aliens afflicted with tuberculosis in any form or with a loathsome or dangerous contagious disease, or with any mental or physical disability which would bring such aliens within any of the classes excluded from admission to the United States under Section 3 of this act."[2] These are known as the *mandatorily excludable* classes. Section 21 here referred to as containing the exceptions, *i.e.*, as specifying the only cases in which the certificate of the medical officer may not be final as the cause of debarment, provides that any alien liable to be excluded because

1. likely to become a public charge, or

2. because of physical disability other than tuberculosis in any form or a loathsome or dangerous contagious disease, may be admitted in the discretion of the secretary of labor upon the giving of a suitable bond. The only appeal of an alien certified for insanity or mental defect is to a board of medical examiners (Section 16). Appeals from the ordinary decisions of the boards of special inquiry are to the secretary of labor. Every adverse decision may be thus appealed. Section 19 provides that aliens who at the time of entry belonged to one or more of the classes excluded by law, or who entered the United States in violation of the law, shall, upon the warrant of the secretary of labor, be taken into custody and deported.

These are the specific provisions of our immigration law with reference to the exclusion of eugenically undesirable aliens.

[2] Section 3 names the excluded classes, as above indicated.

WHY EUGENICALLY UNDESIRABLE ALIENS HAVE NOT BEEN MORE EFFECTIVELY EXCLUDED

Complete and satisfactory as the act of 1917 seems to be, it has not accomplished its purpose. *It has not in the past been rigidly enforced.* Every one who is at all familiar with immigration problems knows that, and especially the aliens themselves, their relatives and friends in this country and the steamship companies. There have been admitted not hundreds but thousands of aliens who were diseased; who were mentally and physically far below par; who had criminal records and tendencies; who could not earn their own living; who were in every way hopelessly undesirable and impossible material for American citizenship.

There have been three main reasons why the many excellent eugenical provisions in our immigration law have not been enforced. These are

1. the lack of enough thoroughly competent and well-paid inspectors;
2. the impossibility of detecting, in the usually hurried and superficial examination at the port of arrival, nearly all the cases which for one reason or another should be debarred;
3. the abuse of the privilege of appeal from the decision of competent medical officers and of the boards of general immigration inspectors, and the far too great leniency in sustaining such appeals in the office of the secretary of labor.

The decrease in numbers and the improvement in quality of our immigrants which will result from the new Immigration Act of 1924 should help greatly to make the medical examination of arriving aliens more thorough, and thus lead to the detection of more of those who belong in the mentally and physically defective classes. In other words, the difficulties noted under 1 and 2 above ought to be lessened. The third difficulty, noted under 3, will remain unless those who are concerned about the future mental and physical condition of our people take hold of this problem and see to it that what has happened in the past shall hereafter no longer be possible. The appeal and bonding clauses of the act of 1917 give the secretary of labor authority, in his discretion, to reverse the decisions of the boards of special inquiry, and also to permit aliens suffering from certain diseases or disability, or likely to become public charges, nevertheless to enter the United States for a limited time, under bonds, for treatment or observation, or to give them opportunity to prove that they will not become public charges. In theory, this is a very humane and just provision. In the opinion of unprejudiced students it is one of the biggest holes in our general immigration law. Under these clauses far too many aliens mentally and physically defective and certain to become public charges have been admitted. Appeals are constantly made on behalf of every class of alien specified in the law as excludable. Immigrant "aid" and charitable societies; immigrant lawyers who prey on the alien; relatives and friends of those liable to be debarred; senators and congressmen of the United States and city and state politicians more interested in securing a few votes from their foreign-born constituents than in the future character of our race; misguided sentimentalists, appeal in behalf of the detained alien. The United States usually has everything to lose and nothing to gain if the appeal is sustained. The only safeguard which the country has is in the honest and patriotic officials of the Immigration Service, who, in the face of terrific pressure, endeavor to uphold the law. The result has been that aliens certified by thoroughly competent expert medical officers as having such mental or physical defects as constitute them potential public charges and highly undesirable elements in our population have been admitted, on appeal or under bonds. As Hon. Robert E. Tod, recently commissioner of immigration at Ellis Island, has said, "It is an insult to the intelligence of the examining boards of medical officers to reverse their decisions over and over again under political pressure."

The situation regarding aliens who are certified as having physical defects which in the opinion of the medical officers may affect the ability of the alien to earn a living needs a few words of comment. The provision adding to the excluded classes (1907) those certified as being mentally and physically defective, the defect being of such a nature as to affect ability to earn a living, has proved of comparatively little value eugenically. Those who drafted this provision intended it to be a medical test, but it was very soon decided that the medical certificate in such cases was only one piece of evidence to be taken account of by the board of special inquiry as bearing on the question of the ability of the alien to earn his living. In other words, the provision became an economic, not a medical test. Most of the cases admitted on appeal have been those of aliens with a medical certificate of this character, but where other circumstances seemed to warrant admission.

The remedy for this situation is obvious:

1. No immigrants belonging to the class of *mandatorily excludable* aliens (*i.e.*, those suffering from idiocy, insanity, imbecility, feeble-mindedness, epilepsy, constitutional psychopathic inferiority or chronic alcoholism) should ever be admitted.[3]
2. There should be no yielding to political pressure for the admission of aliens on appeal over the decisions of the medical examiners and the boards of special inquiry. As a recent writer has said, "any intervention by a politician in behalf of an excludable alien should be regarded as a strong presumption that the case should be dropped at once, and the alien deported forthwith."
3. The whole policy of admitting aliens who are not *clearly* and *beyond question* entitled to land — border-line cases — must be stiffened up all along the line.

Appeals from adverse decisions of the boards of special inquiry should rarely be sustained. Aliens suffering from a physical or mental disability which makes them potential public charges should always be excluded unless there are very strong reasons to the contrary. The appeal and bonding provision as it stands at present can be, and has been, used to nullify many of the excellent eugenical clauses of the law. American public opinion must arouse itself and insist on a rigid enforcement of this law. As things now stand, alien interests and alien influences and alien "pressure" working — to their shame be it said — through American senators and congressmen are active day and night to secure the admission of immigrants whom Congress has declared inadmissible.

One reason for the laxity in the enforcement of the law is that there is a very widespread idea that "the United States should not separate the families of aliens" when an imbecile or a feeble-minded or other excludable member of the family arrives at our ports. But it should be remembered that in the large majority of such cases, the alien family intentionally separated itself overseas, when some

[3] Recommendation of Interstate Conference on Immigration, New York, Oct. 24, 1923.

members of the family, knowing perfectly well the provisions of our law, came over first, established a foothold, and then sent for the feeble-minded or imbecile or diseased son or daughter, mother or aunt, uncle or nephew. The vast majority of our immigrants know our immigration laws far better than most Americans do and deliberately "work" the sentimental plea in favor of the admission of the undesirable child or relative. It is very easy to arouse tremendous sentiment in individual cases of apparent hardship. A brief paragraph in a daily newspaper is all that is necessary to bring that about. The far larger interests of the United States, which suffer through the admission of mentally and physically unfit aliens, are more remote, and hence attract little or no attention.

THE IMMIGRATION ACT OF 1924

Although the Immigration Act of 1924 contains no specific provisions looking towards a more rigid exclusion of eugenically undesirable aliens, it will accomplish a better selection than has hitherto been possible. It will accomplish much more than a change in the racial character of our future immigration, tremendously important as that change will be. It will also bring about a distinct improvement in the mental and physical conditions of our immigrants. As Dr. Wm. J. Mayo truly said in an address at the Boston City Hospital, November 14, 1923, before the new act was passed:

> The alien is a public health problem, just as he is a social problem, and the public hospital sees the dark side of this picture. In the American of several generations, the doctrine of moral obligation has become thoroughly ingrained. In southern Europe the Oriental point of view more or less prevails that no obligation which is not enforcible exists. The laxity of the conduct of the law in the United States, the slowness of justice, and the extraordinary latitude allowed the offender against the community, give the criminal more than a sporting chance to escape punishment and have exposed the administrators of law to the contempt of the class of offenders brought to us in recent years by immigration. And these are the people with whom our public hospitals are overcrowded. Our courts have been filled with alien lawbreakers until the people have arisen in righteous indignation and reduced the number of immigrants to 3 per cent. of the number already here from each country. If the percentage system of immigration in effect in 1890 could be reverted to, as has been

advised, a much more desirable class of citizens would be brought from the countries that gave birth to the United States and its concept of government.

The new Immigration Act will not only bring us

1. a limited, more homogeneous and more easily assimilated immigration, but
2. an immigration of generally higher intelligence than has characterized the bulk of the people who have come here in recent years and
3. greatly reduced numbers of aliens belonging to many of the "socially inadequate" classes.

The original argument in favor of a percentage limitation was economic. The fundamental reason for its continuance is biological.

The act of 1924 contains a new provision — that of immigration visas — so important that if it contained nothing else the time and the labor involved in its preparation and discussion would have been well spent. For many years students of immigration have advocated some sort of preliminary inspection of intending immigrants overseas, before they start on their journey, as a necessary and a humane measure — a benefit to the United States and a means of preventing unnecessary hardship to the alien. The new law embodies the first practical attempt which the United States has ever made to conduct a preliminary selection abroad with a view to weeding out at least some of those who are debarred by our present laws. Complete overseas inspection, general and medical, is impossible owing to the limited jurisdiction of our consular service under the existing treaties, and because foreign governments have objected to our taking such a step. But foreign governments can hardly object to the requirement in the new law of having the intending immigrant fill out a questionnaire before an American consul, showing whether or not, according to his own statements, he is qualified for admission to the United States under our laws.

The essentials in the new plan are as follows: Aliens entering the United States must have passports from their home government, viséed by an American consul. Hitherto the visa could be withheld only if the alien was known or thought to hold views inimical to organized government. Consular officers could exercise no discretion in the matter of giving visas to prospective immigrants, even when it was certain that the aliens would not be admitted or, if admitted, would be most undesirable additions to our population. Under the new law, a consular officer abroad has a real discretionary power of selection, for he may refuse to issue an immigration visa "if he knows or has reason to believe that the immigrant is inadmissible to the United States under the immigration laws." The consul's action is final. Every immigrant must bring with him his passport and its accompanying visa. Before securing the visa, the alien must answer a very full questionnaire, essentially the same as that which he is asked on his arrival here, intended to show whether he is eligible for admission under our laws. This document includes the question whether the alien or either of his parents has ever been in an institution or hospital for the care and treatment of the insane, must also be accompanied by the alien's *dossier* and prison and military record, and must be sworn to before the consul.

While there will undoubtedly be many cases of perjury and of fraud in this connection, there can be no question that a very great many undesirable aliens, excludable by law, will be headed off by our consuls when application is made. This plan will reduce hardships to the absolute minimum; avoid the division of families; save the nationals of other countries the expense, perils and hardships of the ocean trip to the United States only to find that for some reason the immigrant or some member of his family can not enter. Certificates are to be issued only up to the numbers allowed by the quotas, and are good for four months, so that if an alien comes at any time within that period he will not be denied admission as being in excess of the quota allowance. This provision also stops the rush of aliens at the beginning of each month, and makes possible a more deliberate and more thorough medical inspection — an improvement very greatly to be desired. The real inspection, medical and otherwise, will be made at our own ports, as it should be, but many of the aliens who would be excluded on examination here will never start on their journey. The certificate plan, then, will, through the preliminary selection overseas, benefit the United States. It will also very greatly diminish the hardships of the alien. It is selective. And it is humane.

Three other clauses in the Act of 1924 deserve mention because of their eugenic importance:

1. The fines on the transportation companies for bringing inadmissible aliens are very considerably increased and this will greatly help in the enforcement of the law;

2. any alien who at any time after entering the United States is found to have been at the time of entry not entitled to enter or to have remained here for a longer time than permitted shall be deported;
3. alien seamen must be detained on board ship until they have submitted to inspection, including a medical examination. With certain exceptions, alien seamen found excludable are prohibited from landing.

The new law is a long step forward along eugenic lines, and as such deserves hearty support on the part of all who desire that the immigrants who come to us shall be physically, mentally and morally sound and desirable progenitors of future Americans. Various suggestions put forward from time to time by close students of immigration problems who are especially concerned about the eugenical selection of our immigrants have, however, not yet become part of our immigration policy. These deserve careful consideration at this time.

I. CASH BONDS

Reference has already been made to the provision in the act of 1917 which permits the secretary of labor to admit certain classes of aliens under bonds, and to the evils which have resulted from the abuse of this bonding privilege.

The way the bonding provision actually works out is this. The bonds are usually in amounts between $500 and $1,000. They are taken out through a surety company by a relative or friend of the alien, or by some immigrant aid society. For many reasons, in most of which the relative or friend plays the chief part, the alien admitted on appeal has too often been "lost." Change of residence, change of name, and removal to another state have been common schemes for bringing this about. In many cases the relatives or friends have been willing enough to care for the admitted alien for a time, but soon lost interest, and were quite ready to have their bonded fellow-countryman taken care of by the community. The bonds are for too small amounts. They can not always be enforced. They have too often become mere "scraps of paper." A large percentage of all bonded aliens have in the past violated and forfeited their bonds and are now here, some in public institutions; some supported more or less of the time by public or private charity, and most of them at large in the community, a social menace because, themselves in many cases mentally defective, they have been producing mentally inferior children. The "paper" bonding system has worked incalculable injury to our population.

This situation, recognized as such by competent and unprejudiced authorities on immigration, should be remedied.

1. Aliens belonging to the "mandatorily excludable" classes should never be admitted on appeal over the heads of the medical examiners, as has been urged earlier in the present article. And
2. in all other cases when aliens are admitted on appeal *cash* bonds in substantial sums *should be required.*

Section 21 of the Act of 1917, which provides for bonding, expressly states that in lieu of other ("paper") bond, any alien "may deposit in cash with the secretary of labor such amounts as the secretary of labor may require, which amount shall be deposited by said secretary in the United States Postal Savings Bank." If the alien became a public charge, the money would be directly available towards the expenses of his support; and no suit to recover would be necessary. As things stand now, the expense of suing, on the part of any state or municipality or town, is usually too great to make it worth while to institute proceedings for the recovery of the money, the amount of which is usually far too small. A $1,000 bond should be the minimum, and $5,000 would not be too much in many cases.

In connection with cash bonds several points should be kept in mind. Congress has already approved them as an alternative to paper bonds. A cash bond is a perfectly fair requirement in the case of any alien who is given the special privilege of being admitted contrary to law, for the United States is taking a decided risk in admitting him. If, at the end of say five years, the alien appeared and gave proof that he had not become a public charge, the capital sum of the deposit, plus interest, should be returned to him. In case he did not appear, the United States could use the money for hunting him up, and for deporting him if found. As things stand under our present bonding system, the government too often does not attempt to find an alien who has forfeited his bond because of the expense involved and the difficulty or impossibility of locating him. If a cash deposit of a considerable amount were required, the relatives and friends of the alien and the immigrant aid societies would be much less ready than they now are to appeal the cases of excluded aliens. If the alien himself had to put up the cash bond it would be reasonable evidence that he would not become a public charge. Cash bonds, as here urged, would force the steamship companies to be more careful in permitting the embarkation of aliens who would probably be excluded on arrival here, because far fewer such would be allowed to enter on appeal. Another most desirable result of such bonds would be the very great decrease in the harassing and laborious work of hearing appeal cases in the office of the secretary of labor, and would thus also largely do away with the present conditions of political pressure for the admission of aliens on appeal. Finally, cash bonds would, without any doubt whatever, result in the landing of a very greatly reduced number of undesirable aliens.

Cash bonds, of considerable amounts, were recommended by the Sub-Committee on Immigration of the Eugenics Committee of the United States of America in its first report (January, 1924).

II. MEDICAL INSPECTION TO BE MADE DURING THE VOYAGE

The impossibility of conducting thorough medical examinations during the hurried inspection at the port of arrival has led to a demand that such examination should be carried on during the voyage, when there would be ample time for the work, and when the aliens could be observed for several days in succession. Definite action looking towards this end was taken at a conference of alienists and social workers held in New York City, November 16, 1912, at which the most important scientific bodies in the United States then dealing with the treatment and prevention of insanity were represented.[4]

This conference unanimously endorsed the adoption of "a provision authorizing the detail of commissioned medical officers of

[4] American Medico-Psychological Association, National Committee for Mental Hygiene, New York Psychiatrical Society, New York State Charities Aid Association, Committee of One Hundred on National Health, New York State Hospital Commission, Immigration Committee of the Eugenics Section of the American Breeders Association.

the U. S. Public Health Service to any vessels bringing immigrants to the United States, such medical officers being required to examine immigrants, with special reference to their mental condition, on the voyage to this country." This suggestion was later embodied in a section of the Act of 1917, authorizing the secretary of labor to enter into negotiations with the transportation companies with this end in view. So far as the present writer is aware, no action on this matter has ever been taken by our government. The National Republican Club (New York) later passed a resolution to the following effect: "In so far as existing law may be inadequate to permit the placing of inspectors and physicians on vessels bringing aliens to this country, it should be amended." This suggestion, it should be observed, applies to placing American medical officers on the steamships, and would therefore remove the responsibility from the transportation companies, where it would seem properly to belong.

Dr. Spencer L. Dawes, medical examiner of the New York State Hospital Commission, has for some years been a very able advocate of a plan which has been widely and enthusiastically endorsed.[5] Dr. Dawes's proposal is that as a prerequisite to the granting of a visa by an American consul the emigrant shall present a medical certificate (on a blank provided by the Immigration Service) embodying family and personal history, and certifying that the emigrant is not of the excluded classes. This certificate is to be based on a thorough medical examination made by a physician employed by the transportation company which is intending to bring the alien to the United States. Fines are to be provided, as at present, in all cases in which ineligible aliens are brought here. The reasons for such a provision are the necessarily hurried, inadequate medical examinations by our own officials at the port of landing; the impossibility, owing to the attitude of certain foreign governments, of having a medical examination overseas by United States officials, and the very discouraging situation here of seeing thousands of mentally and physically unsound aliens landed, either

1. because the hurried medical examination here can not detect the disabilities or
2. because of the landing of such undesirable aliens on bonds.

[5] By the Interstate Conference on Immigration, the New York State Federation of Women's Clubs, the National Republican Club, the U. S. Chamber of Commerce, the American Mining Congress, numerous district branches of the New York League of Women Voters, etc.

Dr. Dawes's plan places the responsibility directly where it belongs. If the steamship company carries out the physical examination it can not complain if it should be found, on the immigrant's arrival in the United States, that any passenger is, from a medical standpoint, ineligible under the provisions of the statute. On the other hand, if medical examinations were carried out by officers of the United States at the European ports it would be impossible to shift the responsibility to the steamship company for deportation of an ineligible immigrant by reason of physical or mental disability.

A very important part of the Dawes proposal is the inquiry into the personal and family history of the emigrant, which should be minute and thorough.

> If the steamship company is held responsible for the verification of this phase of the applicant's examination, all the hardship cases would be absolutely eliminated. What happens now is that an immigrant voluntarily separates himself from his family, which may be composed of one or more children mentally deficient, and then, when the alien has made enough money to import his family a howl goes up as to the separation of these unfortunates. Unquestionably here is true hardship, but it must be borne in mind that the original separation was the voluntary act of the people who desired to enter the United States.

The plan is simple, feasible and would be highly effective. Canada, which is well in advance of us in the matter of selecting her immigrants, requires a medical examination by the steamship companies' doctors, and aliens found mentally or physically inadmissible after arrival at Canadian ports must be returned at the expense of these companies.

III. HIGHER PHYSICAL STANDARDS

Close students of the eugenical aspects of immigration have for many years felt that too large a proportion of incoming aliens have been of low vitality and poor physique — distinctly undesirable members of our population yet not specifically excludable under existing statutes. The matter has more than once been brought to the attention of Congress, but without result. This whole matter was carefully considered by the Sub-Committee on Immigration of the Committee on National Affairs of the National Republican Club of New York, under the able chairmanship of Mr. William Williams, and the following resolution was unanimously adopted at a meeting of the club held February 17, 1920:

> The general physical requirements for males coming here to perform manual labor should be raised moderately and made somewhat more definite than they now are. While we are not in accord with those who would make these requirements as severe as those governing admission to the Army and Navy, yet we believe that by analogy certain reasonable minimum physical standards should be adopted, either by Congress or by the U.S. Public Health Service under authority of Congress, and applied to male aliens of the class referred to. After observing for a time their operation, the experience gained would show whether it was desirable also to adopt analogous physical standards in reference to other classes. Too many immigrants of indifferent general physique have in recent years been finding their way into the United States. With such standards to serve as a guide, there would be less excuse than there now is for the steamship companies to bring here laborers who, while not suffering from any loathsome or dangerous contagious disease, are nevertheless persons of poor physique or impaired general health.

This would seem to be a reasonable and logical, as it also is a most desirable, step for us to take in this matter.

IV. MENTAL TESTS

In this very able address in Boston, November 14, 1923, already referred to, Dr. William J. Mayo spoke as follows:

> Eugenics as applied to man is still in its infancy. During the World War, tests showed that 18 per cent. of the young men drafted were not developed beyond the mental age of eleven years. Since our form of government must always be controlled by men of average intelligence, the general average of intelligence must be raised if the standards of government are to be raised. This 18 per cent. of citizens in the Boy Scout stage of development, mentally too low to be reached by reason, easily led by an appeal to prejudice, and voting solidly, are within 3 per cent. of controlling the average election. Our great safeguard, general education, will not aid them or us. Nature has fixed their mental status. This substratum of society presents one

of the greatest problems of American citizenship. It will exist long after a proper settling of the immigration question, and will tax the best minds of the future to remedy.

The grave dangers that thus threaten our future race and our institutions have led eugenicists to the conviction that only aliens who attain a certain standard of intelligence should be admitted to this country.

The Sub-Committee on Immigration of the Eugenics Committee of the United States of America, in its first report, made the following brief but inclusive recommendation:

> No alien should be admitted who has not an intellectual capacity superior to the American average. Aliens should be required to attain a passing score of, say, the median in the Alpha test, or the corresponding equivalent score in other approved tests, these tests to be given in the native tongue of the immigrant. Further, if possible, aliens whose family history indicates that they come of unsound stock should be debarred.

The American median here referred to, which is now fairly well known from the Army tests, can be readily worked out for use in new tests to be applied to aliens.

Experts have estimated that had mental tests been in operation and had the "inferior" and "very inferior" immigrants been refused admission to the United States, over 6,000,000 aliens now living in this country, most of them potential fathers and mothers of future Americans, would never have been admitted. It surely is high time for the American people to put a stop to such a degradation of American citizenship and such a wrecking of the future American race.

That mental tests as here recommended would certainly operate to debar large numbers of aliens who are of inferior intelligence is perfectly certain. On the other hand, it is no less clear that the public as a whole is not yet educated up to an acceptance of such tests as a logical part of our immigration policy.

V. REGISTRATION OF ALIENS

With the increasing restrictions which have been put upon immigration, the smuggling and surreptitious entry of aliens across the

Canadian and Mexican borders and by sea have naturally enormously increased. It has been estimated that probably 100 aliens daily enter this country in violation of our laws, and the number may be very much larger. While many of these "bootleg" immigrants are probably mentally and physically up to the very low standards which we have set, the majority doubtless belong to the diseased and defective classes who should most rigidly be excluded. The new Border Patrol, made possible by an appropriation of $1,200,000 for the current year, will help to remedy this very bad situation. But more is needed. Secretary of Labor James J. Davis strongly advocates a plan for registration as an effective way of outwitting the border-jumper and the smuggled alien. Under this plan every alien would be required to register or enroll annually. Failure to register would be punishable by fine. Registration would be carried out by the naturalization service of the Department of Labor and perhaps also by interested individuals and organizations. A final check-up of aliens who failed to comply with the law would occur when an alien applied for his citizenship papers. This plan would not only help in the work of assimilation and education, but, what is of even more importance, would reveal the presence of aliens who had entered the country in violation of the law, in whose cases there would be no record of legitimate admission by immigration inspectors.

SUMMARY

In conclusion, the various methods which have here been discussed for raising the mental and physical standards of our immigrants may be briefly summarized.

1. Our immigration laws should be rigidly enforced all along the line.
2. "Mandatorily excludable" aliens should never be admitted.
3. All border-line cases, which are mostly those liable to become public charges for medical reasons, should be debarred unless there is *very strong* evidence in favor of admission.
4. Appeals from adverse decisions of the boards of special inquiry should rarely be sustained.

5. There should be no yielding to political pressure in the case of any alien who belongs to any of the excluded classes.
6. When, in very rare cases, aliens are admitted under bond, the bonds should be cash bonds, in considerable amounts.
7. As a prerequisite to the granting of an "immigration visa" by an American consul, the alien should present a medical certificate from a physician employed by the steamship company to the effect that such alien is not of the excluded classes. If diseased or mentally or physically defective aliens are found by our examining medical officers, the steamship companies should be fined, and the alien deported.
8. Higher physical standards should be required.
9. No alien should be admitted who has not an intellectual capacity superior to the American average.
10. All aliens should be required to register annually.

7

THE COLLEGE AND MASS CULTURE

No anthology from the magazines of the 1920's would be complete without an excerpt from the *American Mercury.* Alfred A. Knopf, the book publisher, founded it, and H. L. Mencken, the "bad boy from Baltimore," edited it, and its unique mixture of scholarship and irreverence, of acute criticism and heavy-handed exposé, of hard sophistication and unwitting sentimentalism, makes it in some ideal-typical sense *the* American magazine of the Twenties. In addition to the academic writers (Woodbridge Riley, Melville Herskovits), literary people (Conrad Aiken, Dorothy Parker), and Mencken's old newspaper cronies (Virginius Dabney, James M. Cain), who wrote for the *American Mercury,* it also published material by "unknowns" – workingmen, prison inmates, and hoboes. It carried essays by leftists who violently disagreed with Mencken's political point of view, such as Louis Adamic and Emma Goldman, and it published a number of significant essays by American Negroes. For all its catholicity, however, the *Mercury's* mental horizons had certain severe limitations, well illustrated in the slice of life that follows.

Bernard DeVoto had had five years' experience as an English instructor at Northwestern when he wrote this article. Like several other writers included in our anthology – Duncan Aikman, Granville Hicks, Mike Gold – DeVoto was both an actor *in* the Twenties and later a commentator *on* them. His book *The Literary Fallacy* (1944) remains one of the most powerful cases that has ever been made against the intelligentsia of the Jazz Age (although, ironically, many of them would have agreed with the judgment he expressed in 1928 on "English A"). Readers familiar with the passionately democratic tenor of DeVoto's later writings – e.g., *Year of Decision, Across the Wide Missouri,* and his "Easy Chair" editorials in *Harper's* – may be surprised by the elitist tone of this earlier essay, typical though it was of the *Mercury's* ethos; surprised all the more inasmuch as voices sharply disagreeing with this view of the college classroom were also to be heard in the Twenties. (See John Erskine's crisp statement on "Mass Education" in *The Bookman* for September, 1924, and an article by G. R. MacMinn on "Our Serio-Comic Undergraduates," in the March, 1928 number of the *North American Review.*)

ENGLISH A

Bernard DeVoto

In the older colleges of this country, the chairs of English are of comparatively recent origin. The colleges were founded to train parsons and to educate gentlemen. A parson, being concerned with Hebrew and exegetics, had no need of English literature, and a gentleman acquired at home such knowledge of it as was seemly. A certain skill at public speaking was recognized as desirable, however, and the chairs of oratory designed to furnish it to parsons and gentlemen alike were the germ from which the English Department, now usually the largest in every college, developed. This slow development paid little attention to the writing of English, and courses in composition were at first uncommon. Proficiency in writing was supposed to come to well-bred men as a natural result of studying the classics. Such an assumption was by no means absurd so long as college students came from families of established cultivation. Two generations ago the average undergraduate was a literate man and wrote well according to the flowery standards of his day.

But with the increasing vulgarization of American society and the democratization of the colleges that accompanied it, the old assumption became untenable. Passable English could no longer be expected of the undergraduate, who tended more and more to spring up from the towpaths and the sticks with only the James A. Garfield tradition as preparation. The colleges then universally established courses in composition, which attracted those who had leanings toward journalism, the less idiotic kind of orators, and dilettante

FROM *The American Mercury,* XIII (February, 1928), pp. 204–12.

youths who found them a pleasant substitute for requirements in Greek, Hebrew, or the moral sciences. That is to say, they wholly failed of their object, for those who registered for them could already write respectably, whereas the illiterate avoided them.

So, about the time when the nation spontaneously decided that only the college-bred could succeed in business, say thirty-five years ago, the colleges all over the country suddenly realized that they were graduating an annual crop of A. B.'s who could not write a passable business letter, still less a literate report, review or feature article. Harvard was, I believe, the first college to institute the obvious remedy for this defect, and within a few years every other college in the country followed its lead. A course in the writing of English was required of every student before he was certified for graduation. At first some institutions permitted the student to take that course at any time in his undergraduate career, but it became obvious that the faculty at large, which had to read theses and reports, might as well benefit by the increased literateness presumably conferred by the required course. Thereupon the requirement was universally set for the freshman year.

Such was the genesis of English A. It is variously doctored, variously disguised, and variously taught, but it is a recognized institution in the colleges. From the one-building Baptist university in the pineywoods country to the most impressive metropolitan rolling-mill it is a convention and a commonplace. The three thousand bachelors of arts and science that are spawned in June from a Middle-Western university have approached their degrees by many avenues. Some have specialized in the history of art with minor groupings in Sanskrit and the philosophy of Spinoza. More have devoted themselves to the economics of banking, the theory of salesmanship and the psychology of success. More still have records that reflect the problematical frequency of ten o'clock classes and the fraternity check-lists of snap courses. These last have done their work in such diverse fields as the appreciation of music, hotel management, radio announcing, the theory of home-beautification, personnel methods in the movies, and the psychology of handbill-distribution. But whatever avenues they have taken, they lead back to a common plaza. They have all had English A.

This blanket-prescription, it must be considered, performs a double function for the State universities. They are wedded to the democratic theory of education: all students that the high-schools of the State certify for graduation must be admitted on request, no matter how moronic or incompetent they may be. Obviously, even a university whose standards permit it to award the A. B. for courses in bee-culture and embroidery must devise some sort of screening process to sift out those who cannot be educated at all. English A, though perhaps the most elementary course in the curriculum, is a handy tool for the purpose, and everywhere, at midyear or afterward, scores of freshmen troop home to begin a life dedicated to an even humbler culture than that conferred by the State university. Till they die they will cherish a vague resentment of the system that denies a man four years of college on the ground that he cannot learn to put verbs in his sentences – sentences, by God, that he wouldn't have written if they hadn't forced him to. Meanwhile, those whom the screening process has spared plod onward till they have finished English A, and so have demonstrated that they belong in the college scene.

The private institutions, those which can limit their enrollment, never permit the hopeless prospects to register, and so do not need to make a guillotine of English A. Experience has taught them, however, that whatever else they may assume a freshman to possess, they cannot count on his being literate. Therefore they, too, cling to the required course, in various ways modified and humanized, but at best appalling. So diverse are the sources from which they draw and so diversely prepared the freshmen who come to them, that a growing dissatisfaction with the blanket-requirement is everywhere evident. The plight of the well-prepared student is receiving attention – and indeed no greater agony is readily imaginable than that of a man who knows how to write decently and yet is forced to gear his mind down to the inanities of English A. At Harvard and several other Eastern institutions it has long been possible to "anticipate" English A by passing an advanced examination. This practice has recently spread to all the private institutions of the Atlantic seaboard and to their analogues on the Pacific Coast. Before long, at all institutions that admit freshmen by examination only, it will probably become the custom to excuse from the requirement everyone who makes an honor grade, A or B, in English.

II

Such a development will allay immeasurable suffering. It will not, however, have any effect, even in the private colleges, on those who cannot make the honor grade. Nor will it in any way affect the fortresses of democratic education, the State universities and the small colleges that lust after enrollments the size of Columbia's. These must keep the universal requirement. And, however idiotic the system may appear, no improvement on it has been successfully developed anywhere. In effect, English A will go on till Doomsday.

It is a paradoxical and equivocal course. Nothing in the colleges is more grotesquely taught. It is so mechanically organized that any intelligence, student's or instructor's, is caught helpless in the gears. Lately, the Department of Education has been turned loose on it, so that stupendous insanities have been added upon chaos. It is universally loathed by those who teach and those who take it, and it is attacked by all the other departments of the college, which, seeing their own registration lessen as courses in salesmanship and chautauqua technique multiply, resent the English department's prerogative of compelling all comers to register in it. And yet, for all this, it generally gets results. Students do usually write a little better when they have finished it than they did when they began. It requires a vigorous optimism to attribute as much success to any other course in the colleges.

They swarm in from the prairies and the swamps and the farmlands all about, four thousand freshmen newly come to the State university. Some of them come decently prepared from private academies or metropolitan high-schools that know their business, but in the main they are so much leaf lard — sterile, inert, soggy. They are formed into from one hundred to one hundred and fifty sections, each presided over by an instructor. I can attest the paralyzing effect that the first sight of them has on the instructor. Dazed, bewildered, self-conscious, depressed, they sit before him like so many drawn carcasses in a refrigerating room. They are incredibly docile and propitiatory, incredibly stupid, incredibly hidebound.

The sum of the instructor's job is to teach them, in three sessions a week over a semester or a full year, how to write a grammatical sentence. To that end a tremendous machinery has been developed. They are furnished with the specified manuals, grammars, and correction charts. In the more pretentious colleges they are given, besides, an intricate note-book wherein everything they will do in the course has been set out for them, leaving them nothing to do but to fill in the blanks. Their way has been made as plain before them as pedagogy can mark it out.

Perhaps the end I have described, the ability to write a grammatical sentence, seems a lowly one. Surely, one might think, a college freshman may be trusted to write a ten-word sentence according to the conventions of the language. Well, in good years, when the better high-schools of the State send their best students to State U, fully 10% of them can be trusted to do so, and these exceptional ones are in for a weary time in English A. But the rest, though they may have taken honors in English at Waukesha High and edited the *Waukeshan* there, are quite virgin of such knowledge. Many come from city slums or rural foreign colonies, where Yiddish, German or Norwegian is normally spoken and where, perhaps, the early primary grades are conducted in it. Many more, though innocent of foreign tongues, have never heard literate English spoken except by the alumnae of cross-roads normal-schools that teach the high-school classes. Few have been forced to do enough writing to acquire any familiarity with English idiom. That is why English A invariably becomes the very course in high-school composition that is announced as a prerequisite for it.

I quote from a freshman theme – preserved in my notes not because it was exceptional but because the definition it contains amused me. This freshman, given some leeway in his choice of subject, had elected to tell me why it was that his very soul thrilled to poetry, and had found himself obliged to define poetry. He wrote: "I think that Poetry are words Placed in harmony or rhythm, that having an emotionally reaction upon the reader. Usually in the form of Rhythm. It is a defanite arrangement of words. The defanite arrangement not meaning does not mean not flexible but altering to suit the author."

This is, I grant, somewhat worse than the average freshman's work when he comes to English A, but not much worse, for the man was in my section and not the sub-section to which we relegated the impossible ones. The average freshman, reading his theme over, would have crossed out "not meaning" or "does not mean" in the fourth sentence and would perhaps have been faintly troubled by the second. He might even have spelled "defanite" correctly. But on the whole he would have been satisfied with the passage and rather proud of its intellectual content.

III

The problem is, how to teach such students that they must not write such English. Probably the most effective method is the one that may be called evangelical or, in the luncheon-club sense, inspirational. The instructor who daily preaches that such English will result in the freshman's failing to get a job when he graduates will eventually inspire his section with a passion for reform. "Business letters" are a serviceable text: if you keep pointing out that Smith and Brown's "Manual of Composition" fits the college young to dictate to stenographers, you will move them to study it. They will argue, reasonably enough, that it would be better to make the stenographer study it, but you have a sound rebuttal. An executive, you tell them, emphasizing that magical word, an executive likes to be in a position to correct his stenographer. That clinches the matter. You have proved that facility in composition has a cash value. The section warms to its work. You have now only to assign themes.

The theme-system varies with the college. The parent-course began by requiring a short daily theme, the "one-page theme" that has become notorious, on the theory that daily practice was the best means of acquiring skill. The daily theme is preserved in many colleges, but perhaps a greater number, fearing that the system developed an ability to write a paragraph but left the student helpless beyond that unit, have abandoned it. Instead, they require a longer theme every week and, usually, an ambitious effort of four or five thousand words to be written at the end of the course. Here the weekly theme is the basis of instruction.

Theme-subjects are generally uniform in all sections. A professor is usually given executive charge of all freshman English, and he wears himself thin designing an outline for instructors to follow. The department, harassed by the educators, lusts after standardization. The subjects that the head of the course assigns are those which he believes to be as nearly foolproof as possible for both students and instructors. They are usually a devastating bore. Here is a typical one from the outline of a college in the far West: "Write an account of a game (500 words). Include description, but be sure that the description heightens the interest of the narrative. Aim to secure suspense and climax which will surprise the reader." The result, of course, is predeterminable. Thirty to the section, four thousand frantic students sit down to describe how Homeburg High was being walloped by an invading team when, in the last sentence of the theme and the last second of the game, Ole Swenson, though battered and bloody and probably depressed by the faithlessness of his sweetheart, carried the ball ninety-nine yards for the winning touchdown.

The instructor has from two to four sections, and so must be surprised by Ole's heroism from sixty to one hundred and twenty times. Yet the boredom of such an assignment is inconsiderable compared with that which comes when the outline goes on to direct the freshman to discuss his motives in coming to college, analyze his emotions on being pledged to a fraternity, or describe the wondrous beauties of the dawn. Give the freshman a chance for rhetoric and you will understand the statistics of academic insanity. And if rhetoric is maddening, the abstractions of "exposition, argumentation, description and narration" are positively lethal.

Subjects for themes must be assigned. The innocent instructor who tells a section to "write on anything that interests you" quite wastes the week's effort. Not one freshman in thirty has sufficient originality to be anything but saddened and bewildered by such a command. He will pour out his soul on any subject given him, but he dries up when he has to choose his own. Invariably a class so directed will gather round the desk, when the hour is over, and plead for a fixed topic. Tell me what to write about, Mr. Brown! — it is a cry straight from the depths of human despair. If the instructor remains stubborn, half the class will hand in no themes at all, and the other half will avail themselves of last week's topic, old themes from the files of the fraternity, or new productions based on memories of those done in high-school. I should not, however, be quite so sweeping, for in every section there is sure to be one student, always a girl, with a passion for autobiography. Such co-eds revel in the chance thus offered for personal confession, and manage to create chances when none is provided. My five years of teaching English A gave me a full dozen of such specimens.

There was, for instance, a tall bovine creature, distressingly plain, who had investigated the fringe of Chicago's near-Bohemia and, inspired by the feeble radicalism on tap there, had determined to taste life by acquiring a lover. One memorable theme described how she lured a prospective victim to her home, one evening, when the family were out of town. She disappeared for a moment and returned clad in the most sensational nightgown obtainable at Marshall Field's, bearing a pint of gin in one hand and a copy of "The Rubaiyat" in the other. Poor ambitious girl! She explained how the bewildered victim had fled howling, not even waiting for a drink. Nothing on the near North Side had prepared her for that.

And there was the daughter of a Presbyterian minister, homelier even than the aspirant to Bohemia, who had a set of unsatisfied longings that would frighten a psycho-analyst. Nothing I could write on the back of her themes or say to her from the rostrum was biting enough to halt the autobiography — her themes were a weekly catharsis. I learned about her physiological difficulties, her girlhood speculations about the Facts of Life, her search for men who would enlighten her. When she met, at the poetry club, a handsome young man who seemed magnificently amorous, I learned how she sewed feathers to her garters to give her an air of voluptuous mystery. When the garters, and a fourteen-inch cigarette holder desperately adopted, failed to land the young poet, I learned how she wept over his photograph and meditated suicide. And then, toward the end of the year, in a theme somewhat more reticently allusive than usual, I learned how at last she had found a simian truck-driver from the city who was willing to enlighten all she desired.

IV

The theory of instruction in English A is reasonably sound. The student writes a theme. The instructor reads it, calls attention to errors in grammar, rhetoric or taste, and writes pertinent criticism or advice on the back. The student then, using the manual as a guide, corrects the errors or, if the original is hopeless, rewrites the theme. It is a drearily mechanical system, but I do not see how it could be improved. The critic must not suppose that English A attempts, or can attempt, to develop writing ability or teach style. One could not hope to teach four thousand students to write. The standard of achievement is everywhere set as low as possible, but everywhere the English department is under fire for its wildly impractical demands.

At the college that I have just quitted the minimum requirement may, perhaps a little sweepingly, be thus described: the student, at the end of a semester of eighteen weeks, must be able to write a theme without committing what are known as the "period fault" and the "comma fault." The "period fault" may be observed in the second sentence of the passage I have quoted from my poetic freshman: "Placed in harmony or rhythm, that having an emotionally reaction on the reader." It is, in the language of the texts, "a pseudo-sentence, without subject or finite verb." The "common fault" is defined in a learned potboiler as "presenting as a single sentence two or more grammatically complete sentences that are not connected by coördinating conjunctions or separated by semicolons." The same text (I collaborated in the production of it) illustrates the error with this sentence: "He had failed in his career, failed in love, failed in honor, accordingly, he determined to end his worse than useless existence."

One is to understand that the error here would not have been committed if the author had used a semicolon instead of a comma before "accordingly." One may think that these are arbitrary or emptily pedantic requirements, for only the hopelessly illiterate commit the first error, and the second is not an error at all outside the pages of a freshman manual. Still, to ask a student to learn how to avoid them in the course of four months is a moderate requirement. It nevertheless endangers the standing of the whole freshman class. Early in the course the wholly stupid are weeded out of all sections and herded together for spoon-feeding. Of those that remain, about five out of fifty will fail to master the two principles I have mentioned, and from five to twenty more will slide by only because the instructor dares not let his flunk-list get too imposing.

The manual used for correction is a volume of pedagogical rules. A staggering number of such texts are on the market. I have examined about fifty, and have helped to write one. They are signal evidence of the ignorance of the college students to whose instruction they are addressed. The best of them are the work of intelligent men who have taken time off from collating Elizabethan texts to fund a new car or a Summer abroad. The worst are the work of professors of education who have devised a scientific method of eradicating the comma fault. Most of them are reactionary and unrealistic, taking no account of the living language and expending much effort on fine-spun pedagogical abstractions that have no bearing on the actual writing of English. When my collaborators and I prepared to issue to the world a manual that sanctioned the split infinitive, admitted *so* to standing as a "coördinating conjunction," looked untroubled upon the use of *which* as an adjective, declared that some period faults and comma faults were unobjectionable, and admitted that the formal rules of grammar need not always dictate the management of verbs, pronouns, and participles, we felt that we were exposing ourselves to the ridicule of the whole profession.

It is, however, only fair to say that the conservatism of the text-books is not wholly due to professional mulishness. Rather, it proceeds from a hard-boiled experience in teaching college students. The questions of taste that govern the use of *ain't* or of the split infinitive are altogether too mysterious for the freshman. He will only feel himself betrayed and abandoned if asked to consider them. You cannot tell him that *ain't* is sometimes an agreeable and effective way out of a dilemma, but sometimes an atrocity. However you phrase the proposition, it will reach his consciousness and remain there as a blanket permission to use *ain't* in all circumstances whatever. From that day on he will write, "Michigan ain't likely to win the Big Ten championship, for their team ain't what it was last year, and I ain't convinced they ever will be again." And when the instructor protests, he will triumphantly point out the authorization in the text. No, you tell the freshman that *ain't* is never permissible, in any sentence whatsoever. Then you repeat the interdiction three times a week throughout the semester, flunking every theme in which he uses the word. Perhaps, after eighteen weeks, you will have suggested to half the class that the use of *ain't* is sometimes inadvisable.

Themes and the text, then, are the material of class-room work. The instructor uses both as the basis of his lectures. He reads from the last week's themes, carefully adjusting his sarcasm to the limited intelligence of the class. He points out merits and mistakes. He discusses the assigned pages of the text. He labors to give the dreary routine some interest, some faint stirrings of life. If he is inexperienced and hopeful, he lugs in quantities of good writing — accepted classics, contemporary novels, the brighter weeklies and reviews — reads them to the class, and implores them to learn from the example. If he is old at the game, he sticks to the matter at hand, the work done by his own students, and doggedly hammers away at its immense inertia.

His sympathy goes out to the six or seven alert and intelligent students in every section, for he knows that he is desperately boring them. But he must ignore them, who do not need his efforts, and address the inert mass. They sit patiently before him, dazed, bewildered, uncomprehending. They honestly desire to learn, but they resist instruction. Nothing matters much, he decides: they are impermeable. So year by year he abandons more of his forensics and vaudeville, and with them all that is positive in his teaching. He instructs entirely by fiat and negation. Don't say "we was." Don't say "kiddie, girlie, alrightie." Don't say "it is impossible that there is any book written along this line." Don't say "a dull thud was heard." Don't use an adjective when an adverb is called for. Don't get your pronouns crossed. Don't write on both sides of the paper. Don't forget to write your name on your theme.

If he abandons this nauseating method he may save his own

sanity, but a fog will settle over the dim minds from Homeburg High, and they will end the course no better equipped than when they began it. So long as he sticks to it he may justify himself by the reflection that he is doing something to keep the college literate, to raise the standard of business correspondence, and to give his students some return for the trust they have confided to him. Slowly, as the semester goes on, the themes improve. Comma faults thin down to an average of two a theme. Sentences that would not disgrace a country correspondent begin to emerge here and there. A few of the likelier students anticipate the pages of the manual that deal with diction. By the end of the course, the average student wlll be writing as well as he was supposed to write when he was a sophomore in high-school.

V

The able teachers of the department do not, in most schools, have anything to do with English A. The average professor of English, I must assert in spite of the slurs cast upon him, is an intelligent and capable fellow. Several selective processes have operated on him. The rigorous discipline of the Ph.D., though often devoted to trifling subjects, is a test that nincompoops cannot survive, so that the threshold of qualification is high. Promotion is not often conferred upon fools, dullards, or incompetents, and a man who has become an associate or full professor is likely to be a good man. But such men will not waste their time teaching freshman composition. They devote themselves to their private interests, philology, criticism, or the history of literature. The tedious job must be left to instructors, section hands, and assistants.

Here an economic factor operates. A State university, with an annual freshman registration of four thousand, cannot afford to pay eighty thousand dollars for tuition in one course. Still, there are one hundred and fifty sections that have to be taught. The department, acting on the only assumption possible, that anyone can teach freshman English, hires as half-time instructors seventy-five students of the graduate school, who serve for their own tuition and a meager sum in cash. For the most part these budding M.A.'s are captious hayseeds from the sticks — normal school graduates eager to amass enough hours in Education to fit themselves to be principals of cross-roads high-schools, elderly virgins who are taking a year off from teaching the fifth grade to prepare themselves to teach the seventh grade, or, at best, potential high-school teachers too broke to pay for another year of study. Not one in thirty hopes to be a college teacher, not one in fifty ever is.

Their intelligence would hardly turn litmus paper. They are likely to be aware of their own unfitness, and so tyrannical. They are certain to be distracted by the effort to teach others while doing their own studying. With the best will in the world, a man who is trying to write a master's thesis will not be able to give his pupils the attention they require. And so English A is made still more mechanical and arbitrary by the incompetence of its faculty. What little vitality is possible under the system is altogether frustrated. At one university two "comma faults" in the course of the year will flunk a student, however brilliantly he may write. At another, instructors must exchange themes, so that no man reads or grades the work of his own students. At a third, the student's passing depends not at all on his work or his instructor's opinion of it but on the manipulation of a sort of educational slide-rule operated by a committee that never see the freshmen, nor read their themes. These absurdities seem incredible, but they arise from an honest effort to compensate for the incompetence of the doodles that conduct the sections.

The university with which I was recently associated escapes the worst of these follies, but the results are still dreadful. Its freshman class never exceeds one thousand, and it requires four semester-courses in English; therefore it is able to hire full-time instructors who are far better qualified than the neck-shaved drudges of the State U's. The superiority, however, goes no further, for it is still assumed that almost anyone can teach composition. The stiff selection of the Ph.D. has not yet operated on the faculty of English A. They are nearly always literate, but they are usually little more.

There was, for instance, Joe X, who, when a slack season depressed the real estate game, remembered that he had an A. B. It was not one that would be widely recognized in the profession, but still it was an A. B. His first shock was the discovery that in the second half of English A he would have to teach poetry. He inquired just what poets were considered elevating in academic circles and, on being told, decided that they might bear looking into. Did any of us have a book of poetry? he asked. In May he remarked that he had heard of a library on the campus — now, if he'd only known of it earlier he would have used it. He is probably the only college teacher who ever held up a model to his students the prose style of the late President Harding. He had read in a newspaper, he said, that it observed all the classic traditions. In the literary end of the course he was spelling Shakespeare's heroes *McBeth* and *O'Thello,* and his major contribution to scholarship was the identification of Michael Cassio with one Cassidy who, he said, was one of the Irish adventurers that had made Venice great. We lost Joe when the chairman of the department had to bail him out of jail for accosting a woman in a movie.

Then there was Y, a Kansan who had his moments of grandeur. Across his breast hung a double row of keys, crosses, rosettes and dinguses that symbolized all the prizes for distinction in rhetoric, oratory and debate offered by some lean-to university in the hinterlands beyond Wichita. Following his triumph at Cornopolis U, he had taken a year at Harvard, and there had acquired an accent to astonish the prairies, the *Ersatz* New England accent that can always be spotted by its broadening of the *a* in *hand* and *have.*

One-half of his duty, as he conceived it, was the communication of this grace to his students, and the other half, since he was a Kansan, was the preservation of their souls. His classes alternated between drill in swallowing the consonantal *r* and harangues on the moral life. Perhaps once a fortnight he took up questions of composition and there, you were to understand, the blend of Harvard and the Cornopolis Literary Society was omniscient and infallible. The student who ventured to dispute his fiats received an F for the course, and anyone who laughed was fired. Once a stubborn youth maintained that a word which Y had questioned in his theme was spelled correctly. He dragged to class the twelve-pound bulk of Webster's New International Dictionary, opened it on the desk before Y, and awaited action. There was silence for a moment while Y read the entry and the class held its breath. At last, with measured finality, Y drew a fountain pen from his pocket, crossed out the word in the International, and wrote in above it the spelling he had ordained.

Not to forget Z, upon whom a great silence sat. He once called formally on me, coming at one in the afternoon and remaining until six. In the course of those five hours he spoke exactly one word: it was yes, and was to inform me that he would have a highball. For one semester his classes did not differ materially from that visit. He would come into the class-room, sit down at the desk, gather up the day's quota of themes, indicate a half-dozen pages of the text for the class to study, and then sit there motionless and silent while his students worked mathematics assignments, caught up on their geology reading, and chatted sociably. After ten minutes, or a half-hour, or sometimes fifty minutes, he would rise, remark, "I guess that's all today," and amble off.

But at midyear a startling change occurred. Z became energetic and extremely vocal. We now learned that he was a surveyor temporarily down on his luck — and that he was hard-boiled. He began to address his class as "youse guys" and to belabor them with fragrant oaths. His new method was not quite grammatical and it lacked precedent in the Department of Education, but his classes began to turn out work. He hurled a chair at one sprawling freshman and invited another one, a fullback, to "get up out of that there desk, you washout, if you want to get slapped down." We all swaggered a little with this muscular vindication of academic dignity, but his co-ed students grew vaporish and so he too left us.

But such chaps as these at least had color. They gave the day's grind adventurousness. And therein they differed from the average, the patient nonentities who go thrice daily to the class-room and there repeat their memorized discourses. These draw diagrams of modifiers and pick out topic sentences. They quote what Woolley says about commas and what Wendell says about coherence. They devise jingles to illustrate the comma fault. They analyze, they define, they codify. The fog of their lives is filled with shapes of monsters — pronouns that have vague reference, distorted parallelism of clauses, the dangling participle, the "due to" error, the anticipated antecedent, the incomparable absolute. They construct intricate charts for the avoidance of these reefs.

The game they play with such solemnity is a blend of all the philological puzzles that have of late years amused the populace, but they have drained away all possibility of amusement. It is a game less intelligent than crossword puzzles, and less mature than the "This to That" craze that has broken out in the newspapers. It is a silly, tiresome, utterly mechanical charade that has no sense in it. And if the colleges should be reproached for universally offering a course that has no relation to writing and no bearing on education, they have an unanswerable comeback. Does anyone suppose that in any university anywhere can be gathered together four thousand or one thousand freshmen capable of learning how to write a literate sentence or being otherwise educated? If anyone does, let him teach English A for a year.

8

THE REVOLUTION IN LEARNING

The conflicts of the Twenties were nowhere more severe than in education. Lingering from the Theodore Roosevelt era was the brimstone aroma of "social efficiency," which would have ruthlessly subordinated both the student and what he studied to the needs of the state. Sharply opposing that Prussian creed was the concept of the "child-centered" curriculum and school, which won praise for having liberated the learner from joyless formalism, and blame for having in some cases freed him also from rationality. Underneath surface innovations, the old ways often continued. In the schools of the Lynds' *Middletown,* administratively revamped in the Twenties along social-efficiency lines, such things as "square root, algebra, French, the battles of the Civil War, the presidents of the United States before Grover Cleveland . . . sonnets, free verse, and the Victorian novel" still constituted the core of education.

Somewhere in the middle was John Dewey, critical alike of "social efficiency," of conventional education, and of certain tendencies among the progressives. The Progressive Education Association, established in 1919, wanted Dewey as its honorary president; he declined, and the title thereupon fell to the venerable Charles Eliot of Harvard, who himself in his day had been a champion of *avant-garde* educational views. After Eliot's death in 1926 Dewey was again invited to take the honorary presidency. This time he accepted, and delivered to the organization's 1928 annual convention the address that follows, which was published in the Association's lively (and handsomely designed) magazine, *Progressive Education.*

After 1930, by a twist of historical irony, the Progressive Education

Association lost most of its "radical" character. The cover of *Time* for October 31, 1938 pictured its current leader, Frederick Lovatt Redefer, over the caption: "We are no longer a rebel group." But, said *Time's* cover story, "most bandwagon-jumping schools have swallowed chunks of Progressive methods, little Progressive philosophy." Dewey himself lived to see his own anti-dogmatic views venerated as dogma; "It is a commonplace," Reginald Archambault wrote in 1964, "that everyone talks about Dewey and no one reads him" — either in the kinds of classrooms where he is revered or in those where he is reviled.

PROGRESSIVE EDUCATION AND THE SCIENCE OF EDUCATION

John Dewey

What is Progressive Education? What is the meaning of experiment in education, of an experimental school? What can such schools as are represented here do for other schools, in which the great, indefinitely the greater, number of children receive their instruction and discipline? What can be rightfully expected from the work of these progressive schools in the way of a contribution to intelligent and stable educational practice; especially what can be expected in the way of a contribution to educational theory? Are there common elements, intellectual and moral, in the various undertakings here represented? Or is each school going its own way, having for its foundation the desires and preferences of the particular person who happens to be in charge? Is experimentation a process of trying anything at least once, of putting into immediate effect any "happy thought" that comes to mind, or does it rest upon principles which are adopted at least as a working hypothesis? Are actual results consistently observed and used to check an underlying hypothesis so that the latter develops intellectually? Can we be content if from the various progressive schools there emanate suggestions which radiate to other schools to enliven and vitalize their work; or should we demand that out of the cöoperative undertakings of the various

FROM *Progressive Education,* V (July-August-September, 1928), pp. 197–204. Reprinted by permission of the John Dewey Society for the Study of Education and Culture.

schools a coherent body of educational principles shall gradually emerge as a distinctive contribution to the theory of education?

Such questions as these come to mind on the occasion of such a gathering as this. The interrogations expressed are far from all inclusive. They are one-sided, and intentionally so. They glide over the important questions that may be asked about what these schools are actually doing for the children who attend them; how they are meeting their primary responsibility that to the children themselves and their families and friends. The one-sided emphasis is, as was said, intentional. The questions are shaped to take another slant; to direct attention to the intellectual contribution to be expected of progressive schools. The reasons for this one-sidedness are close at hand. It is natural that in your own exchange of experiences and ideas the question slurred over should be prominent. And that pupils in progressive schools are themselves progressing, and that the movement to establish more progressive schools is progressing, I have no doubt. Nor do I think that the old question, once a bugaboo, as to what will happen when the pupils go to college or out into life, is any longer an open one. Experience has proved that they give a good account of themselves; so it has seemed to me that the present is a fitting time to raise the intellectual, the theoretical problem of the relation of the progressive movement to the art and philosophy of education.

The query as to common elements in the various schools receives an easy answer up to a certain point. All of the schools, I take it for granted, exhibit as compared with traditional schools, a common emphasis upon respect for individuality and for increased freedom; a common disposition to build upon the nature and experience of the boys and girls that come to them, instead of imposing from without external subject-matter and standards. They all display a certain atmosphere of informality, because experience has proved that formalization is hostile to genuine mental activity and to sincere emotional expression and growth. Emphasis upon activity as distinct from passivity is one of the common factors. And again I assume that there is in all of these schools a common unusual attention to the human factors, to normal social relations, to communication and intercourse which is like in kind to that which is found in the great world beyond the school doors; that all alike believe that these normal human contacts of child with child and of child with teacher are of supreme educational importance, and that all alike disbelieve in those artificial personal relations which have been the chief factor in isolation of schools from life. So much at least of common spirit and purpose we may assume to exist. And in so far we already have the elements of a distinctive contribution to the body of educational theory: respect for individual capacities, interests and experience; enough external freedom and informality at least to enable teachers to become acquainted with children as they really are; respect for self-initiated and self-conducted learning; respect for activity as the stimulus and centre of learning; and perhaps above all belief in social contact, communication, and coöperation upon a normal human plane as all-enveloping medium.

These ideas constitute no mean contribution: It is a contribution to educational theory as well as to the happiness and integrity of those who come under the influence of progressive schools. But the elements of the contribution are general, and like all generalities subject to varied and ambiguous interpretations. They indicate the starting point of the contribution that progressive schools may make to the theory or science of education, but only the starting point. Let us then reduce our questions to a single one and ask, What is the distinctive relation of progressive education to the science of education, understanding by science a body of verified facts and tested principles which may give intellectual guidance to the practical operating of schools?

Unless we beg the question at the outset assuming that it is already known just what education is, just what are its aims and what are its methods, there is nothing false nor extravagant in declaring that at the present time different sciences of education are not only possible but also much needed. Of course such a statement goes contrary to the idea that science by its very nature is a single and universal system of truths. But this idea need not frighten us. Even in the advanced sciences, like those of mathematics and physics, advance is made by entertaining different points of view and hypotheses, and working upon different theories. The sciences present no fixed and closed orthodoxy.

And certainly in such an undertaking as education, we must employ the word "science" modestly and humbly; there is no subject in which the claim to be strictly scientific is more likely to suffer from pretence, and none in which it is more dangerous to set up a rigid orthodoxy, a standardized set of beliefs to be accepted by all. Since there is no one *thing* which is beyond question, education, and since there is no likelihood that there will be until society and hence schools have reached a dead monotonous uniformity of practice and aim, there cannot be one single science. As the working operations of schools differ, so must the intellectual theories devised from those operations. Since the practice of progressive education differs from that of the traditional schools, it would be absurd to suppose that the intellectual formulation and organization which fits one type will hold for the other. To be genuine, the science which springs from schools of the older and traditional type, must work upon that foundation, and endeavor to reduce its subject-matter and methods to principles such that their adoption will eliminate waste, conserve resources, and render the existing type of practice more effective. In the degree in which progressive schools mark a departure in their emphasis from old standards, as they do in freedom, individuality, activity, and a coöperative social medium the intellectual organization, the body of facts and principles which they may contribute must of necessity be different. At most they can only occasionally borrow from the "science" that is evolved on the basis of a different type of practice, and they can even then borrow only what is appropriate to their own special aims and processes. To discover how much is relevant is of course a real problem. But this is a very different thing from assuming that the methods and results obtained under traditional scholastic conditions form the standard of science to which progressive schools must conform.

For example it is natural and proper that the theory of the practices found in traditional schools should set great store by tests and measurements. This theory reflects modes of school administration in which marks, grading, classes, and promotions are important. Measurement of I. Qs and achievements are ways of making these operations more efficient. It would not be hard to show that need for classification underlies the importance of testing for I. Qs. The aim is to establish a norm. The norm, omitting statistical refinements, is essentially an average found by taking a sufficiently large number of persons. When this average is found, any given child can be rated. He comes up to it, falls below it, or exceeds it, by an assignable quantity. Thus the application of the results makes possible a more precise classification than did older methods which were by comparison hit and miss. But what has all this to do with schools where individuality is a primary object of consideration, and wherein the so-called "class" becomes a grouping for social purposes and wherein diversity of ability and experience rather than uniformity is prized?

In the averaging and classificatory scheme some special capacity, say in music, dramatics, drawing, mechanical skill or any other art, appears only one along with a large number of other factors, or perhaps does not appear at all in the list of things tested. In any case, it figures in the final result only as smoothed down, ironed out, against a large number of other factors. In the progressive school, such an ability is a distinctive resource to be utilized in the coöperative experience of a group; to level it down by averaging it with other qualities until it simply counts in assigning to the individual child a determinate point on a curve is simply hostile to the aim and spirit of progressive schools.

Nor need the progressive educator be unduly scared by the idea that science is constituted by quantitative results, and, as it is often said, that whatever exists can be measured, for all subjects pass through a qualitative stage before they arrive at a quantitative one; and if this were the place it could be shown that even in the mathematical sciences quantity occupies a secondary place as compared with ideas of order which verge on the qualitative. At all events, *quality* of activity and of consequence is more important for the teacher than any quantitative element. If this fact prevents the development of a certain kind of science, it may be unfortunate. But the educator cannot sit down and wait till there are methods by which quality may be reduced to quantity; he must operate here and now. If he can organize his qualitative processes and results into some connected intellectual form, he is really advancing scientific method much more than if, ignoring what is actually most important, he devotes his energies to such unimportant by-products as may now be measured.

Moreover, even if it be true that everything which exists could be measured — if only we knew how — that which does *not* exist cannot be measured. And it is no paradox to say that the teacher is deeply concerned with what does not exist. For a progressive school is primarily concerned with growth, with a moving and changing process, with *transforming* existing capacities and experiences; what already exists by way of native endowment and past achievement is subordinate to what it may become. Possibilities are more important than what already exists, and knowledge of the latter counts only in its bearing upon possibilities. The place of measurement of achievements as a theory of education is very different in a static educational system from what it is in one which is dynamic, or in which the ongoing process of growing is the important thing.

The same principle applies to the attempt to determine objectives and select subject-matter of studies by wide collection and accurate measurement of data. If we are satisfied upon the whole with the aims and processes of existing society, this method is appropriate. If you want schools to perpetuate the present order, with at most an elimination of waste and with such additions as enable it to do better what it is already doing, then one type of intellectual method or "science" is indicated. But if one conceives that a social order different in quality and direction from the present is desirable and that schools should strive to educate with social change in view by producing individuals not complacent about what already exists, and equipped with desires and abilities to assist in transforming it, quite a different method and content is indicated for educational science.

While what has been said may have a tendency to relieve educators in progressive schools from undue anxiety about the criticism that they are unscientific — a criticism leveled from the point of view of theory appropriate to schools of quite a different purpose and procedure — it is not intended to exempt them from responsibility for contributions of an organized, systematic, intellectual quality. The contrary is the case. All new and reforming movements pass through a stage in which what is most evident is a negative phase, one of protest, of deviation, and innovation. It would be surprising indeed if this were not true of the progressive educational movement. For instance, the formality and fixity of traditional schools seemed oppressive, restrictive. Hence in a school which departs from these ideals and methods, freedom is at first most naturally conceived as removal of artificial and benumbing restrictions. Removal, abolition are, however, negative things, so in time it comes to be seen that such freedom is no end in itself, nothing to be satisfied with and to stay by, but marks at most an opportunity to do something of a positive and constructive sort.

Now I wonder whether this earlier and more negative phase of progressive education has not upon the whole run its course, and whether the time has not arrived in which these schools are undertaking a more constructively organized function. One thing is sure: in the degree in which they enter upon organized constructive work, they are bound to make definite contributions to building up the theoretical or intellectual side of education. Whether this be called science or philosophy of education, I for one, care little; but if they do not *intellectually* organize their own work, while they may do much in making the lives of the children committed to them more joyous and more vital, they contribute only incidental scraps to the science of education.

The word organization has been freely used. This word suggests the nature of the problem. Organization and administration are words associated together in the traditional scheme, hence organization conveys the idea of something external and set. But reaction from this sort of organization only creates a demand for another sort. Any genuine intellectual organization is flexible and moving, but it does not lack its own internal principles of order and continuity. An experimental school is under the temptation to improvise its subject-matter. It must take advantage of unexpected events and turn to account unexpected questions and interests. Yet if it permits improvisation to dictate its course, the result is a jerky, discontinuous movement which works against the possibility of making any important contribution to educational subject-matter. Incidents are momentary, but the use made of them should not be momentary or short-lived. They are to be brought within the scope of a developing whole of content and purpose, which is a whole because it has continuity and consecutiveness in its parts. There is no single subject-matter which all schools must adopt, but in every school there should be some significant subject-matters undergoing growth and formulation.

An illustration may help make clearer what is meant. Progressive schools set store by individuality, and sometimes it seems to be thought that orderly organization of subject-matter is hostile to the needs of students in their individual character. But individuality is something developing and to be continuously attained, not something given all at once and ready-made. It is found only in life-history, in its continuing growth; it is, so to say, a career and not just a fact discoverable at a particular cross section of life. It is quite possible for teachers to make such a fuss over individual children, worrying about their peculiarities, their likes and dislikes, their weaknesses and failures, so that they miss perception of real individuality, and indeed tend to adopt methods which show no faith in the power of individuality. A child's individuality cannot be found in what he does or in what he consciously likes at a given moment; it can be found only in the connected course of his actions. Consciousness of desire and purpose can be genuinely attained only toward the close of some fairly prolonged sequence of activities. Consequently some organization of subject-matter reached through a serial or consecutive course of doings, held together within the unity of progressively growing occupation or project, is the only means which corresponds to real individuality. So far is organization from being hostile to the principle of individuality.

Thus much of the energy that sometimes goes to thinking about individual children might better be devoted to discovering some worthwhile activity and to arranging the conditions under which it can be carried forward. As a child engages in this consecutive and cumulative occupation, then in the degree in which it contains valuable subject-matter, the realization or building up of his individuality comes about as a consequence, one might truly say, as a natural by-product. He finds and develops himself in what he does, not in isolation but by interaction with the conditions which contain and carry subject-matter. Moreover a teacher can find out immensely more about the real needs, desires, interests, capacities, and weaknesses of a pupil by observing him throughout the course of such consecutive activity than by any amount of direct prodding or of merely cross-sectional observation. And all observations are of necessity cross-sectional when made of a child engaged in a succession of disconnected activities.

Such a succession of unrelated activities does not provide, of course, the opportunity or content of building up an organized subject-matter. But neither do they provide for the development of a coherent and integrated self. Bare doing, no matter how active, is not enough. An activity or project must, of course, be within the range of the experience of pupils and connected with their needs — which is very far from being identical with any likes or desires which they can consciously express. This negative condition having been met, the test of a good project is whether it is sufficiently full and complex to demand a variety of responses from different children and permit each to go at it and make his contribution in a way which is characteristic of himself. The further test or mark of a good activity, educationally speaking, is that it have a sufficiently long time-span so that a series of endeavors and explorations are involved in it, and included in such a way that each step opens up a new field, raises new questions, arouses a demand for further knowledge, and suggests what to do next on the basis of what has been accomplished and the knowledge thereby gained. Occupational activities which meet these two conditions will of necessity result in not only amassing known subject-matter but in its organization. They simply cannot be carried on without resulting in some orderly collection and systematization of related facts and principles. So far is the principle of working toward organization of knowlege not hostile to the principles of progressive education that the latter cannot perform its functions without reaching out into such organization.

An exaggerated illustration, amounting to a caricature, may perhaps make the point clearer. Suppose there is a school in which pupils are surrounded with a wealth of material objects, apparatus, and tools of all sorts. Suppose they are simply asked what they would like to do and then told in effect to "go to it," the teacher keeping hands — and mind, too — off. *What* are they going to do? What assurance is there that what they do is anything more than the expression, and exhaustion, of a momentary impulse and interest? The supposition does not, you may say, correspond to any fact. But what are the implications of the opposite principle? Where can we stop as we get away from the principle contained in the illustration? Of necessity — and this is as true of the traditional school as of a progressive — the start, the first move, the initial impulse in action, must proceed from the pupil. You can lead a horse to water but you can't make him drink. But whence comes his idea of *what* to do? That must come from what he has already heard or seen; or from what he sees some other child doing. It comes as a suggestion from beyond himself, from the environment, he being not an originator of the idea and purpose but a vehicle through which his surroundings past and present suggest something to him. That such suggestions are likely to be chance ideas, soon exhausted, is highly probable. I think observation will show that when a child enters upon a really fruitful and consecutively developing activity, it is because, and in as far as, he has previously engaged in some complex and gradually unfolding activity which has left him a question he wishes to prove further or with the idea of some piece of work still to be accomplished to bring his occupation to completion. Otherwise he is at the mercy of chance suggestion, and chance suggestions are not likely to lead to anything significant or fruitful.

While in outward form, these remarks are given to show that the teacher, as the member of the group having the riper and fuller experience and the greater insight into the possibilities of continuous development found in any suggested project, has not only the right but the duty to suggest lines of activity, and to show that there need not be any fear of adult imposition provided the teacher knows children as well as subjects, their import is not exhausted in bringing out this fact. Their basic purport is to show that progressive schools by virtue of being progressive, and not in spite of that fact, are under the necessity of finding projects which involve an orderly development and inter-connection of subject-matter, since otherwise there can be no sufficiently complex and long-span undertaking. The opportunity and the need impose a responsibility. Progressive teachers may and can work out and present to other teachers for trial and criticism definite and organized bodies of knowledge, together with a listing of sources from which additional information of the same sort can be secured. If it is asked how the presentation of such bodies of knowledge would differ from the standardized texts of traditional schools, the answer is easy. In the first place, the material would be associated with and derived from occupational activities or prolonged courses of action undertaken by the pupils themselves. In the second place, the material presented would not be something to be literally followed by other teachers and students, but would be indications of the intellectual possibilities of this and that course of activity — statements on the basis of carefully directed and observed experience of the questions that have arisen in connection with them and of the kind of information found useful in answering them, and of where that knowledge can be had. No second experience would exactly duplicate the course of the first; but the presentation of material of this kind would liberate and direct the activities of any teacher in dealing with the distinctive emergencies and needs that would arise in re-undertaking the same general type of project. Further material thus developed would be added, and a large and yet free body of related subject-matter would gradually be built up.

As I have touched in a cursory manner upon the surface of a number of topics, it may be well in closing to summarize. In substance, the previous discussion has tried to elicit at least two contributions which progressive schools may make to that type of a science of education which corresponds to their own type of procedure. One is the development of organized subject-matter just spoken of. The other is a study of the conditions favorable to learning. As I have already said there are certain traits characteristic of progressive schools which are not ends in themselves but which are opportunities to be used. These reduce themselves to opportunities for *learning,* for gaining knowledge, mastering definite modes of skill or techniques, and acquiring socially desirable attitudes and habits — the three chief aspects of learning, I should suppose. Now of necessity the contribution from the side of traditional schools to this general topic is concerned chiefly with methods of teaching, or, if it passes beyond that point, to the methods of study adopted by students. But from the standpoint of progressive education, the question of method takes on a new and still largely untouched form. It is no longer a question of how the teacher is to instruct or how the pupil is to study. The problem is to find what conditions must be fulfilled in order that study and learning will naturally and necessarily take place, what conditions must be present so that pupils will make the responses which cannot help having learning as their consequence. The pupil's mind is no longer to be on study or learning. It is given to doing the things that the situation calls for, while learning is the result. The method of the teacher, on the other hand, becomes a matter of finding the conditions which call out self-educative activity, or learning, and of coöperating with the activities of the pupils so that they have learning as their consequence.

A series of constantly multiplying careful reports on conditions which experience has shown in actual cases to be favorable and unfavorable to learning would revolutionize the whole subject of method. The problem is complex and difficult. Learning involves, as just said, at least three factors: knowledge, skill, and character. Each of these must be studied. It requires judgment and art to select from the total circumstances of a case just what elements are the casual conditions of learning, which are influential, and which secondary or irrelevant. It requires candor and sincerity to keep track of failures as well as successes and to estimate the relative degree of success obtained. It requires trained and acute observation to note the indications of progress in learning, and even more to detect their causes — a much more highly skilled kind of observation than is needed to note the results of mechanically applied tests. Yet the progress of a science of education depends upon the systematic accumulation of just this sort of material. Solution of the problem of discovering the causes of learning is an endless process. But no advance will be made in the solution till a start is made, and the freer and more experimental character of progressive schools places the responsibility for making the start squarely upon them.

I hardly need remind you that I have definitely limited the field of discussion to one point: the relation of progressive education to the development of a science of education. As I began with questions, I end with one: Is not the time here when the progressive movement is sufficiently established so that it may now consider the intellectual contribution which it may make to the art of education, to the art which is the most difficult and the most important of all human arts?

PART III

FAITH OF OUR FATHERS: LIVING STILL?

This is an age of skepticism, cynicism and disillusionment; but it is also, and simultaneously, an age that is wistfully in quest of religious sustenance and religious certitude, and almost pathetically credulous when given half a chance. . . . The attitude of complete incredulity is in fact inconsistent with the quest of self-realization. To demand everything of life without trusting life, to seek a full, rich, colorful existence without yielding to any enthusiasm, is a psychological impossibility. Eventually the youth must and will believe in something. I hasten to add that the object of his faith is likely to be something quite new and strange, as different as possible from the childhood religion which he has learned to mistrust.

WALTER MARSHALL HORTON
Theism and the Modern Mood (1930)

9

THE TRAVAIL OF RELIGIOUS LIBERALISM

In a presidential address to the American Society of Church History, Professor Robert T. Handy of Manhattan's Union Theological Seminary named the decade 1925–1935 "the American Religious Depression." Many mainstream denominations showed a net membership decline; a count of magazines indexed in the *Reader's Guide* showed more articles critical than favorable toward organized religion; and Sinclair Lewis' savagely anticlerical novel *Elmer Gantry* was a runaway best seller. (He dedicated it, incidentally, "To H. L. Mencken, With profound admiration.") What did clergymen themselves think of their calling in the Twenties?

Allan Armstrong Hunter (Princeton, '16; war service, American Red Cross, 1918–19; M.A., Columbia, '25), was pastor of a community church in Palisade, New Jersey, when he wrote the article reprinted here. Later in the Twenties he spent a year in China, teaching for a time in the National University of Peking. Then he was called to a parish in Southern California which combined civic action ("Our church integrated long before the war," Mr. Hunter wrote me in 1968) with the meditative life ("During the war some of us . . . worked with Gerald Heard and Aldous Huxley at least three hours a day"). Active as national vice-chairman of the Fellowship of Reconciliation, and in the Southern California chapter of the American Civil Liberties Union, Allan Hunter has found time also to write a dozen books, ranging from religion (*The Audacity of Faith*) and foreign affairs (*Facing the Pacific*) to marriage counseling and birdlore.

The *Forum* in 1923 – the year in which the following article appeared – acquired the subtitle "a non-partisan magazine of free discussion," resuming a policy which had made that journal great during the Eighties and Nineties. Under the skillful management of Henry Goddard Leach, the magazine ran articles, pro and con, on topics such as Fundamentalism, companionate marriage, the policies of Lenin, cubism, Catholicism in America, and the possibility of war with Japan, from contributors as various as Bertrand Russell, Upton Sinclair, Cordell Hull, Reed Smoot, and William Jennings Bryan. Interestingly, this journal of controversy fared better in Babbitt's America than in FDR's; after a spurt in circulation (to 92,000) by the end of the Twenties, the *Forum's* readership shrank drastically, and by 1950 the magazine was no more.

WHY WE ARE SILENT

THE PROBLEM FACING YOUNG MINISTERS

Allan A. Hunter

While preachers of long-standing dispute the virgin birth, a new generation of ministers and theological students, imbued with modern scientific thought, are bewildered by the much more urgent issue as to what attitude they are to adopt toward the confusing social problems of the day. How are they to find useful solutions? And can they dare, in their pulpits, to give frank utterance to the unorthodox doubts that are assailing them?

Battles now being waged between the older liberals and the fundamentalists seem to center in the issues as to whether the Bible is inerrantly inspired, whether Jesus was supernaturally born, whether his death appeased an otherwise implacable despot-deity, and whether he arose from the dead with the same body that was buried in the tomb. I am a theological student, aspiring to active service in the pastorate, and as I listen to the heated arguments of the opposed camps, I find myself curiously cold, — disappointingly cold. Just one thing in all this theological controversy impresses me. That is the amazing dumbness and diffidence of us younger men who are preparing to be ministers.

I am well acquainted with the popular idea: that we are pin-feathered chanticleers who expect the sun to rise to hear us crow, that we are cocksure and desperately vocal. But in reality we are insufferably shy, painfully out of ease. Not all of us, of course. There are "seminoles," — theological students in hide-bound seminaries who are learning to thunder the urgency of baptism and brimstone, of golden streets and the second coming, with what they convince themselves is conviction. In the pre-millennial Bible Institute of Los Angeles, for example, they will keep up the tumult and the shouting of their elders for at least another generation. But they constitute no more than an eddy in the stream of prophecy. The rising generation of ministers who are eager to interpret the progressive revelation of God to the men of today, have had the advantage of learning enough science in college to assume that the world was made not in six days, nor even, as quibbling conservatives put in "in six aeons."

The problem for us who are preparing to be prophets is that we are overwhelmed with too many situations: the situation in the Ruhr, the situation in Russia, the situation in the oil fields abroad and the coal fields at home, the situation in the divorce courts. Our brains ache with them all; we are bewildered by thus having incessantly to bear the weary weights of this unintelligible world's worries. Day after day, in the class room, at table, and in our "bicker sessions," we pull these cosmic problems up and down in our minds.

FROM *The Forum*, LXX (October, 1923), pp. 1975–82. Reprinted by permission of Allan A. Hunter.

We pull and grow faint, — so faint that we have not the breath to vociferate against the conservatives, nor even against die-hards who insist that the very commas of the Bible are inspired.

It is not that with the sorrowful Matthew Arnold we are wandering between two worlds, one dead, the other powerless to be born. It is rather that our world is born; and it is too big for us. As Chesterton points out, even the trusted laws of gravitation, thanks to Einstein, appear now to be dancing with a lamentable levity. As for evolution, it is not so simple as Darwin and Drummond, Nietzsche and Fiske proclaimed it to be.

The general hypothesis of living evolutionists like J. A. Thompson, that mind is gradually, through the ages, exerting "a stubborn dominance over matter," we accept and preach right gladly, for we are learning that perhaps the supreme principle of religion is growth, or, — to use the phrase of the Columbia University educators, — "activity leading on to further activity." And some of us feel that Jesus corroborates our faith in this principle when he says, "Greater things than these shall ye do," and "first the grain, then the blade, then the full corn in the ear." We do not think that there is any enmity between the hypothesis of evolution and the inspiration of the Bible: God has breathed his spirit into both. But we must admit that it is perplexing, almost bewildering, this necessary effort of ours to work out the full spiritual implications of the more recent expositions of the evolutionary hypothesis. Into what will the human race develop? Will changes take place in our religious standards as well as practises?

And this is our cry that comes from the deepest places of the heart: "O God, lead us to the paths of simplicity! Give us to say 'Nay!' and 'Yea!' without shadow of turning, without any need for qualifying our statements."

The other night at prayer meeting a pastor asked those present if they had any questions for discussion. One young man asked, "How can I be sure of right and wrong?"

"By following your conscience," was the clear cut answer and firm.

"Conscience!" No doubt it is definite and final enough to those long established in the Church. But we of the questioning generation are not so set in our minds. We have studied the origin of conscience, we have watched the effects of following the conscience without reservations; and now we suspect that it is pretty much a matter of environment, of the social group one happens to belong to. Conscience is a good deal like the pinch of discomfort a man feels, wearing pointed narrow-toed shoes when blunt ones are the fashion.

On the positive side, I have seen the pressure of conscience move a happily married woman to leave her home and break up her family. One metaphysician in Los Angeles, arguing with a young woman who had doubts about the righteousness of traveling abroad, on the grounds that perhaps it would be acting selfishly toward her parents, swept aside all scruples with this exhortation, "Go ahead! You should do as you feel like doing. The fact that you want to go so badly shows that it is the *voice of God in your heart.*"

We ministers under thirty really envy the assurance of our betters in the pulpit who are wont to vindicate their stand in the war with this formula: "I am absolutely right. When a ruffian enters my house and attacks my mother, I know I must kill him. When the Germans invaded Belgium, there was no doubt."

It would bring a great peace to our minds if we could settle the war thus promptly, thus completely. But we cannot. Too many problems are tangled up together. What would have happened, for example, if the French in 1914 had listened to their own Romain Rolland, or the Russian Tolstoi, or Jesus of Nazareth, — and harkening had met German violence with the refusal to murder millions of men in return?

It was simple enough intellectually for the Donald Hankeys and the Rupert Brookes and those fellows who fell before disillusion sickened their vision. But to some of us who were not killed then and are not able now to close our eyes to what France is doing to her neighbors, it is not so clear. Our revulsion of sentiment is suggested, but only suggested, in the exclamation of the young English poet, Robert Nichols: "War does not ennoble; it degrades."

Red moments blind us when we clench our fists fanatically with the words, "Well, one thing we know. If there is another war, we'll go to jail in protest, — we'll do anything rather than go out and butcher men that the propagandizers will tell us are our enemies!"

But this is only whistling in the dark. We are sufficiently aware of the tricks that take place in other people's minds and our own to realize that if the flag were unfurled and the ladies started action with white feathers to pin on slackers' breasts, we would gallantly revise our interpretations, — our mollycoddle interpretations as the Roosevelts would term them, — of the sermon on the mount. We would no doubt quote as lustily as the older ones did in 1917 and

1918 the incident of the whip of cords and the money changers in the temple, along with the "I came to bring not peace but a sword" passage. And we would righteously try to get into the flying corps. At least there would be the horrible chance of our relapsing like this.

Again, we envy the brilliant young radicals writing for certain journals and conducting forums, who have swallowed whole the pacifist non-resistance platform. It would be so intellectually restful if we could join them and stop thinking. If we could shout, "No More War!" If we could register only disgust upon seeing a battleship, after the manner of a certain seminary student who likes to debate against war. When this friend beholds a dreadnaught on the Hudson he gets a sudden attack of *mal de mer;* and the mere sight of Grant's Tomb, "that barbaric glorification of militarism," makes him a little queasy. The flag he hates to see in a church; he would abolish militarism.

And he is right: militarism should be abolished. But the majority of us who are on the threshold of the ministry crave more data as to how, specifically, to do it. We have pretty well lost confidence in the efficacy of just preaching goodwill and peace on earth. We want to get at the economic and sociological causes of tension between nations before we start hammering upon our pulpits about it. And frankly, we have not yet got those causes sewed up in our minds.

Many of us have gone to no end of trouble in our effort to deal with war scientifically. We have read and reread Thorndyke, William James, Woodworth, and J. A. Hobson, seeking to understand the part that the various instincts have to play in breeding conflicts. We have taken notes on the lectures of Norman Angell, Bertrand Russell, and John Haynes Holmes on the economic futility of war; we have underlined and digested articles on its spiritual futility. We have even learned to discuss the matter with our older friends in the field of history, pacifically, without losing our tempers; and we have prayed that light might come from Gandhi's non-cooperation movement in India. Some of us have travelled through Europe and Asia interviewing financial and ethical leaders, or attending student conferences, to the end that we might know.

But we don't know. Some of us are coming to the conviction, a few have already arrived at the conviction, that this world is a net of psychological and economic forces with a mesh too small to let any of our pet panaceas slip through to an idealistic solution. "There can be no peace now but a common peace, no prosperity but a general prosperity," — that is one of the few assurances we have.

Almost equally tormenting, in some cases far more perplexing, is the economic issue. A young Congregationalist entering the ministry explodes in a letter: "The business of social injustice lies about me like a bar of heavy lead. I'm not going into churches forever to patter about things that don't matter. This matters, — and yet I am afraid to speak about it. A great deal of time is needed to think about this and reach a point of surety."

To our gray-haired friends who own stock in the United States Steel Corporation, we cannot pretend that our industrial autocracy is a righteous system. On the other hand, our enthusiasm for guild socialism or what-not generally chills after a few months of honest-to-goodness study.

Our hearts burn within us when we talk over the ways of the Utopians as described by H. G. Wells, where the acquisitive instinct is so sublimated that there is no profiteering, no sanguinary competition, not even coinage, and everybody gives full play to the creative instinct out of sheer passion for work and service. Then our hearts grow cold and our minds numb when we realize that not one preacher in this country has a clearly defined platform that appeals to us, on which the needs of employers and employees as well as consumers can be reconciled.

Furthermore, most older ministers are so choked with the mere mechanics of pastoral work, — what Brother Lawrence would call "trivial devotions," — that they utterly fail to face with insight the issue of industrial democracy. By industrial democracy is meant among other things not only sufficient wages and hours of leisure to the working man wherewith to live a decent life, but also a voice in the administration of the occupation in which he is engaged.

A young friend says of his pastor that he is a delightful man, "But he is making no dent, economically speaking, on the world rulers of this darkness, — he has his kids to take care of, you know. Perhaps," concludes my friend, "this social gospel is an idea which we have erected into a Christ. All the same, we are ready to suffer for it."

About divorce, I suppose that most of us entertain views that would make the apostle Paul turn over in his grave, were we to come out with them. Some day we hope to have a science of human relationships, in accordance with which people will not marry until they have thoroughly tested out the compatibility of their temperaments. Meanwhile the Church does little specifically to educate young men and women to marry intelligently and to live together skilfully, happily, hygienically in marriage; and we are inclined to believe that until the Church takes scientific steps to educate against divorce, it has no right arbitrarily to forbid relief from those marriages which have become a crushing bondage.

As regards birth regulation, there may be something in Wells' suggestion that in this age of confusion the fundamental evil is the overcrowding of the planet, and that two hundred and fifty million people are enough. At any rate, to help offset "insensate multiplication of the common life," a classmate at seminary apparently considers it a vital part of his mission work on the foreign field to spread such information among the dense native poor of China as shall encourage them to prevent over-crowding. The fact that a Japanese general has protested against propaganda for birth control on the argument that it will cut off prospective recruits for the Imperial army, corroborates our conviction that in this field lies one of the most vital problems for organized religion to face, — the problem of directing the forces that increase population throughout the world.

At the heart of this problem is the new and urgent necessity of working out a more finely adjusted code between men and women, based on standards of personality and the sanctity of the sources of life.

We wish to avoid being hard and dogmatic. Joseph Conrad says, "At a time when nothing which is not revolutionary in some way or other can expect to attract much attention, I have not been revolutionary in my writings. The revolutionary spirit is mighty convenient in this, that it frees one from all scruples as regards ideas. Its hard, absolute optimism is repulsive to my mind by the menace of fanaticism and intolerance it contains." There are stirring within us new scruples as regards ideas, and a new hatred, — the hatred of intolerance.

These issues, these situations, these problems that have browbeaten us who hope to preach, are so bewildering that we can sympathize a little with one young idealist, who, after doing his stint in the war, joined the American Friends' Reconstruction work in Europe. Disenchanted with such ameliorative efforts, he suddenly jumped into a career of art with this apologia: "It's no use trying to do anything along the present lines in Europe or at home. What is being done now," he explained, standing at his easel in Paris, "is just painting cancer with iodine."

That may be, but despite its shortcomings, the Church is a clinical laboratory dedicated to working out a cure. Its intervening dogmas and bigotries notwithstanding, the Church is pledged to the person of Jesus whose spirit is the only spirit that can solve the problems now leaving us stunned and mute. Jesus valued persons above military successes, above property systems, above social institutions, — infinitely above these things. And we cannot forget that, as our Leader, He puts us under the inescapable obligation to attest our reverence for men by standing ready to pay any price, — even as He paid it, — that they may have the more abundant life.

Under that obligation, somehow and before long, we hope to have something definite if not dogmatic to say. But the word that we shall speak will not be for or against the virgin birth, the blood atonement, the verbal infallibility of Scripture, — issues as dead as those battled over in the Civil War. Rather, the word that we shall speak will be toward the living truth that sets men free.

10 THE OLD-TIME RELIGION IN SUBURBIA

Media coverage of the Scopes "monkey trial" has led us to view the Fundamentalist–Modernist controversy in the Twenties simplistically, as a struggle between rural and urban values. But when John Van Schaik commissioned Granville Hicks to do a series of interviews with youth leaders, to be published in the (Unitarian) *Christian Register,* the (Universalist) *Christian Leader,* the *Congregationalist,* and other liberal religious weeklies, Hicks's quest for a representative young Fundamentalist took him not to Dayton, Tennessee but to West Philadelphia. Further surprises were in store, and the article that follows should be read not only for its subject's views but also for the interviewer's reactions.

Granville Hicks was an instructor in the Bible and in English at Smith College when he wrote up this interview. Nurtured in the humane New England religious culture which had produced the venerable denominational organs that published such articles, Hicks was already beginning to turn more radical; the touchstone, for him as for so many others, was the execution of Sacco and Vanzetti that same year (1927). The Depression deepened his radicalism, and afterward, as a member of the Communist Party (1935–1939), a staff writer for the *New Masses,* and the author of a definitive biography of John Reed (1936), he became a major voice among the "writers on the Left." Hicks's subsequent disenchantment with Stalinism is vividly recaptured in his novel *Only One Storm* (1942).

Of his 1927 interview with Hicks, Hillyer Straton wrote me in 1968 that he "would hate to be remembered for eternity for that." (For perspective, see his essay in the *Christian Century's* series "How My Mind Has Changed in This Decade," October 26, 1949.) The younger

Straton's scholarly articles on his father's ministry during the Twenties are a major contribution toward undoing the stereotyped view of Fundamentalism. In his present pastorate in a Boston suburb, Straton writes, he has dealt with young people of the same social status as those in his first church in West Philadelphia, but he finds the present generation more idealistic than his own: "We tended to take it out in irrelevant rebellion like sporting coonskin coats."

THE SON OF A FUNDAMENTALIST PROPHET

HILLYER HAWTHORNE STRATON GIVES LIVELY EVIDENCE OF KNOWING WHAT HE BELIEVES

Granville Hicks

Waiting outside the door of the Straton home in New York, I found myself a little dismayed. With the people I had hitherto interviewed I had felt that I had a great deal in common, but I did not know about young Straton. I looked forward to the interview, and yet I felt it would be difficult.

He welcomed me cordially in a voice that has a distinctly Southern accent. He looks young, and he is young, this son of the famous John Roach Straton, who is himself on the road to fame; but he is mature and self-assured in his bearing. He asked me to sit down, and prepared to answer my questions.

First I asked about himself. "I did my work at Mercer University in Macon, Georgia," he replied. "I took my A. B. and A. M. there. Last summer I did some work at Columbia summer school. Now I'm in my first year at the Eastern Baptist Theological Seminary in Philadelphia. And I'm also pastor of the New Berean Baptist Church of Philadelphia."

"That reminds me," I interrupted. "What happened in that dispute over your ordination that got into the papers last summer?"

FROM *The Christian Register,* CVI (March 10, 1927), pp. 197–8. Reprinted with permission.

"Why, nothing," he answered in his easy Southern drawl. "You see, I was fighting for a matter of principle. The association of Baptist churches in southern New York had created a standing committee to ordain candidates. I haven't any reason to suppose that they wouldn't have accepted me, but I held that they hadn't anything to do with such matters. Our churches hold to the congregational form of organization, and any church has a right to ordain whomever it wishes. That's been the Baptist principle for four hundred years, and I couldn't see why this particular group should make a change. So I stood out for the historic method. Nothing happened."

"I see. Tell me something. Have you any organization of young Fundamentalists?"

"Not as far as I know. I'm opposed more or less to organizations. You take the conference at Milwaukee, for example; a lot of people went there and talked and talked and didn't do anything. If those two thousand young people had spent the time and money going out in the way that the Lord Jesus commanded, preaching and teaching repentance to the individual, they would have accomplished something that would have resounded throughout Christendom. Organization is one of the curses of the liberals. They don't have anything else to do. Of course Fundamentalists have the vice, too, but not to the same extent. They are too busy saving souls to bother with organization." He spoke with that tremendous earnestness which repeatedly during the interview brought a look of sternness to his sensitive, smiling face. "Here I am in Philadelphia," he went on. "I have my church with two preaching services every Sunday. I'm carrying a full course at the theological school. I have parish calls to make, and I'm mighty happy to be able to say that in my calls recently I've been able to bring several people to a saving knowledge of Christ. What time have I for organizations?"

"Are the Fundamentalists holding their own among the young people?" I inquired.

"They certainly are. In my own church I had a young people's night, and I asked all the young people who wanted to reconsecrate themselves to Christ to come forward. More than thirty responded, and my church is not large."

"But aren't they exposed to Modernism in the colleges?"

"Yes, indeed. Most of the State universities have felt the liberal influence, and even many denominational colleges that pretend to hold to the fundamentals have been tarred by the Modernist stick. But when they're given the gospel religion they respond to it. Why, in my church I have young people who are doing graduate work at the University of Pennsylvania and elsewhere. We're told that we ought to be liberal and give dances, but I've seen too many churches die that way. All I do is to preach the word of God, and it holds the young people as well as of old. It worked in apostolic times — Timothy and Titus were young men. I've seen it in my father's church — he has a fine class of young people. They come there and rejoice. I believe that there are as many young people there as in any church of its size in the country, and last year he had more conversions than the four other leading Baptist churches in New York put together. And I've seen the same thing in my own church. Hicks, that's where the liberal churches are going to lose out. Of course a Fosdick can get a crowd, but there are hundreds of liberal churches that are dying. There is no gospel preached, and the people don't and won't come."

"How do you feel about such organizations as the Y.M.C.A. and the Christian Endeavor?"

"I haven't fully formulated my ideas. You could take the 'C' out of Y.M.C.A. and nobody would ever notice the difference. I suppose that the Christian Endeavor and the Baptist Young People's Union have some value, but I'm getting back to the idea that the Church, the Bride of Christ, is the all-important thing. There's always the danger that the young people will come to the young people's meeting and won't go to church. We have a young people's meeting in my church, but they stay to the service afterwards. Half my crowd Sunday evenings are under twenty-five. And the beauty of the conservative position is that it works, the old-time religion works. I was mighty happy last Sunday night when nine people came forward and accepted Christ. I don't suppose there was anything like it in any other church in America."

"Have you had training in science?" I asked.

"I've specialized in one branch of science. I planned to be an electrical engineer before God called me into the ministry, and I am a member of the Institute of Radio Engineers. At Mercer I designed and built a broadcasting station. I've been to sea as a radio operator. And this year, before I accepted my church, I was supporting myself by working as an engineer at Station WOO, the Wanamaker store in Philadelphia. I didn't take biology in college, for I'd had a good course at DeWitt Clinton high school, but I took physics and chemistry. I've done a good deal of private study, both in geology and in biology, carefully examining the evolutionary as well as the anti-evolutionary point of view."

"How do you feel about anti-evolution laws such as that passed in Tennessee?"

"Certainly a democratic state by a majority vote has a perfect right to make such laws. Evolution isn't a fact; it's a theory. It isn't science; it's the philosophic doctrine of continuity. It's a materialistic philosophy, and it leads to atheism and therefore is a religion. There is no more justification for teaching it than there is for teaching some other form of religion in a State college — the Baptist or the Unitarian or any other form of sectarianism. But personally I am perfectly willing to have it taught and believe that it ought to be taught *if* both sides are presented. In any other scientific field under the sun we get both sides; why not in evolution? You know as well as I that in the average college there is only one side presented, and I ask you or any fair-minded man if it is science to give only one side of a theory, and especially to present that theory as if it were a proven fact."

After we had talked a little about evolution, I changed the subject by asking, "Do you think the modern generation is bound for the dogs?"

He smiled. "That's where Father and I disagree. I don't think they're any worse than any other young people. There always have been some bad ones, and there are to-day. A young person who hasn't been regenerated is bad in any age, but you show me a group of young people whose hearts have been changed and I will show you a group of young people whose peers will never be found. Hicks, you take regeneration out of life and out of the Bible, and there's nothing left. My own experience would convince me of that, even if there were nothing of it in the Bible. If you take the passages out of the Bible that refer to regeneration you have a skeleton left that is not only minus meat but also bones. From the time Jesus was twelve years old, he had the Cross in view. Without the Blood Atonement, there's nothing in Christianity worth bothering with. Give modern youth the old-time religion, and they're all right. Without it they're bound plumb for Hell. They need to know Jesus as their personal Savior. That's the whole point. I'm not interested in dogma; I am interested in the redeeming power of Christ."

"You say you're not interested in dogma; what about the Virgin Birth?"

"The Virgin Birth is not dogma; it is just plain fact, as stated by the Bible."

"Do you mean that a man couldn't be regenerated if he didn't believe in the Virgin Birth?"

"I don't say that. 'With God all things are possible.' But for myself I think that the Virgin Birth is essential. Jesus must be fully

God." And this youth in his early twenties, just out of college, hurled at me a torrential exposition of conservative Christology.

When he had finished I asked, "Are you interested in such problems as war and race?"

"I'm vitally interested — just as interested as the rankest social service worker, but I'm interested in a different way. You've got to regenerate the hearts of men before you can do any good. Once you've changed men's hearts, the social problems will take care of themselves. Social reform alone is futile. Education alone is futile. The worst devil in the world is an educated devil."

"Are you interested in fighting Modernists?"

"Only to this extent: The Book of Jude tells us 'to contend earnestly for the faith once for all delivered to the saints.' I've no interest in fighting them; all I want to do is convert them. But when they get hold of denominational organizations, when they secure control of colleges endowed by the money of God-fearing folk who would turn over in their graves if they knew what was taught, when they corrupt mission boards — then we conservatives must step in. I believe that the Fundamentalist position is the true one, and like any man I'll stand up for what I believe."

"The colleges," I remarked, "are filled with Modernists. What are you going to do about it?"

"Convert them," he shot back. "Give them the truth! The average young person is a Fundamentalist till he goes to college and gets his faith knocked out of him. Get hold of him and give him the gospel message. That's the way to save our generation." I rose to go, and he pondered a moment, formulating a last word. "I want to say this," he said at last. "The great need of the modern age for young people, old people, for Modernists, Fundamentalists, and in-betweens, is the regenerating influence of a personal knowledge of the Lord Jesus Christ."

Straton's face was stern and deadly serious as he spoke, but he was smiling as he accompanied me to the door. As he shook my hand, his face became grave once more. "Good-bye, brother," he said. "God be with you. I hope you may some day come to see the light."

11
PROHIBITION AND THE GENERAL WELFARE

A few institutions seem ageless no matter how profoundly the world is changing. In 1923 the *Ladies' Home Journal* published Zane Grey's "The Vanishing American"; "Our Social Ladder: Its Sound and Rotten Rungs," by Mrs. John King Van Rensselaer; "My Own Story," by Mary Pickford; and other pieces by Florenz Ziegfeld and Edith Wharton. There were essays on "Down East Cookery," and on "Making Last Year's Dress This Year's Length," and advertisements for kitchen cleansers and deodorants. From the outside world, Senator Borah contributed an article on "How the World Court Can Be Perfected," and Charles A. Selden muckraked "The Enemies of Prohibition." The *Journal's* editor, Barton W. Currie, thought that the World Court and Prohibition would be "the two major issues to be fought out in American politics" in 1924.

Many Americans would have agreed with Currie that the Eighteenth Amendment was a major (and divisive) political issue. Some saw it as a generational conflict; "These glad young folk do not like the thing which they know as religion . . . from what they see of the reforming army of the Lord," wrote one Episcopalian clergyman in 1920 apropos of the Volstead Act, "and they say . . . 'We don't want to be like them.' " Others considered Prohibition a humanitarian crusade, in the spirit of the Methodist bishops who declared in 1932 that they had "fought liquor, not because it has made men happy, but because it has made men unhappy." In the editorial reprinted here, Barton Currie judged the liquor question to be a "class issue," but members of the classes involved might well have asked him: *cui bono?*

Currie came to the *Journal* from the *Country Gentleman,* with which he had been associated since 1912. Before that he had worked for the New York *Evening Sun,* the *Times,* and the *World;* following his sojourn with the *Ladies' Home Journal,* he edited the lively news monthly *World's Work.* Barton Currie's avocation was collecting rare editions and manuscripts, a hobby about which he wrote a readable work of his own, *Fishers of Books* (Boston, 1931).

SOFT MORALS

Barton W. Currie

The prohibition embroilment is shaping its course as an inevitable class issue.

The fashionable rich demand their rum as an inalienable class privilege.

"To hell with the benefits to the poor there may be in prohibition! We demand our personal liberty to embellish and grace our social functions with sparkling wines and smooth heady liquors, with high-voltage cocktails to electrify our jaded nerves, with spirits of acid strength to fire our sluggish blood. We prefer bootleggers to horse-faced cranks and reformers and will pour our treasures into their laps no matter what crimes and iniquities they commit in the act of supplying alcoholic needs. We abhor radicals and their theories of anarchy and revolution; we demand that organized society police our mansions and villas and safeguard our wealth; we look for rigid honesty and obedience to established authority and law in our servants and agents, but when it comes to our personal festivities and gala entertainments we are a law unto ourselves in the face of this interfering and sumptuary prohibition statute."

On the theory that action speaks louder than words, the above quoted declaration of privilege or enunciation of "rum rights for the rich" is being iterated and reiterated in hundreds of communities where "society" entertains and bootleggers flourish. In exclusive clubs you hear dull monotonous boasting of overflowing cellars and pet rum runners. In New York City some of the "first families" have gone in for aristocratic bootlegging and one of these families finds several of its members under Federal indictment.

Hollywood, California, has been held up to world-wide scorn and abhorrence for its unlicensed debaucheries, yet if the truth were known the new-rich screen stars and promoters and directors gone berserker with sudden wealth have only taken their cue from Newport and Southampton, where "wet" orgies have been commonly the means of social distinction since the enactment of prohibition.

The "respectable" press of our great cities print thousands of columns of news on the subject of prohibition, but almost invariably with a wet slant. They give vastly more prominence to a hurry-up interview with a brewer than to a carefully considered and fact-elaborated statement of a bishop — that is, unless it be the gentle sophistry and polite cynicism of a fashionable bishop of "broad and liberal" views. There are certain yellow journals, however — still anathema in the home of the fastidious patrons of the rum interests — which have been and still are consistently in favor of prohibition.

Since we began publishing Mr. Selden's series of articles on the Enemies of Prohibition, we have received hundreds of letters of approval and five letters of denunciation. Three of those five letters of denunciation were written on the official stationery of the Association Against the Prohibition Amendment.

So far we have not been accused of a business alliance with the bootleggers, but we are charged with bigotry and narrowness, with sniveling hypocrisy and with failure to quote at length from the crime and drunkenness statistics prepared by and for the agents of the brewers and distillers.

In smart circles — not necessarily fashionable even in the money-mad society of the day — of the great Eastern seaboard cities you hear almost exclusive comment on the grotesque and lugubrious failure of prohibition. It benefits no one save the bootleggers. Every kind and all kinds of liquor are flowing in endless streams through illicit channels, yet the medical profession cannot squeeze out a pint or two to save the life of a patient. The laboring man is deprived of his mixed ale and garbage-distilled "redeye," in which he used so conveniently to drown and deaden his woes and tribulations. Little children are no longer seen tripping gaily and blithesomely to the back doors of saloons to "fill the growler" for their tired parents or for thirsty janitors. "Drunks" who have spent their last nickel are no longer hurled by sturdy bouncers through the swinging doors of saloons to roll bloody and sodden into welcoming gutters. There is no longer any iron in our blood or violence in our kidneys. A new race of milksops tiptoe furtively to some bootlegger's roost and then sneak home with the diluted contraband only to find that they have bought some vinegar mixed with alcohol that nauseates almost before the stopper is pulled. In what dark corridors of gloom can one find a more dismal picture of how the common people of these United States are put upon and victimized by psalm-singing idealists?

Before weeping too bitterly, however, read this letter which found its way into one of the New York newspapers which is "respectably" opposed to the "insidious" Volstead Act:

> Sir:
>
> In your issue of December eleventh you gave us a lurid description of the illegal liquor selling in Chicago, St. Louis, Milwaukee and California. Why not try your home town? It is reported by some papers that the amount of drinking in clubs, restaurants and hotels is something tremendous.
>
> In 1910 one of your reporters came to a church in the 35th Police Precinct to find out about the lax observance of the law on Sundays. We went into ten saloons by the side door on Sunday afternoons, and he was told if he had time we could visit 150 more and find the same lawlessness. In 1910 there were 177 saloons in the 35th Precinct. By investigation they were found to have a trade of $3,250,000 a year, taken out of the pockets of the poor.
>
> At a survey made December 8 and 9, 1922, sixty-eight saloons were found selling — supposedly — one-half of 1 per cent beer and wines. These saloons are owned by the breweries. Ten or fifteen years ago the small shopkeepers had hard work to make a living, many of them just kept their heads above water and a large percentage of them every year went under. Now the butcher and baker, the grocer and shoemaker are thriving and the confectioners are riding in motor cars.
>
> The 35th Police Precinct stretched from Seventy-ninth Street to Ninety-sixth Street and from Fifth Avenue to the East River. Prohibition has closed 190 saloons, over 60 per cent, and made the precinct so orderly that the police station is closed and the force transferred to where there is need of it.
>
> What is true of this East Side district of our city is no doubt true of others where our working people live. Would it not be better to find out what New York is like than wander away to realms you know not of?
>
> It is said by some of our New York papers that anyone can get a drink anywhere in the city. I doubt it, but will be willing to

test it if you will send a reporter to me, not into the so-called residential districts, nor to so-called reputable citizens, nor into the White Light region, but into the places where the common people live.

They are the backbone of this great moral reform, which in time will not only make the United States dry but will drive the evil of the liquor traffic off the face of God's earth and make not only the United States God's country but bring all countries in the Kingdom of God. It makes no difference how long it takes. The patience of God, and of his saints, is proverbial.

James V. Chalmers.

Also read this letter:

The Ladies' Home Journal, Philadelphia:

I read today in your December number an article by Charles A. Selden on the Enemies of Prohibition. In my opinion prohibition is getting more and better results daily. I hear the rabble say it is worse by far than it was before the adoption of the Eighteenth Amendment. I am a passenger-train conductor and have been on busy runs for a good many years, the years before September, 1917. On a certain run when it came just before a Saturday and Sunday or a holiday or circus day or something of that sort, I would lay off and lose the time rather than make the return trip. I left every third day at six o'clock P.M., and on Saturdays and Sundays there were always more drunken persons to encounter than at other times.

I went over to France with the A.E.F. in 1917, and came back in October, 1919, when I went to work on my old run. I have been on it ever since, and in somewhat over three years I do not recall having had more than two drunken men on my train. So if there are so many getting drunk — as some of our people would try to make us believe — they must be staying quietly put in some place until they get over it and not showing up on the trains I run at any rate.

I have heard the argument that the Eighteenth Amendment was put over while two millions of soldiers were out of the country. That is the veriest rot. Had the amendment been put to the vote of the soldiers it would have been a divided vote, I think, with much the larger per cent of them in favor of the amendment.

From my experience, I think it likely that there are comparatively few who get drunk now, while four years ago there were many.

I was at the American Legion meeting in New Orleans in October last. My son — who is also an overseas soldier — was with me. It was, I think, a big boost for the young men of America that there was evidently such an absence of the desire for anything to drink; I am confident that the bootlegger's business with the exsoldiers in New Orleans did not make the rum runners rich.

I am giving you this bit of testimony, as I come in contact with from three hundred to five hundred people every day.

December 23, 1922

The "wet" propagandists are almost unanimous in proclaiming that a revised enactment which will legalize the sale of light wines and beers will not bring back the saloon. They admit that the saloon was a curse; they proclaim that it is gone forever. What then of the thousands of licensed saloons that are still open and doing business in New York, New Jersey, Massachusetts, Pennsylvania, Illinois and many other states? How many of these brewery-owned and distillery-owned dispensaries ever observed the Sunday closing law before prohibition, and how many of them now observe the Volstead Act? Only so many, located in neighborhoods of the poor, as find it profitable to sell "legal" beer. How many of them are headquarters for bootleggers? Practically all.

Could you trust one or any of these still brewery and distillery owned dispensaries to observe a light-wine-and-beer statute? Not a solitary one of them. The liquor interests in the United States are as vicious and as vile as they ever were. They declaim against the law-breaking bootleggers, and yet *they* are the bootleggers. *They* aided and abetted bootlegging before prohibition when they fostered blind tigers and speak-easies in no-license neighborhoods. *They* have always been guilty of scorning and evading the law and they always will be.

What they are up against under prohibition is the high cost of law breaking. The bribery and corruption overhead are a crushing burden. They can keep their saloons going only in prosperous neighborhoods. The patronage of the poor is practically wiped out, and it was from the vast numbers of the poor that they derived their huge profits in the past.

President Harding has made an appeal to the leadership element in the country to support prohibition. The prosperous millions in our population have been giving an alarming exhibition of soft morals and selfish indulgence that invites anarchy and revolution. The organized women of the country have been staunchly supporting the Eighteenth Amendment; indeed, except for the smart and fashionable minority, the women everywhere have been whole-heartedly for the amendment.

We are undoubtedly headed for a national say-so on prohibition at the polls. It is to be hoped that we can force the issue without straddling and equivocation in the 1924 election. We are confident that there is a three-to-one sentiment for prohibition. If it should be the other way round we shall accept the verdict and prepare to begin all over again to fight for a cause that is one hundred per cent sound in what it offers morally and economically for human kind.

PART IV

AN ASSEMBLY-LINE CIVILIZATION?

The idea that men are created free and equal is both true and misleading: men are created different; they lose their social freedom and their individual autonomy in seeking to become like each other.

DAVID RIESMAN, et al.
The Lonely Crowd

At Potomac Park, just a few blocks from the White House, President and Mrs. Wilson and other assorted dignitaries were becoming impatient as an army crew attempted to start the plane which would carry the first air mail from the nation's capital. The plane had been assembled only the day before, and after considerable checking for fouled spark plugs and faulty ignition, some knowledgeable observer discovered the plane had no gas.

"Airmail Celebrates 50th Year," *Northwest Passages*
(St. Paul/Minneapolis International Airport,
June–July, 1968), p. 7.

12
THE KENNICOTTS AND CALVIN COOLIDGE

"To understand Minnesota," Sinclair Lewis wrote in 1923, "you must be an historian, an ethnologist, a poet, a cynic, and a graduate prophet all in one." Lewis' lifelong attempt to understand Minnesota – and America – reached its climax in the Twenties, years which saw the publication of *Main Street, Babbitt, Arrowsmith, Dodsworth,* and *The Man Who Knew Coolidge.* At the end of the decade, Lewis became the first American author to receive a Nobel Prize.

Main Street in particular loomed as a major landmark in the literary landscape of the Jazz Age. But, as often happens, this work has been the victim of its own critical and popular success; whatever Lewis was trying to say has been obscured by arguments *about* the book. Was *Main Street* an indictment of the frontier barbarism that survived in modern America, and thus part of a literary rebellion against the small town? Or was it instead an indulgent and nostalgic recollection of a folk culture that Lewis really loved? There have been partisans of both judgments, and the only escape from the critics' contradictory dogmatisms is to sit down and read the novel afresh for oneself.

A further clue to Lewis' intentions can perhaps be found in the brief sequel, less well known, to *Main Street* that we reprint here. Lewis originally wrote it for *The Nation* during the Presidential campaign of 1924. The magazine was supporting Robert La Follette, an altogether characteristic choice, for these were the "fighting years" when Oswald Garrison Villard was *The Nation*'s editor, assisted by a brilliant and rambunctious young staff. There were important linkages between the "old" *Nation* of E. L. Godkin in the Gilded Age and the "new" *Nation* of Villard in the Twenties – the magazine's hostility to imperialism and its championing of the cause of the Negro, for example. But the old *Nation*'s *laissez-faire* orthodoxy was a far cry from the new *Nation*'s welfare liberalism, and it is difficult to imagine a man of Godkin's bookish gentility printing the articles on Sex, Modern Morals, and the New Woman which enlivened the venerable weekly's pages during the Twenties.

MAIN STREET'S BEEN PAVED

Sinclair Lewis

When *The Nation* asked me to visit Gopher Prairie, Minnesota, and ask the real he-Americans what they thought of the presidential campaign, I was reluctant. Of all the men whom I met in Gopher Prairie years ago, during that college vacation when I gathered my slight knowledge of the village, Dr. Will Kennicott was the one whom I best knew, and for him I held, and hold, a Little Brother awe. He is merely a country practitioner, not vastly better than the average, yet he is one of these assured, deep-chested, easy men who are always to be found when you want them, and who are rather amused by persons like myself that go sniffing about, wondering what it all means.

I telegraphed the doctor asking whether he would be home, for sometimes in summer he loads his wife and the three boys in his car and goes north for a couple of weeks' fishing. He answered — by letter; he never wastes money by telegraphing. Yes. He was in Gopher Prairie till the middle of August; would be glad to talk with me; knew Carrie (his wife) would enjoy a visit with me also, as she liked to get the latest gossip about books, psychoanalysis, grand opera, glands, etc., and other interests of the intellectual bunch in N.Y.

I arrived in Gopher Prairie on No. 3, the Spokane Flier. Many people will be interested to know that No. 3 is now leaving Minneapolis at 12:04, that the St. Dominick stop has been cut out, and that Mike Lembcke, the veteran trainman so long and favorably known to every drummer traveling out of Mpls., has been transferred to the F line, his daughter having married a man in Tudor.

I was interested to see the changes in Gopher Prairie in the past ten years. Main Street now has three complete blocks paved in cement. The Commercial and Progress Club had erected a neat little building with a room to be used either for pleasure and recreation or for banquets; it has card tables, a pool table, a top-notch radio; and here on important occasions, like the visit of the Congressman or the entertainment of the Twin City Shriners' Brass Band, the ladies of the Baptist Church put up a regular city feed for the men folks. The lawns are prettier than they used to be; a number of the old mansions — some of them dating back to 1885 — have been rejuvenated and beautified by a coating of stucco over the clapboards; and Dave Dyer has a really remarkable California bungalow, with casement windows, a kind of Swiss chalet effect about the eaves, and one of the tallest radio aerial masts I have seen west of Detroit.

But quite as striking was the change in Dr. Kennicott's office.

The consulting-room has been lined with some patent material which looked almost exactly like white tiling — the only trouble with it, he told me, is that lint and so on sticks to it. The waiting-room is very fetching and comfortable, with tapestry-cushioned reed chairs and a long narrow Art Table on which lie *Vogue*, the *Literary Digest*, *Photo Play*, and *Broadcasting Tidings*.

When I entered, the doctor was busy in the consulting-room, and waiting for him was a woman of perhaps forty, a smallish woman with horn-rimmed spectacles which made her little face seem childish, though it was a childishness dubious and tired and almost timid. She must once, I noted, have been slender and pretty, but she was growing dumpy and static, and about her was an air of having lost her bloom.

I did not at first, though I had often talked to her, recognize her as Carol, Dr. Kennicott's good wife.

She remembered me, however, by my inescapable ruddiness and angularity; and she said that the doctor and she did hope I'd drop in for a little visit after supper — she was sorry they couldn't invite me to supper, but the new hired girl was not coming along as well as they had hoped, as she was a Pole and couldn't speak a word of English. But I must be sure to come. There would be a really fine concert from WKZ that evening — of course so much of the broadcast stuff was silly, but this would be a real old-time fiddler playing barn-dance music — all the familiar airs, and you could hear his foot stamping time just as plain as though he were right there in the room — the neighbors came in to enjoy it, every Thursday evening. Oh! And could I tell her — There'd been such an argument at the Thanatopsis Club the other day as to what was the *dernier cri* in literature just now. What did I think? Was it Marcel Proust or James Joyce or "So Big" by Edna Ferber?

She couldn't wait any longer for the doctor. Would I mind telling him to be sure to bring home the thermos bottle, as they would need it for the Kiwanis picnic?

She whispered away. I thought she hesitated at the door. Then the big, trim doctor came out of the consulting-room, patting the shoulder of a frightened old woman, and chuckling, "So! So! Don't you let 'em scare you. We'll take care of it all right!"

From his voice any one would have drawn confidence; have taken a sense of security against the world — though perhaps a sense of feebleness and childishness and absurdity in comparison with the man himself; altogether the feeling of the Younger Brother.

I fumbled at my mission.

"Doctor, a New York magazine — you may not have heard of it, but I remember that Mrs. Kennicott used to read it till she switched over from it to the *Christian Science Monitor* — *The Nation,* it's called; they asked me to go around and find out how the presidential campaign is starting, and I thought you'd be one of the — "

"Look here, Lewis, I've got a hunch I know exactly what you want me to do. You like me personally — you'd probably take a chance on my doctoring you. But you feel that outside of my business I'm a complete dumbbell. You hope I'm going to pull a lot of bonehead cracks about books and writings and politics, so you can go off and print 'em. All right. I don't mind. But before you lash me to the mast and show me up as a terrible reactionary — that's what you parlor socialists call it, ain't it? — before you kid me into saying the things you've already made up your mind you're going to make me say, just come out and make a few calls with me, will you?"

As I followed him downstairs I had more than usual of the irritated meekness such men always cast over me.

He pointed to a handsome motor with an inclosed body.

"You see, Lewis, I'm doing all the Babbitt things you love to have me do. That's my new Buick coop, and strange to say I'd rather own it — paid for in advance! — than a lot of cubist masterpieces with lop-jawed women. I know I oughtn't to get that way. I know that if I'd just arrange my life to suit you and the rest of the highbrows, why, I'd make all my calls on foot, carrying a case of bootlegged wood alcohol under one arm and a few choice books about communism under the other. But when it drops much below zero,

I've got a curious backwoods preference for driving in a good warm boat."

I became a bit sharp. "Hang it, doctor, I'm not a fool. Personally, I drive a Cadillac!"

This happened to be a lie. The only mechanical contrivance I own is not a Cadillac but a Royal typewriter. Yet I was confused by his snatching away my chance to be superior by being superior to me, and for the second I really did believe I could beat him at motoring-owning as I can beat him at theories of aesthetics.

He grinned. "Yeh, you probably do. That's why you haven't got any excuse at all. I can understand a down-and-outer becoming a crank and wanting to have Bob La Follette or this William X. Foster — or, God! even Debs! — for President. But you limousine socialists, a fellow like you that's written for the real he-magazines and might maybe be right up in the class of Nina Wilcox Putnam or even Harry Leon Wilson, if you did less gassing and drinking and more work and real hard thinking — how you can go on believing that people are properly impressed by your pose of pretending to love all the lousy bums — well, that's beyond me. Well, as I said: Before we go into politics and Coolidge, I want to show you a couple of things to point out what I mean."

He called to Dave Dyer, in the drug-store. Dave is really an amiable fellow; he used to keep me supplied with beer; and we would sit up, talking science or telling dirty stories or playing stud poker, till a couple of hours after everybody else in town had gone to bed — till almost midnight.

Dave came out and shouted: "Glad to see you again, Lewis."

"Mighty nice to see you, Dave."

"I hear you been up in Canada."

"Yuh, I was up there f'r little trip."

"Have nice trip?"

"You bet. Fine."

"Bet you had a fine trip. How's fishing up there?"

"Oh, fine, Dave. I caught an eleven-and-a-half pound pickerel — jack-fish they call 'em up there — well, I didn't exactly catch it personally, but my brother Claude did — he's the surgeon in St. Cloud."

"Eleven naf pounds, eh? Well, that's a pretty good-sized fish. Heard you been abroad."

"Yes."

"Well. . . . How'd the crops strike you in Canada?"

"Fine. Well, not so good in some parts."

"How long you planning stay around here?"

"Oh, just a couple days."

"Well, glad to seen you. Drop in and see me while you're here."

I was conscious, through this agreeable duologue, that Dr. Kennicott was grinning again. Dave Dyer's amiability had lubricated my former doubtfulness and I was able to say almost as one on a plane of normality with him: "Oh, what are you sniggering at?"

"Oh, nothing, nothing — posolutely Mr. Leopold, absotively Mr. Loeb. (Say, that's a pretty cute one, eh? I got it off the radio last night.) I just mean it always tickles me to see the way you loosen up and forget you're a highbrow when you run into a regular guy like Dave. You're like Carrie. As long as she thinks about it, she's a fierce Forward Looker and Deep Thinker and Viewer with Alarm. But let the hired girl leave the iron on a tablecloth and burn it, and Carrie forgets all about being a Cultured Soul and bawls hell out of her. Sure. You write about Debs, but I'd like to see you acting natural with him like you do with Dave!"

"But really, I'm very fond of Gene."

"Yeh. Sure. 'Gene' you call him — that's the distress signal of your lodge — all you hoboes and authors and highbrows have to say 'Gene.' Well, I notice when you talk to Dave, you talk American, but when you get uplifty on us, you talk like you toted a monocle. Well, climb in."

I considered the sure skill, the easy sliding of the steering-wheel, with which he backed his car from the curb, slipped it forward, swung it about the new automatic electric traffic signal at the corner of Main and Iowa, and accelerated to thirty-five.

"I guess you've noticed the paving on Main Street now," he said. "People that read your junk prob'ly think we're still wading through the mud, but on properly laid cement the mud ain't so noticeable that it bothers you any! But I want to show you a couple of other things that otherwise you'd never see. If I didn't drag you out, your earnest investigation would consist of sitting around with Carrie and Guy Pollock, and agreeing with them that we hicks are awful slow in finally making Gopher Prairie as old as Boston. . . . Say, do you play golf?"

"No, I haven't — "

"Yeh. Thought so. No Fearless Author or Swell Bird would condescend to lam a pill. Golf is a game played only by folks like poor old Doc Kennicott of G. P., and the Prince of Wales and Ring

Lardner and prob'ly this H. G. Wells you're always writing about. Well, cast your eye over that, will you."

We had stopped, here on the edge of Gopher Prairie — this prairie village lost in immensities of wheat and naivetes, this place of Swede farmers and Seventh Day Adventists and sleeve-garters — beside a golf course with an attractive clubhouse, and half a dozen girls wearing smart skirts and those Patrick sweaters which are so much more charming, more gay, than anything on Bond Street or Rue de la Paix.

And in a pasture beside the golf course rested an aeroplane.

I could say only: "Yes. I see. But why the aeroplane?"

"Oh, it just belongs to a couple more Main Streeters from some place in Texas that are taking a little tourist trip round all the golf courses in the country — terrible pair, Lewis; one of 'em is a Methodist preacher that believes hard work is better for a man than whiskey — never would dare to stand up in a bacteriological argument with this give-'em-the-razz scientist friend of yours, DeKruif; and the other is a cowardly lowbrow that got his Phi Beta Kappa at Yale and is now guilty of being vice-president of a railroad. And one other curious little thing: I went into Mac's barber-shop to get my shoes shined this morning, and Mac says to me: 'Afraid you got to let 'em go dusty, Doc — the bootblack is out playing golf.' Now, of course, we're a bad, mean, capitalistic bunch that 're going to vote for that orful Wall Street hireling, Coolidge. In fact, we're reg'lar sadists. So naturally we don't mind playing golf with the bird that blacks our shoes, and we don't mind the hired girl calling us by our first names, while you earnest souls — "

He had forced me to it. "Oh, go to hell!"

He chuckled. "Oh, we'll save you yet. You'll be campaigning for Cal Coolidge."

"Like hell I will!"

"Look, Lewis. May I, as a rube, with nothing but an A. B. from the U of Minn (and pretty doggone good marks in all subjects, too, let me tell you!) inform you that you pulled 'hell' twice in successive sentences, and that the first person singular future indicative of the verb 'to be' is 'shall' and not 'will'? Pardon my hinting this to a stylist like you. . . . Look, I'm not really trying to razz you; I'm really trying the best method of defense, which I believe is attack. Of course you don't think so. If the Japs were invading America, you'd want to have a swell line of soap boxes built along the California coast, and have this bird Villard, and this John Haynes Holmes, and this Upton Sinclair — and prob'ly Lenin and Trotzky and Mother

Eddy and some Abrams practitioners and Harry Thaw — all get up on 'em and tell the dear artistic Japs how you love 'em, and then of course they'd just be too *ashamed* to come in and rape our women. But, personally, I'd believe in going out with one grand sweet wallop to meet 'em."

"Doctor, you have two advantages. Like all conservatives, all stout fellows, you can always answer opponents by representing them as having obviously absurd notions which they do not possess, then with tremendous vigor showing that these non-existent traits are obviously absurd, and ignoring any explanation. But we cranks try to find out what is the reality of things — a much less stout and amusing job. And then, while we admit enormous ignorances, you never try to diagnose anything you can't physic or cut out. You like to do an appendectomy, but an inquiry into the nature of 'success' — "

"I've noticed one funny thing in all your writings and stuff, Lewis. Whenever you have to refer to a major operation, you always make it an appendectomy. Have you a particular fondness for 'em, or don't you know the names of any others? I'd be glad to buy you a medical dictionary. All right. I'll quit. Now I want to show you a few other changes in G. P."

He drove back into town; he pointed out the new school building, with its clear windows, perfect ventilation, and warm-hued tapestry brick.

"That," he said, "is largely Vida Wutherspoon's doing. Remember her and you and Carrie used to argue about education? You were all for having Jacques Loebs and Erasmuses and Mark Hopkinses teaching, and she concentrated on clean drinking-pails. Well, she pounded at us till we built this. . . . Meantime, what've *you* done for education?"

I ignored it, and asked what sort of teachers in this admirably ventilated building were explaining Homer and biochemistry and the glory of God to the youth of Gopher Prairie.

"The teachers? Oh, I guess they're a bunch of dubs like the rest of us; plain ordinary folks. I guess they don't know much about Homer and biochemistry. . . . By the way, in which school are *you* giving your superior notions about Homer and biochemistry, and meanwhile correcting themes, and trying to help the girls that get so inspired by the sort of junk you and Mencken write that they blow home at three G. M., lit to the guards? You hint — of course you haven't met any of 'em but you know it all beforehand — you aren't satisfied with our teaching; we've got a bunch of dumbbells. . . . Willing to come here and teach Latin, math, and history, so they'll be done right? I'm on the schoolboard. I'll get you the job. Want to?"

At my answer he sniggered and drove on. He showed me the agreeable new station — depot, I think he called it — with its flower-bordered park; the old-fashioned English garden put in by a retired German farmer; and the new State fish-hatchery. He demanded: "Well, how about it? Main Street seem to be existing almost as well as the average back alley of some burg in Italy?"

"Certainly. You have them completely beaten — materially!"

"I see. Well, now we've got one other exhibit that we, anyway, don't think is just 'material' — how birds like you love that word! We've got a baseball team that's licked every town of our size in the State, and we got it by hiring a professional pitcher and coach for five months, and going down into our jeans, without any 'material' return, and paying him three hundred dollars a *week!*"

"How much do you pay your teachers a *month?*" was all I had to say, but it provided voluble, inconclusive debate which lasted the twenty-odd miles to a hamlet called New Prague.

Dr. Kennicott stopped at a peasant-like cottage in the Polish settlement of New Prague, and as he knocked I beheld him change from a Booster to the Doctor. What he did in that house I do not know. I do not understand these big suave men who go in to terrified women and perform mysteries and come out — calm, solid, like stockbrokers. During his fifteen minutes within there was the shriek of a woman, the homicidal voice of a man speaking some Slavic tongue — and as he started off he said to me only: "Well, I think I've got her to listen to reason."

"Good Lord, what reason? What do you mean? What happened in there? Who was the man? Her husband or another?"

I have never seen quite so coldly arrogant a cock of the eyebrow as Kennicott gave me.

"Lewis, I don't mind explaining my financial affairs to you, or my lack of knowledge of endocrinology, or my funny notion that an honest-to-God Vermont school-teacher like Cal Coolidge may understand America better than the average pants-maker who hasn't been over from Lithuania but six months. If you insist on it, of course I shouldn't mind a bit discussing my sexual relations to Carrie. *But* I do not ever betray my patients' confidence!"

It was splendid.

Of course it didn't happen to be true. He had often told me

his secrets, with the patients' names. But aside from this flaw it was a noble attitude, and I listened becomingly as he boomed on:

"So! Let that pass. Now, why I brought you out here was: Look at this cross-roads burg. Mud and shacks and one big Ford garage and one big Catholic church. The limit. But look at those two Janes coming."

He lifted his square, competent hand from the steering-wheel and pointed at two girls who were passing a hovel bearing the sign "Gas, Cigarettes, Pop, and EATS"; and those girls wore well-cut skirts, silk stockings, such shoes as can be bought nowhere in Europe, quiet blouses, bobbed hair, charming straw hats, and easily cynical expressions terrifying to an awkward man.

"Well," demanded Kennicott. "How about it? Hicks, I suppose!"

"They would look at home in Newport. Only — "

He exploded. "Sure. 'Only.' You birds always have to pull an 'only' or an 'except' when we poor dubs make you come look at facts! Now, do stop trying to be a wise cracker for about ten seconds and listen to a plain, hard-working, damn successful Regular Guy! Those girls — patients of mine — they're not only dressed as well as any of your Newports or Parises or anywhere else, but they're also darn' straight, decent, hard-working kids — one of 'em slings hash in that God-awful hick eating joint we just passed. And to hear 'em talk — Oh, maybe they giggle too much, but they're up on all the movies and radio and books and everything. And both their dads are Bohemians; old mossbacks; tough old birds with whiskers, that can't sling no more English than a mushrat. And yet in one generation, here's their kids — real queens. That's what we're producing here, while you birds are panning us — talking — talking — "

For the first time I demanded a right to answer. I agreed, I said, that these seemed to be very attractive, probably very clever little girls, and that it was noteworthy that in one generation they should have arisen, in all their radio-wise superiority, from the bewildered peasants one sees huddling at Ellis Island. *Only*, was it Doc Kennicott and Dave Dyer and the rest of Main Street who were producing them? Dr. Kennicott might teach them the preferability of listening to the radio instead of humming Czech folk-songs, but hadn't they themselves had something to do with developing their own pretty ankles, buying their own pretty silk stockings, and learning their own gay manners?

And, I desired to be informed, why was it that to Dr. Kennicott the sleek gaiety of socialistic Slavic girls in New York was vicious, a proof that they were inferior, a proof that no one save Vermont conservatives should be allowed to go through Ellis Island, while the sleek gaiety of movie-meditating Slavic girls on Main Street was a proof of their superiority? Was it because the one part had Dr. Kennicott for physician and the other did not?

There was debate again. I perceived that I had not begun to get my interview; that I was likely to be fired by Mr. Villard. I calmed the doctor by agreeing that his ideas were as consistent as they were practical; and at last I had him explaining Coolidgeism, while he drove back to Gopher Prairie at thirty-five on straight stretches, twenty on curves.

"Well, I hope you're beginning to get things a little straighter now, Lewis. I wanted you to see some of the actual down-to-brass-tacks things we've *accomplished* — the paving on Main Street, the golf course, the silk stockings, the radios — before I explained why everybody around here except maybe a few sorehead farmers who'll vote for La Follette, and the incurable hereditary Democrats who'll stick by Davis, is going to vote for Coolidge. We're people that are doing things — we're working or warring — and in the midst of work or war you don't want a bunch of conversation; you want results.

"Now, first you expect me — prob'bly you've already got it written; darn' shame you'll have to change it — you expect me to pan hell out of Bob La Follette. You expect me to say he's a nut and a crook and a boob and a pro-German. Well, gosh, maybe I would've up till a couple of years after the war. But as a matter of fact, I'm willing — I'm glad to admit he's probably a darn' decent fellow, and knows quite a lot. Maybe it's even been a good thing, some ways, to have a sorehead like him in the Senate, to razz some of the saner element who otherwise might have been so conservative that they wouldn't have accomplished anything. I imagine prob'bly La Follette is a good, honest, intelligent man, a fighter, and a fellow that *does* things. But that's just the trouble. We mustn't be doing too many things, not just now. There's a ticklish situation in the world, with international politics all mixed up and everything, and what we need is men that, even if maybe they haven't got quite so much imagination and knowledge, know how to keep cool and not rock the boat.

"Just suppose a couple of years ago, when Banting was working out insulin for diabetes but his claims weren't confirmed yet, suppose you and all the rest of you Earnest Thinkers, including La Follette, had come to me hollering that I was wrong to go on doing the honest best I could just dieting my diabetes patients. You tell me about Banting — but equally you tell me about some other scientist named, say, Boggs, who had something new for diabetes. What'd I have done? Why, I'd of gone right on being a stingy old conservative and dieting my cases!

"Now, when it proves Banting is right and Boggs is wrong, I follow Banting and kick out Boggs, but I don't do either till I *know.* Boggs might have been a wiz, that took his degree of X. Y. Z. at Jena, but he was premature — he was wrong — he wanted to do too much. Well, La Follette is Boggs, a beaner but plumb wrong, and I and some twenty-thirty million other Americans, we're Coolidge, sitting back and watching, handing it to Banting and such when they prove they've got the goods, but never going off half-cocked.

"The trouble with La Follette isn't that he'd lay down on his job or not understand about railroads and the tariff but that he'd be experimenting all the time. He'd be monkeying around trying to fix things and change things all the time. And prob'bly there's lots of things that do need fixings. But just *now,* in these critical times, we need a driver that won't try to adjust the carburetor while he's making a steep hill.

"So. Not that I mean we're worried — as long as we have a cool head like Cal's at the wheel, with his Cabinet for four-wheel brakes. We ain't been half so worried as you Calamity Howlers. You say that unless La Follette is elected, gosh, the dome of the Capitol will slide off into the Potomac, and Germany will jump on France, and prob'bly my aerial mast will get blown down. Well, far's I can see, most of the folks around here are getting their three squares a day, and the only thing that seems to keep agriculture from progressing is the fact that the farmers can get three bucks a quart for white mule, so they're doing more distilling than manuring.

"Oh, yes, we've had bank failures and there's an increase of tenant-farming. But d' ever occur to you that maybe it's a good thing to close up a lot of these little one-horse banks, so we can combine on bigger and better ones? And about this tenant business; is that any worse than when every farmer owned his own land but had such a big mortgage plastered on it that he didn't really own it at all?

"No, sir, you got to look into these things scientifically. . . . Say, is that left front fender squeaking or do I imagine it? There, don't you hear it now? I do. I'll have Mat fix it. Gosh, how I hate a squeak in a car!

"Now I imagine this sheet *The Nation* tries to let on that the whole country is rising against the terrible rule of Coolidge. And I saw a copy of this *American Mercury* — Guy Pollock lent it to me — where some bird said Coolidge was nothing but a tricky little politician with nothing above the eyebrows. . . . By the way, notice that Ford and Edison and Firestone are going to call on him? Of course those lads, that 're merely the most successful men of affairs and ideas in the country, they're plumb likely to call on a four-flushing accident! Oh, sure!

"Well, now look here. First place, did you ever see a four-flusher that went on holding people's confidence? I never did — Oh, except maybe this chiropractor that blew into town three years ago and darned if he isn't still getting away with it! In the second place, suppose Cal were just a tricky little politician, without a he-idea in his bean. Well, what do you need for the office of President?

"For medicine, and for writing too, I imagine, some ways, you need *brains.* You're working single-handed, no one to pass the buck to, and you got to show results. But a preacher now, all he's got to do is to make a hit with his sermons, and a lawyer simply has to convince the poor cheeses on the jury that his learned opponent is a lying slob. In the same way, for President you need a fellow that can pull the wool over everybody's eyes, whether it's in the primaries back home in Hickville or whether it's dealing with Japan or Russia. If Cal can get by without having any goods whatever, then he's the boy we want, to keep the labor unions in order and kid along the European nations!

"Then, next place. . . . Oh, all this talk is just wasted energy. You know and I know that Coolidge is going to be elected. Be better if they called the election off and saved a lot of money, and damn the Constitution! Why, nobody is interested, not one doggone bit.

"As you ride around the country, do you hear anybody talking politics? You hear 'em talking about Leopold and Loeb, about Kid McCoy, about the round-the-world fliers, about Tommy Gibbons's battle in England, about their flivvers and their radios. But politics — nix! And why? Because they know Coolidge is already elected! Even the unregenerate old Democrats, that would love to have Brother Charlie run the country on the same darned-fool, unscientific, they-say basis on which William Jennings has the nerve to criticize evolution!

"I haven't met one single responsible well-to-do person who's for La Follette. Who've we got boosting him, then? Well, I can tell you — I can tell you mighty darn' quick! A lot of crank farmers that because they don't want to work and keep their silos filled want to make up for it by some one who, they hope, will raise the price of wheat enough so they can get by without tending to business! The fellows that 've always followed any crazy movement — that ran after the Populists and the Nonpartisan League! And a lot of workmen in the cities that think if some crank comes into office they'll all become federal employees and able to quit working!

"But aside from these hoboes — Well, I guess I've asked a hundred people who they were going to vote for, some around G. P. and some on the smoker down to St. Paul, and ninety out of the hundred say: 'Why, gosh, I haven't thought much about it. Haven't had time to make up my mind. I dunno. Besides, anyway, I guess Cal is going to win.'

"Now, about these so-called 'exposures' of the Attorney General and so on. Well, I've always suspected there was a lot more to it than you saw on the surface — lot of fellows trying to make political capital out of it — and the fact that Wheeler is running with La Follette proves my contention, and I for one don't propose to let him get away with it, let me tell you that right now!

"Nope. Unless we have an awful' bad crop failure, and the crops never looked better than they do this year, we've got you licked. Cal is elected. It's all over but the shouting."

I called on Kennicott and his wife after six o'clock supper, but I could not get the talk back to the campaign. Carol hesitated that, yes, she did admire La Follette, and Davis must be a man of fine manners if he could be ambassador to the Court of St. James's, but just this year, with so many bank failures and all, it wasn't safe to experiment, and she thought she would vote for Coolidge; then some other time we could try changes. And now — brightening — had I seen "The Miracle" and "St. Joan"? Were they really as lovely and artistic as people said?

It was time to tune in on the barn-dance music from WKZ, and we listened to "Turkey in the Straw"; we sat rocking, rocking, the doctor and I smoking cigars, Carol inexplicably sighing.

At ten I felt that they would rather more than endure my going, and I ambled up a Main Street whose glare of cement pavement, under a White Way of resplendent electric lights, was empty save for bored but ejaculatory young men supporting themselves by the awning-cords in front of Billy's Lunch Room and the Ford Garage. I climbed to the office of Guy Pollock, that lone, fastidious attorney with whom Carol and I used once, in the supposition that we were "talking about literature," to exchange book titles.

He was at home, in his unchanged shabby den, reading Van Loon's "Story of the Bible."

He was glad to see me. With Kennicott I had felt like an intruder; to Carol I seemed to give a certain uneasiness; but Guy was warm.

After amenities, after questions about the death of this man, the success of that, I murmured, "Well, there've been a lot of changes in the town – the pavement and all."

"Yes, a lot. And there's more coming. We're to have a new water system. And hourly buses to the Twin Cities – fast as the trains, and cheaper. And a new stone Methodist church. Only – "

" 'Ware that word!"

"I know it. Only – only I don't like the town as well as I used to. There's more talk, about automobiles and the radio, but there's less conversation, less people who are interested in scandals, politics, abstractions, gallantries, smut, or anything else save their new A batteries. Since Dr. Westlake died, and this fellow Miles Bjornstam went away, and Vida Sherwin's become absorbed in her son's progress in the Boy Scouts, and even Carol Kennicott – Oh, well, the doctor has convinced her that to be denunciatory or even very enthusiastic isn't quite respectable – I don't seem to be awakened by the talk of any one here.

"And in the old days there were the pioneers. They thought anybody who didn't attend an evangelical church every Sunday ought to be lynched, but they were full of juice and jests. They're gone, almost all of them. They've been replaced by people with bath-tubs and coupés and porch-furniture and speed-boats and lake-cottages, who are determined that their possessions of these pretty things shall not be threatened by radicals, and that their comments on them shall not be interrupted by mere speculation on the soul of man.

"Not, understand me, that I should prefer the sort of little people you must find in Greenwich Village, who do nothing but chatter. I like people who pay their debts, who work, and love their wives. I wouldn't want to see here a bunch of superior souls sitting on the floor and dropping cigarette butts in empty hootch glasses. Only – "

He scratched his chin. "Oh, I don't know. But it depresses me so, the perpetual bright talk about gas-mileage and mah jong here. They sing of four-wheel brakes as the Persian poets sang of rose leaves; their religion is road-paving and their patriotism the relation of weather to Sunday motoring; and they discuss balloon tires with a quiet fervor such as the fifteenth century gave to the Immaculate Conception. I feel like creeping off to a cottage in the Massachusetts hills and taking up my Greek again. Oh, let's talk of simpler things!"

"Then tell me your opinion of the presidential campaign. I suppose you'll vote for Coolidge. I remember you always liked books that the public libraries barred out as immoral, but you wanted to hang the I. W. W. and you thought La Follette was a doubtful fellow."

"Did I? Well, this time I'm going to vote for La Follette. I think most of the people who resent, when they go calling, having good talk interrupted by having to listen to morons saying 'Well, good evening, folks!' amid the demoniac static from the loud-speaker – most of them *must* vote for La Follette, and if we don't elect him this year, some time we shall. I have faith that the very passion in the worship of the Great God Motor must bring its own reaction."

"Kennicott feels he has us beaten forever."

"If he has, if the only voice ever to be heard at the altar is Coolidge on the phonograph and the radio, then our grandsons will have to emigrate to Siberia. But I don't believe it. Even the Kennicotts progress – I hope. His ancestors ridiculed Harvey, then Koch, and Pasteur, but he accepts them; and his grandsons will laugh at Coolidge as Kennicott now laughs at the whiskers of Rutherford B. Hayes.

"But meanwhile I feel a little lonely, in the evenings. Now, that the movies have, under the nation-wide purification by fundamentalism and the rigid Vermont ideals of the President, changed almost entirely from the lively absurdities of cowpuncher films to unfaithful wives and ginny flappers in bathing suits, I can't even attend them. I'm going – and, Lord, how I'll be roasted by the respectable lawyers! – I'm going out to campaign for La Follette!

"We must all do it. We've been bullied too long by the Doc Kennicotts and by the beautiful big balloon tires that roll over the new pavement on Main Street – and over our souls!"

13

A NEWSMAN'S JOURNEY INTO AMERICA

In 1923, the year the *American Mercury* was born, *Harper's Magazine* was already seventy-three years old. The Twenties were for the venerable monthly a period of transition. Gone were the serials by Thomas Hardy and George DuMaurier, handsomely illustrated by Howard Pyle and Frederic Remington, which had graced the magazine in the Nineties; yet to come were the post-Depression years when *Harper's* would become, in the words of one of its editors, "almost an organ of politics, economics, and sociology." "During the nineteen-twenties," Frederick Lewis Allen wrote in 1941, "our most successful articles were on family questions, matters of personal conduct, sex and marriage, or personal belief. Business was booming too well, apparently, to offer burning issues; politics seemed dull, except for the always fascinating prohibition question."

Nevertheless, it was possible within this format to write searchingly and informatively about America, as the following essay attests. The familiar image with which it opens, of a man on an American train, could have been developed in either of two conventionally hackneyed directions: a mystical identification with the vast landscape, or a diatribe against its monotony, both physical and social. Happily, Mr. Aikman followed neither of these well-worn trails.

Duncan Aikman, a newspaperman-essayist in the great Broun-Mencken-Morley-Reston tradition, has been strangely neglected by cultural historians. *The Nation* (December 31, 1955) called him "part of the never-written, anecdotal history of American journalism which survives only in memories and half-forgotten episodes" — an unfortunate oversight indeed, as the reader of the article reprinted here will realize if he turns to Aikman's more extensive discussion of the American mind in *The Turning Stream* (1948), which the *Saturday Review's* Norman Cousins considered a book ahead of its time, or to the splendid unsigned reports on Latin America which Aikman wrote for the *Atlantic Monthly* while serving in Washington during World War II as Information Program Adviser, Press Division, for Nelson Rockefeller's Office of Inter-American Affairs. Aikman began his career on the Springfield *Republican* and thereafter worked for newspapers as diverse as the Baltimore *Sun,* the Los Angeles *Daily News,* the El Paso *Times,* the New York *Post,* and *PM.*

NOT QUITE STANDARDIZED YET

Duncan Aikman

FROM *Harper's Magazine,* CLVII (September, 1928), pp. 507-15.

On a pleasant June evening I found myself traveling through Kansas. Friends gifted in sociological reproaches had informed me that the state was the power house of modern American standardization. Now, in half an hour of uninterrupted twilight ratiocination it was easy to see why.

With every whistle the train buried itself deeper in the strictly uniform prairies. Right and left beyond each car window, fields of the same shade of green and the same sleepily rich clover scents heaved in regular swells. At equal intervals the same frame farmhouse careened by, on varying arcs of distance, manifesting, whether from a treeless hill or from its clump of creek-fed willows, the same angular aversion to beauty.

Each dozen miles the same little town crashed down about us with the same roar of sidings and corral fences, the same electric sunbursts summoning attention from the charms of the deepening dusk to those of "The City Hotel," "The People's Store," and "The Palace Theater." Along the highways motor headlights began pricking the dark with slender cones of light — all, it seemed, of the same depth, color, and intensity. The very farm horse whom our train clatter frightened now and then from his track-side grazing seemed in the gloom always of the same shade of brown.

Might not mere scenic repetition, I reasoned, explain the Kansas passion for re-molding society in Kansan images? How expect a people exposed to the lifelong hypnosis of such a landscape to believe that variation from their cheerful complacent average was possible in themselves or desirable in others? Why should they not come to feel that sharing with one another the same prejudices, pleasures, enthusiasms, and inhibitions, the same types of friends, enemies, gossip, and theology was a positive virtue, while the appreciation of anything outside their range of habitual experience was a dangerous and probably criminal vice? When their comfortable world was so obviously made up of one similarity after another, how could they help believing that it was the salvation of all non-Kansan worlds to come, and pattern themselves upon Kansan perfection? Why, when others temporized or resisted, should they not believe that it was the mission of Kansans to pass a law about it, making conformity compulsory?

Their very wit, one reflected – the justly famous banter of a few Kansas editorial pages – partook of this well-meaning leveling quality. Its "line" consisted mainly of stripping ideas, the arts, and persons of all foreign affectations on the theory that a non-Kansas viewpoint *must* be an affectation, and raising a laugh by proving the outside world's humorous identity with themselves. Obviously, whether by ridicule, prohibition pioneering, anti-cigarette laws, small-town dress-reform ordinances, or evangelically fierce codes of private respectability, Kansas had dedicated itself to the sanctified labor of making the human race as alike as two prairie swells.

Across the aisle two young business men, who had got on at a station a hundred miles back, droned into the theme like a chorus. One praised the standardizing efficacy of the high-pressure salesmanship of low-priced automobiles – a process with which he evidently had some important inspirational connection.

"Of course, our agents say we overload 'em with cars and bullyrag 'em until they have to pull in customers by the ears," he was saying. "But what of it? The average American family is happier and healthier for having a good little car even if the old man was bluffed into buying it. As I see it, our company's just helping these folks enjoy life the way folks ought to enjoy it."

"The idea exactly," the other man seconded. "Now I sell home refrigerating plants." And fervently he hoped that soon his company would insure the swifter progress of domestic comfort in Kansas by putting in an agent-bullyragging system of its own.

Plainly, even a Pullman traversing Kansas might become automatically a kind of temple of standardization in which the most innocent over-the-toothpicks gossip of lay worshippers might prove a weaving of priestly spells. Even now it seems incredible that on such an evening anything heterodox could have existed nearer than the Santa Fe art colony or Jim Reed's Missouri.

But the porter broke in upon their conversation to give me the standardized Pullman brushing. The train ground its brakes in a broader sprawl of light, and a higher circle of buildings betokening a five-county metropolis. The man with whom I had come to talk about a curious phase of Western history was waiting for me on the platform.

Knowing that he was Kansas-bred and an expert on dry farming, I half dreaded that he would blame the West for using irrigation or the East for not needing it. Instead, when we reached his house he commanded without preliminaries, "You may think this is a fool idea, but you come from the cow country, and I've got to catch you fellows on the fly. Now sit down and whistle or sing or play me the air of every cowboy ballad you know."

He grinned at his wife for encouragement. "There's no use making any bones about it, is there, May?" he explained. "I'm just a dusty-footed farm hand, but at night when we're being ourselves we're trying to write the frontier opera. And I want just a bushel and a half of this cowboy stuff for refrains. Come on now, tune up."

II

I have no idea of how good or how bad the opera was. The passages they played on an exceptionally well-tuned grand piano bore the properly cadenced energy of galloping cowboys and Indian tom toms welded into recognizably correct technical composition. But they fell upon uncritical ears. I do know, though, that between my chantings, whistlings, and stumbling one-finger exercises on the piano we produced something resembling the scores of "Oh Bury Me Not," "Sam Bass Was Born in Indiana," and the unprintably pastoral "Little Black Bull" for a Kansas musical note book. The standardization menace, I observed, as I sought bed long after the traditional Kansas curfew, was failing to standardize.

I made all the excuses possible for an impression so disarming to a student of standardization menaces. Home opera-composition was so rare and private a vice that even the worst harpies of Kansas conformity might not have thought to frame a fiat against it, or my host might have made it a rule never to confess his aberration except to aesthetically vouched-for strangers.

But no. He had already confided in me that his banker and the Presbyterian minister and one or two other obvious pillars of the town's conventions were among his most helpful critics. When by all the books – especially the novels – of the standardization baiters he should have been a secretive and frustrated aesthete ready to console himself with bank robbery or an elopement to Paris with his best friend's wife, here he was openly and cheerfully juggling with opera themes and ingenuously telling the world about it. Plainly, the way to probe the Kansanization menace was to specialize still further in eavesdropping on high-pressure salesmen.

But although the Kansas excursion was one which opened up for me a year of coast-to-coast travels, it was not practicable to be so exclusive. My journeys have been made in search of information on subjects not involving salesmanship, or even the conventional virtues and repressions. So while they have led me to communities revered and reprehended alike for being the very foci of intolerance and standardization, while standardization has been cooed and thundered at me in its various degrees of seduction and violence across dining-car tables and Pullman aisles, in the intimacies of family living rooms, and in the dim cathedral light of our most pompous hotel lobbies, I have also been unable to escape the equally impressive evidence of the republic's casual but effective resistance to standardization.

No sane traveler, of course, could come home from such a trip doubting that standardization still flourishes. The swarms of constructive thinkers whose chief civic passion is to make their home towns as nearly as possible indistinguishable from Cleveland have not abated appreciably since they were first discovered by alarmed post-war sociologists. Not even a recluse could entirely escape contact with the large class of staunch and aggressive Americans who genuinely believe that all who question their ideas on theology, the marriage relation, musical comedy, or national-defense programs are guilty of intellectual poses and villainous social subversiveness, if not of secret bonds with communism.

I myself, for the bad judgment of being dragged into a prohibition argument by an enthusiastic dry demanding, "Don't you admit I'm right?" was sentenced, in February, 1928, to permanent exile in Russia by an informal moot court of Texans on a train approaching Houston. In a Long Island suburban gathering, all suavity and cocktails, I have learned what it is to be attacked for my Al Smith preferences by ladies and gentlemen murmuring reproachfully, "But he's not of your class." And on a loftier, if less personal plane, the D. A. R.'s defense of its blacklist suggests that our best people's attachment to the idea that whatever is different is dangerous may be still as impassioned as it was at Dayton.

Nevertheless, I beg leave to report that, except in a few small and persecutingly homogeneous communities it makes no difference. My fellow-citizens who enjoy standardization continue to standardize themselves according to one another's patterns with such unction of self-approval as their souls demand. For their further pleasure they continue to clap the more obstreperous rebels against their codes and prescriptions harmlessly, and with occasional publicity advantages, into their black books. No doubt, Hebrews who at the Exodus chose to remain behind to enjoy the sophisticated pleasures of Egyptian city life were punished by not being mentioned in the Old Testament; and medieval scoffers who jeered at the Crusades as picnics of sentimentalists wanting a change from home cooking, were put into the black books or tapestries of the Daughters of the Wars of the Robber Barons. In any case, America's nonconformists of 1928, whether or not profitably advertised by the enemy, seem to be successfully and almost universally foiling the standardization menace by the simple expedient of going about their business.

They may be indifferent to the standardizing codes, they may be seriously and constructively in opposition to them on specific issues. They may be merely engaged in practicing a new and more or less standardized conduct of their own, like the "arty" colonies of our metropolises and the wild, wild coeds of the conventional newspaper spreads, in order to shock the standardizers. Or, like my Kansan operatic agriculturist, they may be so unconscious of the standardization menace surging around them that when one mentions it they imagine it has to do only with prohibition. Whatever their methods and motives, they are leading their own lives in the United States of Calvin Coolidge by the light of such originality and individuality as God gave them, and without, so far as the naked eye can judge, suffering legalized tortures for it, or even any unendurable stings from neighborhood criticism. It seems, in fact, appropriate to suggest that standardization as the great American social menace was never weaker than in the present era of America's greatest intellectual outcry against it.

III

Take, for example, another famous power house of standardization — Tennessee. I rode into Nashville on a balmy April morning some three years after Mr. John Thomas Scopes had agreed with his cronies in a Dayton drugstore to test the malicious qualities of the state's new anti-evolution law. The law had been pronounced constitutional and had ended Mr. Scopes's career as a Tennessee teacher. Hence, according to the visions of all specialists in standardization horrors, Tennessee was a place where a serious professional interest in evolution led to prosecution, where a polite dilettante interest led to ostracism, and where a mere flippant reference to fundamentalist doctrine and legislation might lead to a ride on a rail or a fight. Here standardization had already established itself as a legalized theocracy and was half way to an inquisition.

Yet I approached Nashville amid a small volley of wise-cracks on the forbidden subject from a smoking-compartment assemblage whose members prior to 1925 might conceivably have imagined that Darwin was the name of an English motor car. "No monkeys allowed; park your ancestors outside," was the burden of these witticisms. But a comfortably stout Tennesseean replied by reminding them without rancor that boys coming to see the sights of lively cities like Nashville usually had a better time when they left their grandparents at home.

In the city and surrounded by Tennessee standardizers presumably of the deepest dye, I found the frowning bastion of religious intolerance a good deal of a joke even to its ostensible defenders. With cheerful grins which insinuated that their mischievous little by-play was over, fundamentalists admitted that the law would probably never produce another prosecution. They struck the pose of all properly sophisticated Americans and boasted that they now saw through its politics. The law had gone through, not on the wings of pious ecstasy at the state house, but because certain canny Democratic leaders wished to "sell" themselves to the church vote. It had been signed by a governor who probably did not believe in it, in order to jam through his pet appropriations for schools and highways. Tennessee might never repeal it, since to do so would seem to be letting down the oldtime religion. But the fact was — they stated this a little more indirectly since they evidently did not care to face facts too objectively — that the law didn't mean much.

It naturally meant even less to those who detested it on principle,

I found. The deluge of orders and requests for evolutionary works at Tennessee bookshops and public libraries is only now beginning to decline, three years after the Scopes cataclysm. Apparently rumors of faculty bootlegging of evolution in high schools and the state's higher institutions have been exaggerated. But there are plenty of Tennessee teachers willing and competent to guide the outside reading in evolution of students who are interested.

The situation has even brought about its currents of counter-standardization. Undergraduates defending the Bryan position openly, I was told by a high official of Vanderbilt University, have suffered so much from campus humor that it has become one of the things which are "simply not done." "I have seen signs," a Nashville lawyer and devout modernist church member told me with a smile, "that some of our young people going out of the state to college have been put under an almost irresistible temptation to establish themselves as the campus atheists in order to take the curse off."

Moreover, the very challenge of the law seems to have stimulated all other brands of latent liberalism. Fundamentalists and their opponents both boast that Protestants and Catholics, whites and Negroes get along better in Tennessee than elsewhere in the South, that the state quickly took the measure of the Ku Klux Klan's political effort several years ago as a bit of village horseplay. "Just let theology alone," I was told at least a dozen times daily during my stay there, "and there's no state in the union where you can come nearer to doing and saying as you please than right here."

As yet no visitor seems to have tested this by advocating a communist revolution from the pedestal of the Andrew Jackson monument; but supporting symptoms of a subtler sort are in evidence without resort to coarse heroics. The fugitive group of poets and prose stylists has flourished in Nashville both before and since the anti-evolution outbreak without being sniffed at by the police for an occasional frankly erotic production and without being made to feel that the young Vanderbilt instructors and bond salesmen who compose it have lost caste by declining to become Kiwanis pep stirrers. When the city's leaders of taste convinced the community several years ago that a charming Greek portico would provide a rare aesthetic value to the state capitol annex, and that a literal and exquisite duplication of the Parthenon would be a fitting ornament for Nashville's chief public park, nobody protested that Greek art should be outlawed because pagan, or that it was the duty of Tennessee architects to be one hundred per cent American in design and specifications.

And not only is variation from the orthodox tolerated but it is actually praised. A Nashville newspaper columnist, in a recent black hour, manhandled the four horsemen of Southern backwardness, which he described as timid lawyer politicians, timid newspaper proprietors, one-crop cotton bankers, and the fundamentalist clergy. To Nashville's amusement, his syndicate contributions were thenceforth banished from the less venturous *Atlanta Constitution,* but from Tennessee he received hundreds of letters, most of them approving, and from his own office neither a discharge nor a caution.

The time is coming when even politicians may treat the sacred "monkey law" with the lese majesty of deprecatory humor. The present governor did this, a little gingerly, at a 1928 Nashville gathering, admitting besides that it had won for the state an undue share of undesirable publicity. A few weeks earlier, before the convention of the American Association for the Advancement of Science, a supreme court judge, who had recently pronounced for the law's constitutionality, treated it with scarcely merciful sarcasm.

See how liberal we are — the Tennesseeans eagerly justify themselves to the presumably critical stranger. And as final testimony to the state's almost idyllic tolerance I was informed on several occasions — I do not know how accurately — that side by side with the anti-evolution crusade the state authorities had virtually abandoned all efforts to enforce prohibition, leaving this duty, while Tennessee's freedom increases, to the quite ineffective resources of the federal agents. It was almost as though my hosts had said, "Those Eastern fellows who got so excited about our intolerance ought to realize that New York hasn't got anything on us."

Before I left I heard the anti-evolution law defended on the ground that it is in its way a wholesome protest against standardization itself. The young university instructor who took this surprising stand has made a name for himself in American letters already, and he loved the law neither for its own sake nor for the theology it sought to protect. But the country's real refuge from a dreary social sameness, he declared, was not in sophisticated fads and individualistic poses, but in a healthy and cherished provincialism. Southern provincialism, though it might have its blind spots and archaic intolerance, was on the whole glamorous and worth preserving. "Monkey laws" were Tennessee's crude and ineffective but, nevertheless, wholesomely aroused efforts to preserve it. So long as they remained largely ineffective little harm was done, and that little might in time be repaired. They were, he insisted, far less dangerous to variety of taste and custom than the crusade of a group of Tennessee educators to have their charges, native born white and colored public-school pupils, taught a nondescript cosmopolitan accent in place of the gracious elisions and charming soil-sprung phrases of the oldtime Southern brogue.

He was promptly jumped on by others in the group — Tennesseeans all — and informed that provincialism must be growing too feeble to be worth saving when it has to pass a law to keep itself alive; and that self-conscious provincialism, as represented in the professional Southerner, was no less a pose than the advertised promiscuities of the wilder art colonies. But while he sadly admitted all this, it was easy to see that neither his argument nor its rebuttal was standardized. Whatever mystical triumph the anti-evolution law may represent to Tennessee's "kiver to kiver" religionists, it was not functioning as a strait-jacket for free Tennessee minds.

IV

But in measuring resistance to standardization it is desirable to know what type of standardization one has in mind. The Kansas type seems mainly concerned with preserving small-town taste and customs in private conduct. By its own legal admission, the Tennessee brand busies itself chiefly with belief.

But the other brands are practically numberless. Park Avenue and Epworth League standards, Greenwich Village and lodge-joiner standards, speedy young married set, Catholic-shunning, extravert, Yale-and-Harvard, Country Club, introvert standards, and scores of others pass and re-pass one another daily on parade in nearly every American city large enough to support three national banks and a racing season. The confusions created by their mutual scorn and jostlings may bewilder the investigator, but scarcely interfere with the average citizen's freedom to choose which type of standardization he prefers; or, for that matter, with the eccentric citizen's freedom to stand apart in Thoreauvian aloofness from the turmoil, publicly wishing a plague on all their standards.

This morning, for instance, the Grandopolis Ministerial Alliance may have passed a resolution demanding fines for feminine knee exposures, chaperons for parking parties, life-imprisonment for Mann Act violations, and the extinction of speak-easies by the firing squad. But none of these pronouncements will keep the young wastrels of the Grandopolis Pandemonium Club this evening from staging a revel which would interest, if not scandalize, the court of Charles the Second.

Each group is pursuing pleasure as it sees it and each, no doubt, is hopelessly standardized. But, being unable either to convert or exterminate its opposite, neither succeeds in creating a standardized world. On the contrary, their very stalemate helps American society to get along on a reasonably effective let-alone basis. It may still be difficult to practice avowed companionate marriage in rural Alabama or to stop the neighbors' gin-drinking in New York. But from evangelical atheism to oriental mysticism, practically everything else in 1928 America goes.

Moreover, even in most of the standardized groups certain individuals manage to live by their own views and consciences without suffering ostracism, reproach, or even loss of standing.

One assumes, for instance, that when the prospering American reaches a certain stage of traveled sophistication and worldly outlook he and his family abandon the ancestral Sabbath restrictions in favor of Sunday golf. Yet in a certain Southern metropolis I encountered a circle within the larger circle of gay Babbittry whose birth, breeding, and affluence would have entitled them to practice any fashionable diversion gracefully but who, nevertheless, did their golfing on week days. On the Sabbath they went to church and offered their guests magnificent, old-fashioned Sunday dinners. Later, over excellent but illicit cordials and between snatches of repartee about last week's bridge luck, they would discuss the sermon with the relish their more standardized friends might have bestowed on the latest Will Rogers wise-crack.

They did this, apparently, without the slightest ill-will toward their friends who were busy on the golf links or the slightest feeling that these were hell bound. They merely expected outsiders to accept it tacitly as their own choice of the way to act.

For a long Sunday afternoon I wondered whether they were conscious of their well-bred singularity. Then a middle-aged matron with a persistent whimsical inflection related how on a recent New York visit she and her husband had vainly struggled to create in themselves the frame of mind that would sanction just one Sunday theater attendance.

"My dear," she explained with a definitely mischievous accent, "I know it was simply ante-bellum of me and it almost broke me up because it was our last day. But it just couldn't be done." And suddenly I gathered from her mild self-ridicule that the standardization pressure in a pleasure-loving generation could make piety itself seem slightly rakish.

Again, is it the theory of standardization-menace experts that Americans no longer can converse understandingly or profitably with one another across grooves of antipathetic standardized thought? Yet I have charming recollections of a cheerful contentious evening last summer with a woman evangelist – not Mrs. MacPherson! – in a Pacific coast city, when for four hours her emotional necessity of faith was pitted in honorable sword play against my intellectual agnosticism; while our host, an excommunicated Roman Catholic, tried vainly to break in with his favorite theory that all effective religious leadership proceeds from frustrated nymphomania.

Or, side by side with the conservative folk belief that the wild young generations are standardizing the world to perdition, must we believe the bathetic legend of the novelists that young rebel genius is being daily stultified, at the rate, say, of six muted Miltons per year per Main Street, by the austere conformity demands of small-town Philistines? In rebuttal, I summon as witness a studio party of the spring of this year in another Southern city's five-year-old art quarter.

The festivities had reached the point when the young woman who simply could not express her personal rhythm with shoes on had gone barefoot. Then someone called out, "Where's Jane?"

Jane, it appeared, had gone to a country club dinner dance with her lawyer. This in itself was scarcely a blow at the conventions; but Jane, it further developed, had given her lawyer this "date," hoping the slight condescension might help her to get her divorce cheaper. And in order to please the lawyer while pleasing was important, she had broken an engagement to attend our party with her husband. Incidentally, the description of her strategy was received with a general burst of indulgent laughter, including that of the young man Jane was divorcing her husband to marry.

Now Jane's being twenty-three and a regional minor poet may explain many things. Even so, her conduct suggests that she suffered no really crushing repressions through having lived twenty of her years in a Gulf Coast village where the chief social forces were the Baptist and Methodist churches.

It is possible, however, to find standardization resisted with less Bohemian emphasis. Take, for instance, the assumption of the "menace" exponents that all conventionally minded Americans consider all aesthetic impulses "cockeyed." Yet after a dinner in – of all hopelessly American places — Brooklyn, I have seen with my own eyes the middle-aged and highly efficient woman secretary of a national civic organization — a veritable corps commandress of standardizers, so to speak — lure a Middle-Western manufacturer and his wife away from the bridge tables for a walk across Brooklyn Bridge to see the Manhattan towers under a full moon.

Nor, as a recent instance at a college-class reunion shows, does the magic of prosperity always keep a man in his groove. A stout and shamelessly contented-appearing alumnus arrived to meet a barrage of questions on how the "old bank" was getting along in Omaha.

"All right, I guess," he admitted; "but I suppose you know I'm just finishing my third year at medical college."

The family bank, it appeared, was something his relatives had persuaded him to go into at graduation against his better judgment. Now, having banked long and successfully enough to acquire a competence, he was stolidly taking up the profession he had wanted to enter all along.

Finally, as I discovered in Los Angeles, one may even see the thriving modern cult of standardized loose-speaking thwarted. Lunching with an old friend of the city's pre-Hollywood aristocracy, I found him evidently disturbed.

Eventually with some circumlocution the cause of his annoyance came out. He did not hanker for the role of a male gossip, so he would not mention the name of a certain motion-picture actress who, though probably unknown to me socially, I should certainly recognize as a personage. Anyway, at a ball the night before, he had danced with this nameless hussy and, right after their introduction she had treated him to a mildly off-color jest which nine-tenths of the country club circles of the land might have received with guffaws.

But my friend was still indignant about it. "I don't care who belongs to it," he raged, "I am through with any group when its wit grows swinish."

I asked him, perhaps maliciously, what he proposed to do about it and whether he thought Hollywood could bear its punishment.

"Do?" he exclaimed. "I can retire to circles where women still expect their men to expect them to be ladies. And I know where to find them."

I have no doubt that, even in a world about to be standardized out of its once standard conversational inhibitions, he does.

V

So, I suspect, the standardization menace may for the present be laughed into the limbo of ancient perils along with its predecessors, the Masonic and the white-slavery menaces. Perhaps for brief periods of mob emotional outburst, as during wars and their aftermath, the accompanying deluges of patriotic oratory and pulpit billingsgate may render it mildly dangerous to professional rebels with a martyr complex. But in calmer times the plain people, even including the standardized, tend to dismiss the persecuting urge for the delights of indolence. When companionate marriages are proposed in the neighborhood or novels attacking their favorite brands of ecclesiastical verities are brought to their attention they may disapprove. But they are much too occupied with their own concerns – including the rather difficult maintenance of proprieties in their own lives – to bother with passing laws against the heretics or with enforcing them when they do.

So when the discontented citizen resists by the force of such individualism as fate inspires him with, he is likely to find resistance rather easy. After all, when the market for works of eccentricity and protest in the arts, literature, and opinion was never better, it is difficult to support the charge that American standardization is murdering talent. When university education and the society of emancipated spirits is practically free in every minor regional metropolis, it can hardly be said that standardization, even in our Bible Belts of greatest infamy, is fatal to the individual development of young men and women with ambition enough to buy Fords and leave home. On the contrary, if less romantically, may it not be suggested that the young man, with nascent poetical talents, who becomes a "realtor" and Kiwanian in order to avoid a row with father, and the young woman of vague agnostic sympathies who teaches a Sunday school class because "mother could never understand her viewpoint" are earning their frustration, such as it is, by spinelessness? For though the standardization impulse goes on and continues to content its devotees, it is rarely strong enough to extinguish those its own size.

That it does go on seems, furthermore, quite as it should be. Its presence insures a comfortable place in society for the enormous class of highly useful citizens who are type-conforming, rather than atypical, by nature. In their own element they can set up their little standards and please themselves by conforming to them, doing meanwhile a negligible amount of harm to working nonconformists. Meanwhile, also, the very temptations to conformity which they set up form an excellent device for separating the dilettantes of individualism and originality from the genuine practitioners. Finally, in a properly contentious society, originality and individualism perhaps need stout wooden flag poles of conformity all about them to keep their claws whetted for the action rightly expected of them.

Indeed, the standardized republic with plenty of the antitoxins of resistance in its social body is, I suspect, vastly to be preferred to a society whose members in all classes were constantly and praiseworthily occupied in stimulating and admiring their neighbors' atypicalness. Such Utopias of individualism may furnish profitable daydreams for literature. But as a practical mode of social organization the risk of converting the republic into a one-hundred-and-fifty-million-strong Greenwich Village and the entire voting population into posturing asses would be too terrible to take.

14

TOWARD A HUMANE TECHNOLOGY

Architecture in the Jazz Age was in a state of creative ferment. In Germany Mies van der Rohe, with his austere dictum that "less is more," had already designed the prototype for his later Chicago towers in glass and black-painted steel. In Tokyo, Frank Lloyd Wright built his Imperial Hotel, on a site consisting of "sixty feet of liquid mud overlaid by eight feet of filled soil . . . about the consistency of hard cheese" – and saw it survive the great earthquake of 1923. But the Twenties was also an era of small-town banks disguised as Greek temples, of university libraries in "college Gothic," of real estate tracts crowded with "Cape Cod cottages," and of blighting urban sprawl that prompted H. L. Mencken to argue that Americans had a positive *Libido for the Ugly.* Such was the self-contradictory situation when Lewis Mumford wrote the essay that follows.

Mumford's "Machinery and the Modern Style" appeared in *The* enlivening many a dull issue of *The New York Times* with one of his vigorous letters to the editor, that it may come as a shock to recall that he was a major voice of the Twenties as well. Four of his books date from that decade: *The Story of Utopias, Sticks and Stones, The Golden Day,* and *Herman Melville.* Lewis Mumford's judgments on Man and (or versus) the Machine have changed with the years. The article reprinted here, as its author pointed out in his 1954 revision of *Sticks and Stones,* was written before he had had his intellectually crucial encounter with the pioneering "urban ecologist" Patrick Geddes – but it also contains the seeds of ideas Mumford later would articulate more fully, notably in his impressive Bampton Lectures at Columbia (published in 1952 as *Art and Technics*).

Mumford's "Machinery and the Modern Style" appeared in *The New Republic* in that journal's seventh year, and that magazine, like Mr. Mumford, has shown a basic self-consistency: "It is remarkable," wrote Gilbert A. Harrison in 1964, "how many of the controversies that engaged the moral concern of *The New Republic* twenty-five or fifty years ago still do."

MACHINERY AND THE MODERN STYLE

Lewis Mumford

It has taken our architects and interior decorators a long time to realize that there is a modern style in building, as well as a classic and mediaeval style. By far the greater number of edifices that have been put up within the last hundred years have been patterned in a mold with which neither the current materials nor the methods of workmanship have had very much to do. There have been, it is true, such grand monstrosities as the Crystal Palace, whose architectural significance has not, I believe, been fully appreciated: but the Crystal Palace is the frozen bud of a plant that has hardly had the opportunity to flower. The modern building has not dared to be itself. Our early skyscrapers, for example, were not designed on the assumption that skeletons of steel could reach higher into the air than buildings had ever before reached: they were constructed on the theory that a tall building was a solid pillar, and that it must therefore have a base, a shaft, and a capital. As a result of this stuffy misconception years passed before the extravagant aspirations that steel had made possible were even faintly realized in the Woolworth and Bush Towers.

The outcome of the failure to develop a modern style is that the contemporary city has the air of a ransacked museum, with all its various rooms and periods placed on exhibition. Up to the present all that we can call a modern style consists of misappropriated fragments of antiquity. What our contemporary buildings represent of modern life is its encyclopaedic acquaintance with the past: what they fail bravely to exhibit are the characteristic achievements of

FROM *The New Republic*, XXVII (August 3, 1921), pp. 263–64. Reprinted by permission of Lewis Mumford.

technology by which our daily activities have been molded into a hundred new patterns. Quite frequently the incongruity between our architectural "styles" and our secular habits is so flagrant as to constitute an aesthetic misdemeanor. Perhaps the best examples of ineptitude are the water fountains in the New York Public Library: from the mouth of the conventional marble lion there spouts, not water, alas! but a patented, sanitary drinking device with a hard nickeled surface. That is the sort of hole in which a classically trained architect finds himself when he begins to fill up his Greek and Roman frame with apparatus designed to meet strictly modern requirements. Without any hope of persuading the community to live a Roman life, he attempts to make the community live in a Roman building.

Yet, although our more ostentatious architecture has not developed a modern style, a fresh tradition has been stealing in upon us, like the proverbial thief in the night. In the fulfillment of some peculiarly contemporary purpose the modern style has here and there been introduced; and since the difficulty of creating a new structure is not so great when the functions it performs are themselves new, there is nothing strange in the fact that the two main sources of the modern style at present are the subways and the cheap popular lunchrooms. Because our subways and lunchrooms have been constructed with as strict an eye to ways and means and ends as a mediaeval guild hall or a Roman amphitheatre, these modern structures have come increasingly to possess that intelligibility of purpose and that integrity of execution which mark what can properly be called a "style." There is, indeed, perhaps finer promise of a living art behind one of those white-rimmed glass fronts, where white-winged chefs pour white batter upon an immaculate griddle, than there is, for example, in the Cathedral of St. John the Divine, which it has taken so much labor and reconsideration to build. This will very likely seem a malicious paradox to those who fancy that "style" is nothing more than a pleasing superfluity that can be added to or withdrawn from a work of utilitarian art at will — like a sheet of veneer. Those who appreciate the sociological insight of Ruskin and Morris, however, believe that a "style" is fundamentally the outcome of a way of living, that it ramifies through all the activities of a community, and that it is reasoned expression, in some particular work, of the complex of social and technological experience that grows out of a community's life. From this latter point of view a Child's restaurant is nearer to the source of a contemporary style than a building by Richardson, White, or Cram.

Let me disarm criticism by confessing that we are only at the beginning of a modern style, and that the beginning is crude. Lured into the void of a modern lunchroom by the vision of thick disks of golden batter basking on the griddle, one is struck immediately upon entrance by a cacophonous chorus of china and metal. From the polished tiles of the white interior comes a frigid glare, and it is difficult not to associate this surgical immaculacy with that of a ward in the better sort of hospital. The cleanliness is, in fact, blatant: the restaurant is like a soap which not merely removes the dirt efficiently but adds a gratuitous odor of antiseptics by which, as it were, to call attention to its performance. These defects of overstatement have discredited the modern style; they have drawn attention away from the fact that there *is* a style. Yet here is an equipment, harmonious in almost every detail, which could not possibly have exhibited itself in the world before 1880. If one looks carefully at the floors, the cutlery, the tables, the chairs, and the rest of the fixtures one discovers that there is not an object in the place which is not a machine product. What does that mean? Cheapness, standardization, monotony, ugliness one is perhaps tempted at first to answer; but this is by no means all.

Of its kind every article in the modern lunchroom is excellent, and its excellence is due to the fact that it has been made by a machine, and that it exhibits the accuracy, the fine finish, and the unerring fidelity to design which makes machine work delightful to everyone who knows how to take pleasure in geometrical perfection. If there are no surprises in a modern scheme of decoration and equipment there are likewise no disappointments. The whole structure is as neat, as chaste, and as inevitable as a demonstration in Euclid. There is no messiness, no "more-or-less" in the economy of the machine: once it has achieved a certain level of workmanship it can remain there, if the materials hold out, forever. Other ages have recorded great achievements in manufacture; but it has remained for the modern age to attain a hair's breadth perfection. We do not readily complain of monotony when an object is genuinely perfect. It is only an imperfect form that makes us long for a change, or, as we pregnantly say, an alteration. One can wander for hours through a forest of beeches, each tree a lean pole reaching up into a green vault, without the slightest sense of monotony; whereas one cannot walk for five minutes through the by-streets of a Philadelphia or a London suburb without wishing to destroy the mechanical sameness of the ugly little hutches the jerrybuilder has erected. It is not the monotony of a machine product that hurts, but some manifest inadequacy to human uses.

Now the test of a living style is its ability to beget new forms and fresh variations. The imitative "period" decorations that are made by machine in a Grand Rapids furniture factory fall within limits that are defined by the patterns which have survived from other ages: they are as incapable of yielding fresh designs as a mummy is of begetting a family. One of the things that should cause us to be hopeful about the naive modern style is that it is already undergoing improvements: the Bronx subway extension in New York is as great an advance over the old-fashioned system, aesthetically, as the first American subways were over the Piccadilly tube. In the restaurants a similar development has been going on. Recently a couple of lunchrooms were opened on Fifth Avenue whose scheme of decoration has retained the fine congruity with the machinery of cooking and service that marks a genuine style, and at the same time has a mellowness and a refinement which brings a grateful relief from the jangling whiteness of the earlier regime. These new restaurants are as good, on their scale, as the trainhall of the Pennsylvania Station in New York, and they are good in the same way — they perform a necessary purpose with urbanity, distinction and grace. In them the modern style has reached a mature development through which the logic of the machine is reconciled with the decent aesthetic requirements of humanity.

How is it that the modern style has been so slow to realize itself — is still so timid, so partial, so inadequate? Is its crudity not due to the fact that our architects have thought that true art lay elsewhere, in Greek temples and Roman baths and Adam residences and what not, and so they have not given the lunchroom and the subway station the degree of passionate attention which would make them perfect in design as well as in execution? This "division in the records of the mind" accounts, I believe, for the peculiar barrenness and frigidity of the early machine style: its vices were due not to the presence of machine work but to the absence of a vivifying human imagination.

Up to the present the machine style has fallen short of its possibilities largely for two reasons. In the early part of the industrial period the designer attempted to qualify the mechanical rigidity of his materials by introducing forms which were antipathetic to the functions which they performed. The iron cornucopias and flowers that Ruskin railed at, for example, typify this weak attempt to mollify the machine; and the flowery decorations that one can still see on some old model of the typewriter arose out of the same pathetic fallacy. The second reason for its frustration was that when the designer paid due attention to mechanical efficiency, he neglected to carry out those final developments of form and material which – so far from being vague excrescences, like ferrous foliage – were essential to their human enjoyment beyond the mean requirements of use.

To create designs which will respect the logic of the machine and at the same time have regard for the vagaries of human psychology is the problem whose solution will give us a satisfactory, genuine modern style. We have yet to see what humane fulfillments the machine may bring about when we finally come to grips with it, and neither allow ourselves to be overridden by a crude and boisterous utilitarianism nor turn a repugnant, ineffectual face completely away from the instrument which promises – at least promises! – to liberate the community.

PART V

THE TWENTIES INTERPRET THE FUTURE

In America as in Europe a phase of fragmentation set in. It was not a smash to which one can give a definite date, but every day there was something happening in the direction of dissolution. In America as in Europe State governments became insolvent phantoms making feebler and feebler efforts to collect taxes, and the Federal authority in Washington faded away, if not as completely as the League of Nations in Europe, at any rate in a comparable manner. We have the same phenomena of municipalities becoming autonomous, and provisional councils, Citizens' Unions, Law and Order Societies, Workers' Protection Associations and plain Workers' Soviets (in New Mexico and Arizona) springing into activity here, there and everywhere . . . The President was carrying on although his term had expired because his successor elect had disappeared on his way to the capital in the Allegheny Mountains. There had been considerable confusion about the last election, and two Secession Presidents who were disputing possession of the State of New York . . .

The President received his visitor very cordially and asked many very sympathetic and intelligent questions about the European situation. He spoke very hopefully of the American outlook. The 'return to Normalcy', he said, was at last in sight.

H. G. WELLS
The Shape of Things to Come (1933)

15
THE BURDEN OF URBAN CIVILIZATION

In its first issue, dated November 12, 1924, *The Commonweal* greeted President-elect Calvin Coolidge with a staggering list of national and world problems awaiting his attention, complex enough to make even leadership of a nation in wartime seem comparatively simple. On May 1, 1925, Coolidge made public mention of one of them: urban crowding. As far as social amenities were concerned, said the President, modern technology was cutting both ways. "The apartment house, the skyscraping commercial building and the elevator have tended to increase congestion. Electric railways, subways and motor cars have tended to diffusion of the people" – but thus far, Coolidge conceded, in curious agreement for once with Lewis Mumford, the victories had all been on the side of the skyscrapers and the elevators.

In response to this speculative effort by the Yankee in the White House, *The Commonweal* published the following editorial. The problem has even greater pertinence today than in the Twenties, which were not, for the technically advanced Western nations, a time of "population explosion"; quite the contrary. But forty years later, just prior to Paul VI's *Humanae Vitae* and "the Pill," America's population was growing at a rate comparable to India's.

Although firmly Catholic in point of view, *The Commonweal* was in no sense a "voice" of the Church; its first issue contained an announcement that it would be "the independent, personal product of its editors and contributors, who, for the most part, will be laymen." Michael Williams, the magazine's editor from 1924 through 1938, had been a lay newspaperman, working as a reporter for the Boston *Post,* the New York *World* and *Telegram,* as city editor of the San Francisco

Examiner (starting the day before the 1906 earthquake!), and as a correspondent for the International News Service, before going full time into religious journalism. As *Commonweal's* editor, Williams maintained his ties with the secular press, covering the Nazi persecution of the Jews for the New York *Herald Tribune,* the Spanish Civil War (on which he and the rest of *Commonweal's* staff disagreed) for the New York *American,* and the election of Pius XII for *The New York Times.*

THE TERRIBLE SUPER-CITY

A topic of the most serious importance and complex nature was brought to the surface once more by President Coolidge, in his speech on what is pleasantly spoken of as the national highway crisis. The range of the President's thought included much more important matters than the group of automobile club secretaries, to whom he spoke, had gathered to discuss. Indeed it is rather absurd to talk of the traffic conditions, even in cities, as constituting a crisis. Common sense, and a growing power of self control, will go far toward remedying existing evils. At worst, new expenditures for roads and viaducts are in sight, and the gains in wealth from intensification of traffic surely prevent these from seeming a crushing burden. Anyway, if the prophets are to be believed, the crisis or problem or whatever it is, may at any time take a new — and, indeed, a more alarming — turn in the sudden development of aviation. Street rules for aeroplanes do look like a strain on the regulators of the near future.

But President Coolidge's thought leaped out beyond the mere matter of getting about. The size of cities, as a huge complex of the near future, worried him. He was right; it is one of the biggest subjects calling for the consideration of practical politicians. The President's broaching it is an instance of a certain quality of the super-commonplace in his imagination. He has a habit of starting discussion on something which is more or less in everyone's mind — which, in fact, is not new at all — yet is of commanding novelty

FROM *The Commonweal,* II (May 13, 1925), 1–2.

and supreme importance. In the present case, it may be said that the stupendous growth of cities and the menace of its continuance are in everybody's mind. Yet who, with authority, has invited the public attention to the danger, or suggested serious consideration of the resultant evils and means of averting them?

The fact is, that when the growth of cities is spoken of — say the growth of New York to 20,000,000 inhabitants by the year 1950, or 50,000,000 by the year 2000 — the common popular reaction is a sort of fatuous pride — as if mere numbers made greatness. Even enlightened leaders of thought, instead of asking what the life of such a community would be, materially or spiritually, indulge in dreams of marts and markets, air lanes and subterranean passages, electrical homes, and art peddled by radio from municipal stations to the convertible bed-dining-sitting-working-room, of which the ultimate home of the too, too many millions would have to consist. We have all seen the diagrams and pictorial layouts in the Sunday newspapers — map of New York in nineteen-something, taking in all Long Island and New Jersey as far as Trenton, with the Hudson Valley as far as Newburgh thrown in. The Caruso of the day sits in a steel cell, singing at a telephone receiver; while to one side, a pair of boxers in a padded room, thump each other in front of an airless cinema machine. A note adds that at nine o'clock in the evening, the news of the day will take the place of the song — with twenty-four hour weather forecast — and the principal paintings of Raphael or Picasso or Charles Dana Gibson will replace the prize fight.

Presumably, the exploiters of these grandiose ideas never really think of the misery and essential loneliness of the wretched millions, who will, or may, have to endure these fearful luxuries. It is true we are told that they will be scientifically fed, mostly with synthetic foods — as the purveying of any ordinary commodities in the necessary quantities will be impossible with the best possible organization. They will all think the same things, provided by the Mental Direction Bureau of the central government. They will be taught how to walk at the same uniform pace by the experts of the Pedestrian Control. Their lives in all other details will also be strictly regulated — especially their outings — for if they were not, no adequate means of locomotion could be provided. They will all go to work, of course, and home again; but they will do it at their assigned hours and prescribed routes, so as not to tangle up the machine. Probably occasional departures from routine will be allowed for social purposes and for special occasions; but they must be strictly limited so as to avoid absolute deadlock. All amusements will be turned on, as well as religious exercises and sermons on Sundays.

Of course, argues the optimistic sort of super-citizen, the cities will not be really overcrowded, in spite of their gigantic size. The Eugenics department of the super-government will control the births. Also, they will breed for slimness and elasticity, so that the people may be packed tighter and closer in the cars. Perhaps, after a time, the Euthanasia department will take care of the deaths. Painless and even pleasurable gusts of gas will be let loose among the inferior citizens — the poorest, of course — whenever there seems to be a danger of serious congestion of population. Standardization, efficiency, organized, scientific control — worked out after the unimpeachably practical ideas of such eminent reformers as H. G. Wells, Henry Ford, Dean Inge, Bernard Shaw, Professor Getitdone, Dr. Nordical, Andrew Volstead, Margaret Sanger, Trotzky, and associates — these be the new gods of the coming dispensation, as we glimpse its dreams and revelations in the magic mirror of the press.

It seems too bad to object to the glowing vision of the super-city — and the super-state — shall we add, this superstition? This worshipping of the silly idol of mechanism has proceeded to a perilous degree; yet, after all, as soon as men begin to understand the wretched thing, they will laugh — and the wind of their mirth will blow the evil fog away. Meanwhile, common sense suggests that even in so wonderful a machine as is imagined for the super-city, there might still remain some hitches. Some fool will always drop a monkey wrench into the cogs, and the more elaborate the mechanism, the greater the disaster when anything does go wrong. President Coolidge was evidently impressed with this feature of the whole conception — the difficulty of making it work, perhaps; of making it fool-proof.

But in fact its worst evil, its direct tragedy, does not lie in its inevitable malfunctioning upon occasions. Its success would be the real disaster. It is impossible to conceive of these teeming millions in their physical multiplication, and in their spiritual loneliness, without repulsion. It needs but a little thought to show that in these regimented crowds, all the essential qualities and enjoyments of citizenship and civilization must be lost. It is a question today whether the limit of numbers permitting the community sense has not already been surpassed. In the dream city of the future, one feels that the intimacy of feeling and interest which makes the spiritual bond, would be attenuated to the danger point. Multiply the appeal by three, or four, or twenty — and we arrive at a stage where a public-spirited man may perhaps have an affection for his borough or his ward, with an understanding of its advantages and needs, but is repelled even to anger by the exigencies of a rival quarter, which he has never visited, and whose people he regards with suspicion and dislike.

Social intercourse has greatly diminished in American cities, at least as regards the home. The multiplication of obligations leads to even the best and finest being ignored; and the mechanical difficulties of getting together, the enormous rivalry of other duties and attractions, have completely changed the lives of the people in the last twenty-five years. The end of New-Year-calling, is an illustration. New York is too big and too hard to circulate in for mere casual observances. A result already felt is the loneliness of the young people and the isolation of the old. How much more hopeless the mechanism of community living, how vain the hope of any genuine social intercourse among 20,000,000 people without common idea or purpose, and living often fifty miles apart!

President Coolidge has raised a very large question — and it may be a tragic one of the future — in turning the public eyes upon the problems of the super-city of the future. He had the mechanical ones in mind mainly, it would seem; but they are simple as compared with the cultural and moral ones. So devious are these that the true question for civic leaders is — whether it is not time to call a halt? Can it be done? Is it possible to stem the creation of monster communities with no soul, and work back to groups who know each other — who have ideals as well as subways, and inspirations as well as airless entertainment? At bottom, the question is one of soul — but the practical problem is one of better distribution of population.

16
A PREVIEW OF ARMAGEDDON

"Man alone, among the higher animals, seems characteristically to fight his own kind to the death," declared Will Irwin in his book *The Next War* (1921), anticipating some of the somber biological insights of Robert Ardrey and Konrad Lorenz. The slaughters of 1914–1918 generated a literature of the coming war almost as extensive as that of the previous one. The *New Statesman* called one such study, *What Would Be the Character of a New War?,* written cooperatively by Swedish, British, American, Swiss, Japanese, Danish, French, Greek, and German military and civilian experts and published in 1933, "the most terrible book which has ever been written."

At the end of the Twenties, Roland Hugins, an associate of the Brookings Institution – a privately endowed, government-related research center in economics, public administration, and the social sciences – surveyed some of this next-war literature in the article printed below. One year previously the Kellogg-Briand Pact, renouncing war as an instrument of national policy, had been ratified by all the major nations of the world. At the same time, however, the American Legion was doggedly campaigning for compulsory military training in the schools, and the officer-students at the Naval War College were writing term papers on the probable strategy and tactics of a future war with Japan.

World Tomorrow, in which Hugins' article appeared, reflected the viewpoint of the Fellowship of Reconciliation. Socialist as well as pacifist, this magazine (founded in 1918 as *New World*) had had Norman Thomas for its first editor. Kirby Page, a forceful "social gospel" spokesman, became chief editor in 1926, and in 1928 Reinhold Niebuhr left an inner-city parish in Detroit to join the editorial board, dividing his time between *World Tomorrow* and a teaching appointment at Union Theological Seminary. Contributing editors in 1929 included Thomas; Paul H. Douglas, then an economist, later a Senator from Illinois; the Quaker historian Rufus Jones; the liberal Methodist bishop Francis McConnell and the radical Episcopal bishop Paul Jones; the Christian labor organizer A. J. Muste; and the poetess Zona Gale. Divisions within the F.O.R. were reflected in the magazine, which suspended publication in 1934.

THAT NOTORIOUS NEXT WAR

Roland Hugins

Few persons have failed to notice the emergence of a copious literature on the Next War. Doubtless no other war in history has been so thoroughly described and debated – in advance. If all the books on the subject which have appeared during the last ten years in English, German, French, Russian, Italian, and other languages were placed side by side, they would require a considerable shelf; and the magazine articles and newspaper discussions would fill several bulky portfolios. The writers of these books and articles are not content to deal in broad outlines: they go into details concerning weapons, tactics, strategy, and results. They have given full rein to the "scientific imagination," and the pictures they have drawn for us are, of course, gruesome and horrifying.

For the most part the authors who have discussed the next war are in agreement. They foresee a vast and terrible intensification of the methods and horrors of the late World War. For example, Mr. Will Irwin has described an air raid on New York City undertaken by a great fleet of aircraft raining down unlimited quantities of gas-bombs, incendiary bombs, and high explosives. Mr. Henry W. Nevinson has described a similar raid over London. In both instances the anticipated results are appallingly similar: buildings and houses a twisted mass of ruins, acres of corpses, and after a few days, a smoking, silent, lifeless desolation. All the resources of a mechanical and scientific civilization, it appears, are to be

---

FROM *World Tomorrow*, XII (July, 1929), pp. 309–12.

employed for the purpose of mutual annihilation both on land and sea. Only in minor matters do these dire prophets differ among themselves. Some of them maintain that the coming struggle will be, like the last, a static affair of trenches and attrition, while others contend that an extensive use of tanks, great and small, will restore mobility to armies in the field. Some assert that novel weapons, such as the death-ray, disease-bacteria, and new chemicals will decide the issue, while a more conservative school argues that for efficient slaughter we must depend on arms and methods already well developed, in particular, on gunfire, aircraft, lethal and asphyxiating gases, armored ships and submarines. But none of them doubts that all these dreadful engines of war will be brought to comparative perfection, and will work infinitely more havoc than they did from 1914 to 1918.

All true, doubtless. The intellectuals and the experts who have predicted and analyzed the course of the next war have brought to the business so much acumen, imagination, and technical knowledge that their general conclusions cannot be gainsaid. And yet the truth is that not one of them has gone to the pith of the matter. So far as I know, each and all have been so engrossed in the technological and material aspects of the subject that they have failed to see that the modern world has developed quite a new kind of war, and that this change has come about not because of scientific inventions but because of social and institutional attitudes.

To describe in a phrase the kind of war to which we are coming is difficult; perhaps it may best be designated as uncontrollable warfare. Once started, it gets completely out of hand. No section of the nation, whether the army, or the government, or the public, seems able to guide it or to terminate it. It is war *à outrance,* but it is more than that. It is not only war to the finish; it is war without finish. As it goes on, its causes and purposes are lost to view. It becomes war for itself: war-for-war's-sake. It can be ended, on one side or on both sides, only by revolution or by annihilation. And this new species of conflict, appropriate to the machine age, brakeless, unstopable, unrestricted, arises naturally out of our modern ideas and institutions. It is the result, not primarily of machines, explosives, and chemicals, but of the new ideas in our heads. These ideas, centering around the concepts of organization, regulation, and efficiency, have a firm grip on the modern mind. There was once a useful expression: "the fog of war." On the field of battle this fog has been partially dispelled, chiefly by the scouting airplane. It is now no longer possible to move forward secretly large masses of troops. But a different and novel "fog of war" has moved back over the nation itself, over millions of minds, until it has come quite to transform an ancient activity and pastime.

II

Around the question whether other great wars are possible or probable I shall for the most part detour, since it is not really germane to this argument. It is enough to note that among thinking people the number of optimists has diminished.The World War taught most of us to look beneath national proclamations and international pacts to concrete deeds; and a survey of contemporary actualities is not reassuring. The expenditures of the Powers for armaments steadily increase. Never before in history were so many men under arms, or were so many fighting craft ranging the seas. The nations are busy modernizing and improving their fortresses, and in building new strategic roads and railways toward their frontiers. In forcing small countries to obey their will the great Powers quickly resort to relentless coercion, and this is equally true of Russia in dealing with Georgia, of the United States in dealing with Nicaragua, of Great Britain dealing with Irak or Egypt, and of France in dealing with Syria or the Riff. The big empires are not yet sated with territory, and the leaner empires, like Italy and Japan, make no concealment of their appetites. Nearly every realist in Europe expects a major war not later than some time in the decade 1935–1945. Inevitable it is not; but few people would declare another great conflagration to be "impossible."

Let us merely say that the world may have a chance to see an exhibition of modern, scientific warfare at full intensity. This will differ if it comes from all past warfare, I think, chiefly through operation of three social and institutional factors, namely:

1. conscription, completely, logically, and universally applied from the very outbreak of hostilities;
2. censorship in the inclusive sense, with its positive counterpart, propaganda, developed with all the resources of human ingenuity and of modern means of communication;
3. dictatorship, meaning the suspension of all forms of democratic control, and the concentration of all power over war aims and

war methods in the hands of a small clique of energetic men, official and military.

All of these institutional forces were employed in 1914–1918, but crudely and hesitatingly. A huge volunteer army was raised in Great Britain before conscription was applied, and in Australia, indeed, compulsory service was defeated at the polls. Both in Britain and the United States exemptions were granted, rather grudgingly, to a few categories of conscientious objectors. Even on the Continent of Europe the civilian population was not thoroughly sifted into the most helpful economic and quasi-military tasks; and everywhere women were allowed to do about what they liked, directed only by that ardent patriotic fervor which seizes the human female in wartime. Censorship was not systematically complete. In nearly all countries some brave minority and dissentient groups were able to make their protests heard. And even the official propagandists themselves were occasionally restrained by lingering vestiges of respect for truth and honor. Dictatorship was only partial. It is true that no elections were held during the World War in Britain, Germany, Austria, France, or Italy, and that as the conflict progressed supreme power was more and more tightly gathered and exercised by a handful of outstanding rulers and generalissimos. But outside of Europe ordinary political processes were for the most part maintained, and it was generally recognized that the suspension was temporary — "for the period of the emergency."

In the next war all these hesitancies, inadequacies, and illogicalities will be remedied and erased. At the very beginning of the conflict "universal service" will be applied, and all "slackers" will be rounded up forthwith. Conscription is simply enforced labor in wartime: labor on the firing line or labor in the rear. It is a device to override any reluctances to serve which the citizen may entertain; and why, logically, should one kind of a reluctance, sincere or insincere, be respected more than any other kind of a reluctance? Conscription was invented in France, during the Great Revolution, and its beginning is usually fixed at the date of the Jourdan Law of 1798. France introduced conscription for one reason only: that her leaders wanted more soldiers than the methods of volunteering would supply. In full bloom, the system of conscription makes every man who is able-bodied and not too young or too old, available for fighting in the field. In modern nations such armies are huge affairs, and require the full effort of the rest of the population for their equipment, ammunition, clothing, and feeding. Conscription requires that each belligerent nation become an articulated fighting machine, and more than any other factor wipes out any significant distinction between combatant and non-combatant.

The modern man, accustomed to his daily newspapers, his movies, and his radio, must be fed a constant stream of words and images if his "morale" is to be maintained at fullest intensity. In wartime this stream of words and images can be almost completely regulated. Censorship and propaganda will attend to that. The ancient and natural passions of war can be readily whetted and reënforced by the reiteration of accusations and lies. This enterprise does not need to be conducted with any unusual degree of skill or cleverness, for credulity in wartime seems to be boundless. Restricted to only one side of the story, and that side sounded daily on a hundred drums, the citizen of today believes every infamy and depravity attributed to the enemy. It is no accident that during the war of 1914–1918 the United States, which entered the conflict with divided mind, became in less than a year the most hysterical consumer of the atrocity-fictions. America in its system of public intelligence is the most modern of the nations, and presages the possibilities of propaganda, censorship, and espionage in the future.

And lastly, the Next War will be quite definitely run from "above." The conscripts in the army cannot have much to say about it; they are themselves to some degree suspect, and under the constant surveillance of the Military Intelligence. The rest of the nation, the Reserves behind the lines, the men and women who toil in offices, factories, mines and on railroads and farms, in order that the boys in the trenches may not falter — these are the puppets of national policy, not its commanders. A few men at the top of the heap, the Victory Makers or those who promise Victory, shall rule all. During the last World War and after it there was some talk of disagreement and dissension between "the frocks" and "the brass hats," that is to say, between the politicians and the generals. This dispute was largely fictitious. The officials, whether civilian or military, who sponsored force to the uttermost and the knockout blow, rode the tide; and in the Next War their sway will be undisputed.

III

That the new wars of the Machine Age will be politically and humanly out of hand, with unlimited objectives and uncontrolled purposes is certainly true, and true in a sense never quite paralleled previously in history. Many people imagine that since the earliest ages the practices of warfare have been growing steadily more moderate and humane; and that since the time of the ancient Assyrians, who slowly flayed their prisoners alive and relished the long hours of screaming, the grosser barbarities have been progressively eliminated. The fact is, however, that there have been numerous ups and downs in the business. In pre-Christian times the conquered enemy, men and women alike, were put to the sword, and spared only for enslavement; and the babes were dashed on the rocks. In the Middle Ages chivalry introduced some amenities, so that battles were often conducted according to rules of etiquette, with only a few warriors slain, and those all professionals. But the ferocious religious wars which marked the end of mediaevalism brought about a recrudescence of ruthlessness and another submergence of the distinction between combatant and non-combatant. For example, after the capture of Magdeburg the entire town was burned to the ground, and of the 36,000 inhabitants, 30,000 were butchered forthwith. In the modern period, after Grotius, an elaborate code of international law came into being for the regulation of methods of fighting. To cite a few instances: prisoners were always to be granted quarter, and were not after capture to be "subject to intentional suffering or indignity"; non-combatants were never to be killed; unfortified cities were not to be bombarded; dum-dum bullets and saw-toothed bayonets were not to be used in battle; water and food supplies were not to be poisoned; and land-hospitals and hospital ships were granted immunity from attack. This international code was, on the whole, respected throughout the nineteenth century. Not all of it was scrapped during the World War, but parts of it were cast aside as incompatible with up-to-date efficiency. The tendency then was clear enough: such rules are hampering to the "pitiless logic of modern warfare." In future wars, no doubt, "logic" will come into its own.

Modern war, the warfare of the future, has an outer and an inner aspect, an external and an internal character. The first is really a reversion to an ancient form of strife, while the second is something quite new under the sun. In its outer or external aspect the war of tomorrow will be essentially a *siege* with a whole nation, rather than a city-state, the object of investment. Since nations now mobilize their entire human resources for conflict, it is natural that the "nation in arms" should find itself beleaguered. In the World War Germany attempted to cut, with submarines, the overseas communications of

Great Britain; and the Allies, with rather more success, threw a starvation blockade around Germany. In the post-war years the French effectively surrounded and isolated the Riff, keeping out, indeed, even medical supplies. In the next war, fleets of aircraft will help in making the investment more effective. Of course, so long as a country with any seaports can insure that merchantships may enter her harbors, she cannot be hemmed in. But we know that in up-to-date war all international law on the "freedom of the seas" is treated as a joke. Not only are embargoes and blockades applied with full vigor, but neutral ships are seized anywhere on the high seas, and, most important of all, the distinction between contraband and non-contraband is obliterated. If belligerents can prevent it, wheat and pork and cotton are no more allowed to enter the enemy's ports than rifles or gunpowder.

From time immemorial a siege has always been a desperate matter — for the besieged. Slaughter and destruction have ordinarily been the lot of the fallen city. Some commanders like Alexander may have been for the most part more compassionate than others like Tamerlane. But the general rule has been that an enemy who resisted in a fortified place was entitled to less mercy than one who fought in the open field. A community which behind its walls refused to surrender was, if at last overcome, pillaged and laid waste like Troy, like Tyre, like Carthage. As late as 1820, indeed, the Duke of Wellington summed up the matter in the statement: "I believe it has always been understood that the defenders of a fortress stormed have no right to quarter." In future wars the "fortress stormed" will be a nation or a group of nations. And the warring hosts which stand about this nation or group of nations will be bent, with every means within their power, on annihilation.

One ultra-modern idea, in particular, increases the likelihood of wholesale sieges. This is the idea that in each war one side or the other is the "aggressor" and is, consequently, clearly in the wrong. Once the aggressor has been determined, by some brittle rule or other, it becomes the duty of all members of the League of Nations or of all signatories of the Kellogg Pact to pitch in upon him, and by various embargoes and encirclements, economic and military, to bring him to terms. Such a plan might work splendidly if some one small country, say Turkey, could be caught red-handed in an act of militaristic aggression. But imagine a clever schemer like Mussolini being surprised in such a compromising position! No great nation will now go to war unless (a) it has a "moral" case which looks plausible, and (b) it is certain of the sympathy and support of powerful friends. Of course, any statesman may miscalculate — perhaps that is what a statesman normally does; but the inequalities of numerical and economic strength will become apparent only after the conflict is well under way. When all the dubious issues of belligerency and neutrality have been settled, one side will begin to hem in the other. Then we shall see siege warfare on the grand scale. The ultimate results are certain to be rather unwholesome and appalling.

IV

The inner essence of modern warfare is *morale* — not the morale of the troops alone, but of the whole population. The military front on the frontiers has been supplemented by a psychological front at home. In the first stages of the conflict, national morale is all too easy to achieve and sustain. At the outbreak of hostilities all liberties are abrogated, and each man and woman is assigned his and her place in the common function of "defense." All the avenues of information and intelligence are brought under a unified control. The entire national mind becomes fluid and is directed into the channels dug by the governmental censorship and propaganda. Every white lie about itself and its purposes and every black lie about the enemy and his iniquities are readily swallowed by each belligerent country. The war spirit, indeed, rises to a pitch of hysteria and continues at a level of abnormal intensity for months, perhaps years.

But if the conflict is long continued, as it is certain to be whenever the opposing sides are not grossly unequal in strength, a second stage in the national psychosis is reached. What is usually called "war weariness" sets in. The strain begins to tell, and popular doubts begin to stir beneath the surface of national unity. More and more people begin to see through the official exaggerations, misrepresentations, forgeries, and myths. Seditious ideas find currency, if little open expression. In the summer of 1918 Winston Churchill declared: "The war on both sides has become a race between revolution and victory." That phrase was a flash of genius. Revolution is the shadow which stalks all modern war. After a time the only question is, which side shall crack first in its morale and heave its leaders overboard. Of course, these leaders are not, in any ultimate sense "to blame." They too are the victims of the national self-hypnosis. But the leaders, in places of power, enjoy the struggle or at least their leadership, and insist on hanging on to the bitter end. They envision themselves as the mighty directors of national destiny.

And so the Next War is likely to end, like the last, with revolution on one side and abortive victory on the other. But there is a possibility that it will come to a different and more horrible conclusion. Provided that it can be postponed long enough to allow the delusions of the Age of Efficiency to come into full flower and the progressive deterioration of moral, social, and political ideals to overtake all humanity, the world may see holocaust on a scale never before witnessed, and the annihilation of millions of people. The winning side, after withstanding bombardments, blockades, and drenchings of gas, will be ready to exact its revenge, and will throw a relentless pressure around its beleaguered and doomed opponent. When at last it beats down all resistance it will proceed to exterminate every man, woman, and child, and to devastate the territory of the enemy nation from border to border. Of a whole continent, perhaps, these victors will make a waste and silent land, and in that blackened desert they will erect a great monument, fittingly inscribed with the ancient motto: *Dulce et decorum est pro patria mori!*

BIBLIOGRAPHICAL ESSAY

To conserve space, data concerning the publisher's name and place of publication have been omitted for all but a few titles.

Books available in paperback editions are shown with an asterisk [*] following the title.

We begin with the magazines. In the Twenties as in our day they made up a large fraction of our total mass-media environment. Into the 9200 homes in the Lynds' *Middletown* came 35 subscription copies of the *Atlantic*, 20 of *Harper's*, 15 of the *New Republic* – and nearly 1500 of the *Saturday Evening Post*. Magazines were bound into the national market economy by the institution of mass advertising (in the Twenties, even some of the most editorially independent of them had to change their page-sizes to accommodate the advertisers' plates), and, like the rest of the national economy, they prospered. Their bulky bound volumes stand on library shelves today with an air of durability, like gold certificates. Some of them stand alongside other volumes that carry the same title forward to the present and backward to the Gilded Age (the *National Geographic*), or to the Civil War (*Harper's*), or to the Transcendentalists (the *Atlantic Monthly*), reminding us of continuities in history. Others stand in ranks which abruptly end, reminding us of the inevitability of historical change (where now are the *Smart Set*, *Scribner's*, the *Bookman*, *World's Work*? and where then were *American Heritage*, *Commentary*, the *National Review*, and *Playboy*?)

One historian very much aware of the cultural importance of this medium has been Frank Luther Mott. The fourth complete volume of his *A History of American Magazines* (1957) reached only as far as 1905 in the chronology of his subject, but fortunately Mott added a four-hundred-page supplement, "Sketches of certain important magazines which flourished 1885–1905," carrying the story of selected titles down to what was then the present (1957), or to the date of the magazine's demise. We thus have detailed, accurate, and perceptive coverage of many magazines of the Theodore Roosevelt era which flourished also in the Twenties, ranging from the *Saturday Evening Post* and the *Ladies'*

Home Journal to the *Journal of the American Medical Association* and the *Sewanee Review.* A fifth volume, comprising twenty-one comparable sketches of magazines that were active between 1905 and 1930 – for example, *Current History, Poetry,* the *Yale Review,* and *Time* – was published in 1968, but Mott did not live to write the broader historical narrative that was to have accompanied them. Ten of the planned individual magazine sketches also remained unwritten, and we can only guess what the Master of Magazines (as Howard Mumford Jones called him) would have made of the *Masses,* the *Reader's Digest,* the *Saturday Review,* and *Physical Culture.*

Fortunately, there is broad coverage for the years since 1905 in Theodore Bernard Peterson, *Magazines in the Twentieth Century* (1964). Peterson focuses more than Mott did upon magazine publication *as an industry,* an emphasis which gives his survey both strengths and weaknesses. He strives to do justice to what he calls "magazines for cultural minorities" – e.g., *Nation, New Republic, American Mercury,* and the "little" magazines – but a magazine does not really "turn him on" until its circulation hits one or two million, at which point his descriptive prose begins to glow. For an example of the difference between Mott's and Peterson's approaches to their subject, compare their respective treatments of the Curtis and the Crowell-Collier families of big "slick" magazines.

There exist also useful studies of individual "books," as magazine editors like to call them. For an admirable model of how to write such a monograph, see M. K. Singleton, *H. L. Mencken and the American Mercury Adventure* (1962) – with the warning that not even as good a secondary study as this one can absolve the student of the Twenties from his obligation to go back into the stacks and *read* the *Mercury!* There are also biographies of men who edited magazines (and did much else), such as the treatment of the editor of *The Crisis,* in Francis L. Broderick's *W. E. B. Du Bois: Negro Leader in a Time of Crisis** (1959). Briefer essays are sometimes more informative than full-length studies. On the editor of the *Nation,* for example, I found much more insight in a six-page reminiscence by Lewis Gannett than in one entire book specifically on Villard's work during the Twenties [Gannett, "Villard's 'Nation,'" in Henry M. Christman, (ed.), *One Hundred Years of* THE NATION (1965), pp. 35-40; D. Joy Humes, *Oswald Garrison Villard: Liberal of the 1920's* (1960)]. Sometimes an editor himself is the best available commentator upon his own magazine; see Max Eastman's account of *The Liberator* in his memoir *Love and Revolution: My Journey Through an Epoch* (1964), especially Chapters 10 and 20. Or we may learn from a colleague and competitor in an editor's own general field; for example, Frederick Lewis Allen, of *Harper's,* on "Sedgwick and the Atlantic," *Outlook and Independent,* CL (December 26, 1928), 1407.

In their accessibility for the modern reader, these magazines vary greatly. Some of them can more easily be found by walking among the shelves of an old, small-city public library than by presenting a request through the formidable red tape in the library of a large metropolitan university. Others, such as *The Liberator,* are hard to find in complete files anywhere, and all are subject to the ravages of decay, theft, and mutilation. Fortunately, offset printing, xerography, and film have given librarians in our time an equivalent of the plaster-of-paris and other materials used by museum paleontologists to repair dinosaurs' bones.

Like the magazines in which their articles appeared, the authors, also, who are represented in this anthology vary in accessibility. Some have attracted the attention of biographers, in works of the caliber of Mark Schorer's massive and definitive *Sinclair Lewis: An American Life** (1961). Others have written useful memoirs of their own, such as Granville Hicks, *Part of the Truth: An Autobiography* (1965). Still others wrote enough of the public record of their time that they have received extensive treatment in books seeking to interpret a portion of that record; thus the name and work of Michael Gold are a recurrent *leitmotiv* in Daniel Aaron's *Writers on the Left** (1961). Quite a few of these writers, however, are more elusive; the reader in search of further information must pursue his man through the pages of reference works such as James M. Ethridge et al., *Contemporary Authors* (20 vols., Detroit, 1952–1968); Matthew Hoehn, *Catholic Authors* (2 vols., Newark, 1947 and 1952); *American Men of Science;* the *Biography Index;* the *Reader's Guide;* the *International Index;* or the volumes from the Twenties of M. N. Ask, (ed.), *Who's Who in Journalism.*

Correspondence has cleared up some of my own investigative questions. Hillyer Hawthorne Straton, for example, called my attention to two articles he had written for the Baptist historical quarterly *Foundations* [V (1962), 3–24, and X (1967), 137–49] on his father, John Roach Straton. Well researched from the senior Straton's papers, these essays present both father and son in a light by which historians of the Twenties, myself included, had never previously viewed them. I am indebted in particular also to Mrs. Lonnelle Aikman, of the senior staff of *National Geographic,* for her assistance, which included an extensive and informative set of clippings on the work of her late husband. What was said in the body of my text should be repeated here: Duncan Aikman has been unduly neglected. Perhaps the republication here of one of his essays from the Twenties will prompt someone into doing a full-dress monograph on him.

As to our authors' subject matter, the many concerns of the Twenties have generated an enormous historical literature, particularly during the decade and a half since the publication of Henry F. May's stimulating paper "Shifting Perspectives on the 1920's," *Mississippi Valley Historical Review,* XLIII (1956), 405–27. Burl Noggle, in "The Twenties: a New Historiographical Frontier" [*ibid.,* renamed the *Journal of American History,* LIII (1966), 299–314], bore witness to the abundance of this literature in his luxuriant footnotes, which the student in search of further reading in that period should consult. Unfortunately, there remain some writers on the Twenties who seem unaware that any of this research has happened. In a letter to me dated June 5, 1968, Abraham Eisenstadt wondered "how far we have moved along in our perspective of the twenties – from a sentimental reminiscence of modes and life-styles, to a more disinterested sociology, and thence to a more traditional history"; when the same poignant paragraph by the Imperial Wizard of the Ku Klux Klan, the same breathlessly salacious motion-picture ad, the same famous-last-words of Herbert Hoover, and the same profound pronouncement by Walter Lippmann, begin to pass from textbook to textbook and from historian to historian – and I have done, it must be confessed, my share of this sort of thing – the reader begins to wonder if the Twenties have not become some kind of petrifact, instead of an exciting new frontier.

Granted, reminiscence as an historical method has one powerful advantage: even after allowance is made for the many tricks which a memory can play upon its owner, that way of doing history bases itself upon evidence even more "primary" in nature than the letters, diaries, and newspapers (and, in the present case, magazines) which are the research historian's normal stock-in-trade. I have found autobiography, ordinarily the most suspect of historical sources, peculiarly rewarding for the study of the Twenties. "History, unfortunately, is often written by men and women who have access to secondary sources alone, who have never known their subjects personally," declared Charles Angoff in *The Tone of the Twenties* (1966); "and thus they commit gross errors of fact and of judgment" – errors which may then become institutionalized as their efforts win acceptance as doctoral dissertations. The comment is just; nevertheless, the writer of history who is himself too young to have known his subjects personally cannot therefore rest from his own labors, content to take Angoff's – or Cowley's, or Eastman's, or Hemingway's, or Krutch's, or Edmund Wilson's – testimony on the Twenties as final.

Let me illustrate. All of the firsthand, "first generation" histories of the Twenties, as for example Frederick Lewis Allen's *Only Yesterday** (1931), made at least a descriptive mention of the so-called "new psychology" which was one of the motive forces, or at least rationalizations, of the Revolt of Youth in the Twenties. But only in our own day has this movement received the kind of thorough rethinking, and of working through previously unused sources, which the historical study of the Twenties in general so sorely needs; for example, John Chynoweth Burnham, "The New Psychology: From Narcissism to Social Control," a chapter in John Braeman et al., *Change and Continuity in Twentieth-Century America: the 1920's* (1968), pp. 351–98. The popularized science of psychology with which Burnham deals shades gradually into a pseudo-science, or religion, of "mind-cure" with which it basically has nothing to do, and there are important and frightening insights into that movement also during the Twenties in Donald Meyer, *The Positive Thinkers . . . from Mary Baker Eddy to Norman Vincent Peale** (1965), pp. 159–214 – insights of a kind which have only become possible from a longer, younger perspective.

Political history, likewise, has lately had the benefit of reassessment by writers "with the advantage of being too young to lose objectivity through [their] own recollections" [Daniel Boorstin, Editor's Preface to William E. Leuchtenburg, *The Perils of Prosperity, 1914–32** (1958), p. vi]: presidents, presidential candidates, Congressional leaders, and election campaigns of the Twenties are seen quite differently by historians today from the way they seemed to their contemporaries. How far this process can go is exemplified in Robert K. Murray, *The Harding Era: Warren G. Harding and His Administration* (1969). Other presidents once held in low esteem, such as Grant and Buchanan, have found their champions, so perhaps we ought not to be surprised that Harding scholarship has of late turned pro-Harding. Murray himself is aware of, and conscientiously avoids, the pitfall of "historical revisionism for revisionism's sake"; still, one cannot help wondering: Who is next? Franklin Pierce? Fillmore? It is well, therefore, to temper one's revisionist reading with older, more conventional interpretations, such as William Allen White, *Masks in a Pageant* (1928), Arthur Schlesinger, Jr., *The Crisis of the Old Order** (1957), and John D. Hicks, *Republican Ascendancy** (1960).

In economic history, brilliant recent studies such as Irving Bernstein's *The Lean Years: A History of the American Worker, 1920–1933** (1960) and David Brody's "The Rise and Decline of Welfare Capitalism" (Braeman et al., *op. cit.*, pp. 147–78), both take genuinely fresh looks at their subjects; Brody considers seriously a movement which suspicious liberal historians of the first generation since the Crash had been inclined to view as little more than an elaborate "put-on," and Bernstein announces in his preface that he has "sought to break with the tradition that has dominated the writing of American labor history." For an overall picture of the American economy in the Twenties, however, we still fall back in the classroom upon George Soule, *Prosperity Decade: From War to Depression, 1917–1929** (1947), a work now more than two decades old. *Somehow* American business evolved from the "robber barons" of the Gilded Age, however one defines them, into the "new entrepreneurs" of today, however one judges them, and surely in that evolutionary process the Twenties are as pivotal as the New Deal, or even the much-studied Progressive Era. Are even the youngest of our historians still psychically too close to the Crash to generalize as confidently about our grandparents' dollars as we have begun to do about their votes? Or – as graduate professors in this field are wont to say – are there no graduate students who have *read* the T.N.E.C. reports?

In addition to the warm reminiscence of yesterday and the cool monograph of today, other kinds of historical writing on the Twenties should be consulted. Books were written during and immediately after the 1919–29 decade which sought to flesh out the otherwise impressionistic skeleton of events and trends with carefully amassed statistics. Much the most important such work is the President's (Hoover's) Research Committee on Social Trends, (eds.), *Recent Social Trends in the United States* (1933). I entirely agree with the judgment of Henry F. May (*op. cit.*, p. 411) that this remarkable book "is in places a work of art as well as of social science." Still another sort of assessment can be found in the writings of persons whose mind-set was essentially complete *before* the Twenties, and who therefore saw the period from an "older," rather than a contemporary or a younger perspective. One delightful instance is the chapter on "The Country Town" in Thorstein Veblen's *Absentee Ownership** (1923), pp. 142–65 [also available in Wesley C. Mitchell (ed.), *What Veblen Taught* (1936), pp. 394–422]. Veblen by that time had read *Babbitt,* but the outlook is still recognizably that of the author of *The Theory of the Leisure Class** (1899), and the essay is Veblen at his sarcastic best.

Finally, as Clarke Chambers has reminded us [*Journal of American History,* LVI (1969), p. 424], in studying the Twenties we must subdue the temptation to erect that thin ten-year slice of history into a "period," neglecting its antecedents and its consequences. The generation of the Jazz Age had a tendency to forget the social and spiritual roots it had in its own immediate past, but *we* must not make the same mistake. To study the Twenties soon involves us in a longer reach of American history. Indeed, was it an accident that a generation bent on rejecting the experience and advice of its elders should at the same time have managed to rediscover such all-but-forgotten elders as Melville and Emily Dickinson? The search for a usable past, with its inevitable sorting and selecting, finding and forgetting, never ends. In the last analysis the student is back on his own, and I leave you in this essay at the place where we began: on the steps of the library.